Snort For Dummies

Useful Snort Command-Line Options

✔ Starting Snort as a packet sniffer:

snort -v -i *interface*

Where interface is the name of the Ethernet device under Linux, such as "eth0", or the interface number under Windows, such as "1".

✔ Getting available interface numbers under Snort for Windows:

snort -W

✔ Starting Snort in test mode (tests your configuration file options):

snort -T -c *full_path_to_snort.conf*

Where *full_path_to_snort.conf* is the full path to your snort.conf configuration file, for example "/usr/local/snort/etc/snort.conf".

✔ Starting Snort as an IDS under Linux or Windows:

snort -c *full_path_to_snort.conf* -i *interface*

✔ Starting Snort as a daemon under Linux:

snort -D -c *full_path_to_snort.conf* -i *interface*

✔ Installing Snort as a service under Windows:

snort /SERVICE /INSTALL -c *full_path_to_snort.conf* -i *interface*

Important snort.conf Configuration File Settings

Setting	Description
var HOME_NET	The place to put hosts or networks that you administer.
var EXTERNAL_NET	Networks that are hostile or foreign. Usually set to "any".
var RULE_PATH	The path to your Snort signature rules.
output alert_syslog	Set this if you want Snort to alert to Syslog.
output database	Set this if you want Snort to alert/log to a database.
output alert_unified	Set this if you want Snort to alert to a unified binary format for later processing with Barnyard or other tools.
output log_unified	Set this if you want Snort to log to a unified binary format for later processing with Barnyard or other tools.

Snort For Dummies®

Snort Alert Classifications to Watch For

Classification	Priority	Description
attempted-admin	1	An attacker tried to gain administrator/root-level access to your computer.
attempted-user	1	An attacker tried to gain user-level access to your computer.
successful-admin	1	An attacker was able to gain administrator/root-level access to your computer.
successful-user	1	An attacker was able to gain user-level access to your computer.
shellcode-detect	1	An attacker tried to run shellcode (get a command prompt) on your computer.
suspicious-login	2	An attacker is trying to use brute-force methods to log into your computer.
attempted-dos	2	A denial-of-service attack has been detected against your network or computer.
denial-of-service	2	A denial-of-service attack has been detected against your network or computer.

Layers in the OSI Model

Layer #	Layer Name	TCP/IP Stack Equivalents
1	Physical	Your network card and cable.
2	Data Link	Ethernet MAC addresses.
3	Network	The Internet Protocol (IP) and IP addresses.
4	Transport	TCP and UDP protocols and ports.
5	Session	Not used.
6	Presentation	Not used.
7	Application	Familiar protocols like HTTP and SMTP.

Copyright © 2004 Wiley Publishing, Inc.
All rights reserved.

Item 6835-3.

For more information about Wiley Publishing,
call 1-800-762-2974.

For Dummies: Bestselling Book Series for Beginners

Snort™

FOR

DUMMIES®

Snort™ FOR DUMMIES®

by Charlie Scott, Paul Wolfe, and Bert Hayes

WILEY

Wiley Publishing, Inc.

Snort™ For Dummies®

Published by
Wiley Publishing, Inc.
111 River Street
Hoboken, NJ 07030-5774

Copyright © 2004 by Wiley Publishing, Inc., Indianapolis, Indiana

Published by Wiley Publishing, Inc., Indianapolis, Indiana

Published simultaneously in Canada

No part of this publication may be reproduced, stored in a retrieval system or transmitted in any form or by any means, electronic, mechanical, photocopying, recording, scanning or otherwise, except as permitted under Sections 107 or 108 of the 1976 United States Copyright Act, without either the prior written permission of the Publisher, or authorization through payment of the appropriate per-copy fee to the Copyright Clearance Center, 222 Rosewood Drive, Danvers, MA 01923, (978) 750-8400, fax (978) 646-8600. Requests to the Publisher for permission should be addressed to the Legal Department, Wiley Publishing, Inc., 10475 Crosspoint Blvd., Indianapolis, IN 46256, (317) 572-3447, fax (317) 572-4355, e-mail: brandreview@ wiley.com.

Trademarks: Wiley, the Wiley Publishing logo, For Dummies, the Dummies Man logo, A Reference for the Rest of Us!, The Dummies Way, Dummies Daily, The Fun and Easy Way, Dummies.com, and related trade dress are trademarks or registered trademarks of John Wiley & Sons, Inc. and/or its affiliates in the United States and other countries, and may not be used without written permission. All other trademarks are the property of their respective owners. Wiley Publishing, Inc., is not associated with any product or vendor mentioned in this book.

For general information on our other products and services or to obtain technical support, please contact our Customer Care Department within the U.S. at 800-762-2974, outside the U.S. at 317-572-3993, or fax 317-572-4002.

Wiley also publishes its books in a variety of electronic formats. Some content that appears in print may not be available in electronic books.

Library of Congress Control Number: 2004102600

ISBN: 0-7645-6835-3

Manufactured in the United States of America

10 9 8 7 6 5 4 3 2

1O/SS/QW/QU/IN

WILEY

About the Authors

Charlie Scott is an Information Security Analyst for the City of Austin, where he helps maintain the City's network security infrastructure and helps analyze intrusion detection data. He has nearly ten years of experience in the Internet industry and has been an avid user of open source security software that entire time. Charlie is a Certified Information Systems Security Professional (CISSP) and a Cisco Certified Network Professional (CCNP).

Bert Hayes is a Security Technical Analyst for the State of Texas, where he maintains network security for a medium sized agency. In Bert's ten years of IT industry experience, he has done everything from managing a corporate IT shop during a successful IPO to performing white hat penetration tests for corporate and government offices. He has long been a proponent of open source solutions, and is a Red Hat Certified Engineer (RHCE).

Paul Wolfe is an independent information security consultant and author, specializing in open source security.

Authors' Acknowledgments

This book benefited greatly from the research and writing contribution of Mike Erwin, an early collaborator on this project. Mike is the president and CEO of Symbiot, Inc., a developer of intelligent security infrastructure management system designed to interoperate with intrusion detection systems and other pieces of security infrastructure. Mike has fifteen years of experience in network operations and security, has co-authored over a half-dozen books, and is a Certified Information Systems Security Professional (CISSP).

The authors collectively bow to the developers of the myriad of security tools covered in this book, especially Marty Roesch, for answering our questions and creating Snort in the first place!

The authors also thank Melody Layne, Pat O'Brien, and the rest of the Wiley team for their hard work and prodding, and our agent Carole McClendon of Waterside Productions. They also thank Jamie Pugh of Symbiot for his incisive technical review.

Bert dedicates his portion of the book to everyone who would rather build his or her own system than buy one off the shelf. He also acknowledges the unwavering love and support of his wife Kate, the loyalty of his pets, and the wisdom of his parents.

Paul thanks Nikolaus, Lukas, Rayna, Jesse and Brenda, whose support make his work possible (and necessary . . .). And finally, thanks to Charlie for ruling this project with the iron grip of a dictator. Bastard.

Charlie dedicates his portion of the book to everyone who has ever had to clean up a cracked system — may it never happen again. He thanks his wonderful wife, Mary, and his co-workers at the City of Austin for their support.

Publisher's Acknowledgments

We're proud of this book; please send us your comments through our online registration form located at www.dummies.com/register/.

Some of the people who helped bring this book to market include the following:

Acquisitions, Editorial, and Media Development

Project Editor: Pat O'Brien

Acquisitions Editor: Melody Layne

Copy Editor: Barry Childs-Helton

Technical Editor: Jamie Pugh

Editorial Manager: Kevin Kirschner

Media Development Manager: Laura VanWinkle

Media Development Supervisor: Richard Graves

Editorial Assistant: Amanda Foxworth

Cartoons: Rich Tennant (www.the5thwave.com)

Composition

Project Coordinator: Courtney MacIntyre

Layout and Graphics: Andrea Dahl, Stephanie D. Jumper, Lynsey Osborn, Heather Ryan

Proofreaders: Laura Albert, David Faust, Andy Hollandbeck, Brian H. Walls, TECHBOOKS Production Services

Indexer: TECHBOOKS Production Services

Publishing and Editorial for Technology Dummies

Richard Swadley, Vice President and Executive Group Publisher

Andy Cummings, Vice President and Publisher

Mary C. Corder, Editorial Director

Publishing for Consumer Dummies

Diane Graves Steele, Vice President and Publisher

Joyce Pepple, Acquisitions Director

Composition Services

Gerry Fahey, Vice President of Production Services

Debbie Stailey, Director of Composition Services

Contents at a Glance

Table of Contents

Part III: Moving Beyond the Basics *241*

Introduction

Welcome to *Snort For Dummies.* This book introduces you to the world of detecting and responding to network and computer attacks using the Snort intrusion detection system (IDS). Intrusion detection is a fascinating, important, and sometimes harrying subject — after all, we're talking about someone trying to breach all the network defenses you have in place and attack your computer systems! For network and systems administrators, very little is more worrisome than network attacks. Fortunately, the goal of intrusion detection is to remove some of that worry by letting you know when an attack is in progress.

The Snort IDS is one of the most popular intrusion detection platforms available. Snort is an open-source IDS solution, meaning that the source code is free for anyone to use or modify. It's released under the GNU General Public License (GPL) open-source license, which means that it's also free for anyone to use. That's right, it won't cost you anything except time and computer hardware. Interested? You should be. Used in conjunction with your firewall and other layers in your security infrastructure, Snort helps you to detect and respond to worms, system crackers, and other nasty beasts that aim to take down your network and computer systems.

Who Should Read This Book?

This book is for you if you're a network administrator, systems administrator, information security manager, security consultant, or anyone interested in finding out more about running a Snort intrusion detection system to watch for attacks against your network.

About This Book

Snort For Dummies is a reference guide for installing, configuring, deploying and managing Snort IDS sensors on your network. This book covers everything from why you need an IDS, to installing Snort, to dealing with network attacks, to deploying multiple Snort sensors. There are thousands of ways that Snort can be deployed and a myriad of databases, logging systems, and tools it works with. We focus on the tools and techniques that are widely deployed and known to work *best* with Snort, all the while remaining generic enough that the information should be helpful no matter what your situation.

Whether you're watching for attacks on a home network, a small company network, or an enterprise network, *Snort For Dummies* provides you with the information you need.

How to Use This Book

This book is modularly designed so you can jump right in to the information you need, rather than read it from cover-to-cover. You can refer directly to individual chapters that pertain to the information you're looking for. If a concept from an earlier chapter suddenly becomes important, we tell you which chapter to refer to so you can refresh your memory. If you're new to intrusion detection or have never installed Snort before, we recommend that you read Part I. If you already have a Snort sensor and just need to know the best way to manage it, you can skip to Part II. If you're already managing your Snort IDS and want to know about tools and practices that can enhance its ability to detect attacks (and your ability to respond to them), then hit Part III.

What You Don't Need to Read

Depending on your computer and network configuration, you may be able to skip chapters. For instance, if you're running all Linux systems on your network, you can skip the chapter on installing Snort for Windows. Or, if you're only interested in deploying a single Snort sensor, you can skip the chapter on scaling Snort.

Foolish Assumptions

We make a few assumptions about you, a soon-to-be IDS master, so that we can focus this book as much as possible on intrusion detection with Snort:

- ✔ You understand basic computer-, network-, and information security-related concepts and terms. You don't need to have worked for the NSA (known for its security geniuses) but you do need to know what a firewall is.

- ✔ You have a computer that is available, or can become, your Snort sensor.

- ✔ You understand basic software installation and system administration on the system you're working on, be it Linux or Windows.

- ✔ You have access to the Internet in order to obtain the software used to run your Snort IDS.

✔ You're allowed to run Snort on the network you plan on putting it on. This is important because Snort's a network packet sniffer, and there might be privacy implications, or you might violate your organization's own network security policy.

How This Book Is Organized

This book is organized into four parts: three regular-chapter parts and a Part of Tens. There's also an Appendix. These parts are modular, so you can jump around from part to part if needed. Each chapter provides practical installation, configuration, and administration information on running a Snort IDS and its more useful components.

Part 1: Getting to Know Snort and Intrusion Detection

This part covers the basics of getting Snort up and running. It starts by showing you what Snort is capable of and why it's one of the best intrusion detection systems out there. It then shows you where to put Snort on your network. Finally, it shows you how to install Snort on both Linux and Windows systems.

Part II: Administering Your Snort Box

This part covers the day-to-day tasks of running your Snort IDS. It starts by showing you how to use Snort's primary output: logs and alerts. Once you have that down, it takes you through installing the ACID console for getting visuals. Snort's intrusion detection rules are at the core of its operation, so it shows you how to create new rules and tweak them to reduce alerts that don't pertain to you. Finally, it shows you how to deal with an actual attack against your computer systems!

Part III: Moving Beyond the Basics

This part takes you into some of those more advanced features of Snort. It starts by showing you how to send yourself real-time alerts when your network is being attacked. Upgrading your Snort rules or Snort itself can seem like daunting tasks, but we show you how to do both. If you have a large network, you should take advantage of Snort's scalability and run multiple Snort sensors. Finally, this part shows you how to use Snort's unified logging feature and Barnyard to offload log processing from your Snort sensors.

Part IV: The Part of Tens

This part points you to tools and resources to help you get the most out of your Snort IDS. It starts by showing you the top ten coolest tools for Snort, many of which help you visualize what Snort's telling you, or e-mail you convenient summaries of Snort's alert information. Finally, it tells you where you can go for extra Snort help and information.

Icons Used in This Book

 This icon points out technical information that's interesting but not vital to your understanding of the topic being discussed.

 This icon points out information that's worth committing to memory.

 This icon points out information that could seriously impact your ability to run your Snort IDS or companion programs, so please read it!

 This icon points out advice that will make it easier to install or run your Snort IDS.

Where to Go from Here

This book is designed to be modular. Read through the table of contents and decide where you are in the process of installing, configuring, deploying, and managing your Snort IDS. Choose which part or chapter most applies to you and go for it!

Part I

Getting to Know Snort and Intrusion Detection

The 5th Wave   By Rich Tennant

"We take network security very seriously here."

In this part . . .

This part covers the basics of getting Snort up and running. It starts by showing you what Snort is capable of and why it's one of the best intrusion detection systems out there. It then shows you where to put Snort on your network. Finally, it shows you how to install Snort on both Linux and Windows systems.

Chapter 1

Looking Up Snort's Nose

- -

In This Chapter

▶ Understanding network and computer attacks

▶ Understanding intrusion detection

▶ Understanding the Snort intrusion detection system

- -

*Y*our boss left a magazine article on your desk about a company whose customer database was cracked by a hacker. What's worse, the intruder had been pulling credit-card numbers out of the database for months, and all the while the company had no clue it was the victim of a high-tech robbery. The company's customers stopped trusting, and the company lost money. Attached to the article was a Post-It note in your boss' handwriting: "Can this happen to us?" How can you assure her you'll know if an intruder attacks your database? How can you be sure it hasn't already happened?

You did some research and discovered that adding an Intrusion Detection System (IDS) to your network will give you the information you need to detect network attacks. You looked around at some of the commercial IDS products and found these products slick and beautiful, but also found their price tag equals a few months of your salary. Ouch! Despite your boss' concern about hackers, you know that money is tight, and the security budget is small.

Open source software projects have gotten a lot of press because they're often inexpensive, or even free. You found an open source IDS software package called Snort. It looks like a good choice, but you're not a computer security guru, and open-source software isn't known for having an easy "three clicks and you're done" installation process. You want intrusion detection alerts and reports, but you don't have a lot of time to figure out on your own how to build or maintain an IDS.

You've come to the right place! In this book we tell you how to get your Snort IDS up and running, and how to use the information it provides to keep your network secure.

Why All the Hubbub about Security?

It used to be that every computer network was an island unto itself. Network security? All you needed were guards and keys to keep people who didn't belong on your computers out of your building. Sure, some computers were broken into over phone lines, but that was rare and only done by brainiacs like the kid from the movie *WarGames*, right? Computer viruses spread, but only when someone brought in a floppy disk from home. Worms? Only your dog got those.

Then, companies, governments, organizations, and individuals across the globe began connecting to the commercialized Internet, and a couple of things changed for network security.

✔ All those separate islands were connected by bridges (*routers*, technically speaking). It became much easier for one computer to talk to another, across town or across the globe.

✔ Network penetration and computer cracking tools became much easier to obtain and use. It takes hardcore programming skills to build computer-cracking tools, but you don't have to be a Über-hacker to run them. Programmers who know how to create cracking tools can make them available on the Internet, where anyone from a curious 12-year-old to a corporate spy can download and use them.

Some of the threats you have to watch out for include the following:

✔ **Worms:** These little attack-bots are everywhere these days. Worms exploit known holes in computer operating systems and applications to spread automatically from one machine to the next.

✔ **Script-kiddies:** Only slightly smarter than worms, script-kiddies are real people that use someone else's aforementioned cracking tools to do their dirty work. Because they tend to use well-known hacking tools and go after low-hanging fruit, they are usually easy for IDS systems to spot.

✔ **Denial-of-Service and Distributed Denial-of-Service attacks:** These attacks rob you of your computer and network resources (such as network bandwidth, CPU cycles, network connections, memory, and disk space). DOS and DDOS attacks can bring a computer network to its knees.

✔ **Black-hat hackers and crackers:** Black-hat hackers and crackers are usually very skilled at network penetration and exploiting system vulnerabilities. They often go to great lengths to evade IDS systems.

With threats like these on the Internet, information security is a concern for everyone.

What Is an IDS, and Why Have One?

An IDS is an application that detects attacks against your computer or network, and lets you know when the attacks occur. How can an IDS help you deal with the threats against your network and computer systems? What follows is a quick rundown of some of the benefits of running an IDS:

- **Detecting attacks.** Attack detection is what an IDS is there for. An IDS can tell you if a worm is attacking your network, or if a computer system has been compromised.

- **Enforcing policies.** An IDS can monitor an internal network for behavior that violates your organization's network security or acceptable use policies. For instance, if users are chatting on AOL Instant Messenger, when IM use is prohibited.

- **Providing an audit trail.** An IDS can provide an after-the-attack audit trail for seeing how far an attacker got, and where it came from.

- **Resource justification.** An IDS can provide information on how well your firewall is working and exactly how many people are "out to get you." This is useful when the suits want justification for the firewall upgrade, extra staff for the security team, or your pay-raise.

All of the preceding benefits are good reasons to install an IDS as part of your security strategy.

Key IDS concepts

Every aspect of information technology has its own lingo, and intrusion detection is no exception. What follows is a breakdown of key concepts and terms that are important to running an IDS.

False positives and false negatives

False positives are alerts generated by an IDS because it thinks it has detected a valid attack against a monitored system, but the attack really isn't valid. False positives are problems because they create alert noise that can hide a real attack, and then can send you on wild goose chases for attacks that never really happened. A false positive occurs when an IDS generates an alert on either

- Network traffic that looks like an attack to the IDS, but isn't an attack.
- A real attack that attack doesn't apply to the system being monitored.

A *false negative* is a real attack that was missed by the IDS, and therefore not alerted on. An IDS might miss an attack because the attack is not one it recognizes, because the IDS is overwhelmed, or because the attacker has successfully used a method of evading the IDS. The implications of this are obvious: An attacked missed by your IDS is an attack you're not aware of!

Signatures and anomalies

There are a couple of ways IDS solutions can detect attacks:

- **Signature detection.** An IDS that uses signature detection matches the network traffic it sees against a list of attack signatures. These signatures are typically important bits and pieces of the attack that the IDS should look for in incoming network packets and flag as "bad" traffic. The downside of signature detection is that it only knows to look for attacks that it has signatures for, and therefore can miss newly developed attacks. A properly tuned signature detection IDS might be low on false positives, but can be high on false negatives.

- **Anomaly detection.** An IDS that uses anomaly detection works in a different manner. It learns what "normal" traffic for your network looks like, and will then alert you when it sees something that looks "abnormal." Unfortunately, anything new or different might have the chance of being labeled abnormal, so a properly tuned anomaly detection IDS might be low on false negatives, but higher on false positives.

Some IDS solutions use signature detection, some use anomaly detection, and some use both. Snort uses signature detection.

Network-based IDS (NIDS)

A network-based IDS (NIDS) analyzes packets coming across a network connection for data that look like its part of an attack. NIDS perform the following tasks:

- NIDS analyze network traffic for attacks, using signature or anomaly detection (or both). Its network interface card (NIC) runs in promiscuous mode, which means that it captures *all* network traffic that goes by its NIC, not just the traffic destined for the IDS system itself.

- Generates alerts to notify you of an attack in real-time.

- Generates logs to drill down deeper into an attack, typically after the attack has occurred.

NIDS can often be distributed to different parts of your network infrastructure, yet can send alerts to one central console. Snort is a fine example of a NIDS.

Host-based IDS (HIDS)

While a NIDS looks at all the traffic on a network to detect intrusions, a host-based IDS (HIDS) only monitors for intrusions on the system it's running on. HIDS perform one or more of the following tasks:

✔ HIDS look at incoming network traffic for attacks, using signature or anomaly detection. Typically, the NIC on a system running a HIDS is not in promiscuous mode.

✔ HIDS examine system logs for unusual events, such as multiple invalid login attempts.

✔ HIDS check the integrity of files on the system. This has nothing to do with the files' moral character, but rather whether or not a file has been modified. Integrity checking will also let you know if files have been created or deleted. This is useful for detecting when backdoor or Trojan programs have been installed on your system.

The lowdown on layers

While you don't have to be a networking genius to use Snort, there is one concept that is important for the discussion about how Snort works and how to read its output: the Open Systems Interconnection Reference Model (called the OSI Model for short). The OSI Model is an International Standards Organization (ISO) standard for how networking protocols relate to each other. The OSI Model sometimes is referred to as the OSI/ISO or ISO/OSI Model.

The OSI Model is comprised of seven layers that make up the bits and pieces of a networking protocol. So do you have to memorize every single one of the OSI model layers? No. In fact, the TCP/IP protocol suite (which makes up all Internet traffic) only loosely fits into the OSI Model. But we refer to the other OSI Model layers in numerous parts of this book, because describing Snort's output relies on them. What follows is a listing of the layers of the OSI Model that are important to our purposes:

Layer 1 (Physical): Layer 1 is your physical network connection. For instance, your Ethernet network interface card (NIC).

Layer 2 (Data Link): Layer 2 is the binary data that rides over the physical connection. For example, the 802.2 Ethernet protocols operate at this layer. Ethernet Media Access Control (MAC) addresses are also at this layer.

Layer 3 (Network): Layer 3 provides the addressable routing of packets. The Internet Protocol (IP) operates at this layer, so IP addresses are known as Layer 3 addresses.

Layer 4 (Transport): Layer 4 provides end-to-end networking communications. While Layer 3 tells data where it needs to go, Layer 4 tells it how to establish a connection. The Transmission Control Protocol (TCP) and Universal Datagram Protocol (UDP) perform this function in TCP/IP. Layer 4 communications over TCP/IP is done through numbered "ports" over which network applications and network services run. Web servers, for example, typically run over TCP port number 80.

Layer 7 (Application): Layer 7 provides for the end-to-end communication between applications. An example of this is the Hyper-Text Transport Protocol (HTTP), used by Web servers and Web browsers to communicate between each other.

The layers we refer to most in other chapters of this book are Layer 3 (Network), Layer 4 (Transport), and Layer 7 (Application).

Using HIDS is another way to defend your network, and contributes to a defense-in-depth posture by adding yet another layer of security. If someone gets past your firewall and sneaks by your NIDS, there's a chance your HIDS can still catch him.

Don't put all your eggs in the firewall basket

If you don't already have a firewall between your computer network and the Internet, then put down this book and go set one up right now!

Done? Good. A firewall is a basic requirement for a network connected to the Internet these days; without a firewall, you're not even doing the minimum to protect your network and computers. A firewall is your network's bouncer, only allowing certain people in or out. A firewall protects computer resources that you don't want outsiders to reach (for example, your file servers), while allowing access to resources you do want outsiders to reach (your Web server, for example).

You need *both* a firewall and an IDS. A firewall is not a replacement for an IDS, it's just a layer of the total security onion. Although some firewalls have intrusion detection capabilities, they are typically able to detect fewer attacks than a full-fledged IDS.

Why Snort?

Snort (affectionately known by its designers and users at "the Pig") is a network based IDS that uses signature detection; it sniffs and examines network data packets for content that matches known attacks.

Snort is not the only NIDS option available. Security is a hot topic, and there are many big-name manufacturers with IDS products on the market these days (ISS RealSecure and Cisco IDS are two examples). There are also a number of free, open-source IDS projects (the Prelude IDS for Linux and BSD operating systems is one example). With all of these options, why pick Snort to monitor your network for intrusions?

  ✔ **Snort is configurable.** All of Snort's inner workings, configuration files, and rules are laid bare to you, so you can tune Snort to your specific network architecture. Not only that, but you can create your own rules for new attacks.

- **Snort is free.** Snort is released under the GNU GPL, which means you can use it for free, no matter if you're a company or just a curious hobbyist.

- **Snort is widely used.** There are tens of thousands of downloads of Snort each month from the `http://www.snort.org/` Web site.

- **Snort runs on multiple platforms.** Snort not only runs on all the major Unix and Unix-ish operating systems (including Linux), but also runs on Microsoft Windows.

- **Snort is constantly updated.** Maintenance releases for Snort come out as needed, typically once every few months. The Snort rules are regularly updated with new attack signatures and can be downloaded from `www.snort.org/`.

When it comes to network intrusion detection systems, nothing gives you more bang for your buck than Snort.

Snort's Components

Snort's designers set out to create a top-notch open-source IDS, and in our opinion they've certainly succeeded. In the process of designing Snort, the developers focused their energies on taking an existing tool and greatly expanding its abilities to make it something new; again, we see how the open-source model works for *you*. In this case, the existing tool was tcpdump, the ubiquitous packet capturer found on many Unix systems (and available at `www.tcpdump.org/`, by the way). Marty Roesch, Snort's creator, took tcpdump's ability to grab packets, and added the ability to analyze those packets against a set of attack signatures.

Snort is an elegantly designed little beast, made up of several components that each perform a specific task. Figure 1-1 breaks Snort down.

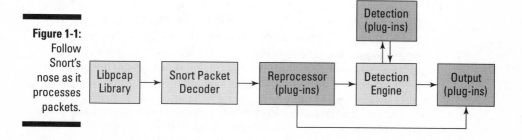

Figure 1-1:
Follow Snort's nose as it processes packets.

Understanding CIDR notation

When you configure Snort to monitor IP addresses and networks, it wants you to use something called CIDR (Classless Inter-Domain Routing) notation to represent the network mask. You're probably familiar with seeing a network and netmask pair such as this for a Class C network:

    192.168.1.0 255.255.255.0

Using CIDR notation, the same Class C network is represented like this:

    192.168.1.0/24

The number 24 after the slash is called the IP network prefix, and basically means the same thing as a netmask. This number is derived from the number of bits that are turned on (starting from the rightmost bit) in a 32-bit IP address.

If you don't already know how to calculate CIDR notation, don't worry — you don't have to calculate the address yourself. Even hardcore network geeks don't calculate it every time — they eventually just memorize which prefixes match up to the netmasks they most often use. The easiest way to map CIDR notation to netmasks and number of hosts is to freeload off of the security wizards at the SANS Institute. The SANS complete CIDR table is found at this Web address: www.sans.org/dosstep/cidr.php.

Whenever a network packet hits an Ethernet wire that Snort is sniffing, it takes the following path:

1. **Packet capture library.** Illustrated as "Libpcap library" in Figure 1-1, the packet capture library is a separate piece of software that tosses Snort network packets from the network card. There are unprocessed Data-Link Layer (Layer 2 of the OSI model) packets, such as Ethernet frames. On Linux and Unix systems, Snort uses libpcap (covered in Chapter 4). On Windows systems, Snort uses WinPcap (covered in Chapter 5).

2. **Packet decoder.** The packet decoder takes the Layer 2 data sent over from the packet capture library and takes it apart. First it decodes the Data Link frame (such as Ethernet, TokenRing, or 802.11), then the IP protocol, then the TCP or UDP packet. When finished decoding, Snort has all the protocols information in all the right places for further processing.

3. **Preprocessor.** Snort's preprocessor has several plug-ins that can be turned on or off. Preprocessing operates on the decoded packets, performing a variety of transformations making the data easier for Snort to digest. Preprocessors can alert on, classify, or drop a packet before sending it on to the more CPU-intensive detection engine. We tell you more about Snort's preprocessors in Chapter 9.

4. **Detection engine.** The detection engine is the heart of Snort. It takes information from the packet decoder and preprocessors and operates on it at the transport and application layers (Layers 4 and 5 of the OSI

model), comparing what's in the packet to information in its rules-based detection plug-in. These rules contain signatures for attacks, and we cover them in-depth in Chapter 8.

5. **Output.** When a preprocessor or rule is triggered, an alert is generated and logged (optionally along with the offending packet). Snort supports a variety of output plug-ins, including its own text- and binary-based logging formats, a number of databases, and syslog. Chapter 6 covers Snort's output methods.

At the network layer (OSI model Layer 3) and above, Snort can only decode packets that are part of the TCP/IP protocol suite. This means it cannot decode packets or detect attacks that are carried out over other network protocols, such as Novell's IPX/SPX or AppleTalk. For the most part, though, this is no big deal, as many network operating systems have already migrated to TCP/IP. And don't worry about someone attacking you with IPX from the Internet — because they can't!

Glancing at Snort's Output

Just to give you a brief taste of what Snort will tell you whenever you're under attack, here's an alert generated when a packet matching the MS-SQL Worm propagation attempt rule, also known as the Slammer worm, came across our wire (the IP addresses have been obfuscated with Xs and Ys to protect the guilty):

```
02/26-17:59:01.635549  [**] [1:2003:2] MS-SQL Worm
        propagation attempt [**] [Classification: Misc
        Attack] [Priority: 2] {UDP} Y.Y.250.124:1162 ->
        X.X.2.27:1434
```

The alert tells us the following:

✔ The date and time the attack occurred

✔ Signature identification information to match the alert to a specific Snort rule

✔ A description of the alert

✔ What type of attack the alert is classified as

✔ The alert's priority (the lower the number, the more serious the attack)

✔ What protocol the attack came over (in this case UDP)

✔ The source IP address and port number, and the destination IP address and port number

All of this information is potentially useful to us to track down an attack. We give you more information on Snort's alert output, and show you other ways of logging alerts, in Chapter 6. We tell you how to track down an attack in Chapter 10.

Visualizing with Consoles

As you can see in the preceding section, Snort's output isn't much to look at. While a flat-text Snort alert file contains a whole lot of useful information, and is great for parsing with a script, staring at Snort alerts scrolling by will make you go blind before your time.

Fortunately there's ACID (Analysis Console for Intrusion Detection), a Web-based helper application for viewing and analyzing Snort alerts. Figure 1-2 shows a snapshot of alerts on an ACID console.

Much better, eh? Not only does ACID give you a more pleasurable alert-viewing experience, but ACID also allows you to drill down into the guts of an alert, track where the attacker came from, and search on alerts using a number of criteria. We cover installing and using ACID in Chapter 7, and show you how to use ACID to investigate an attack in Chapter 10.

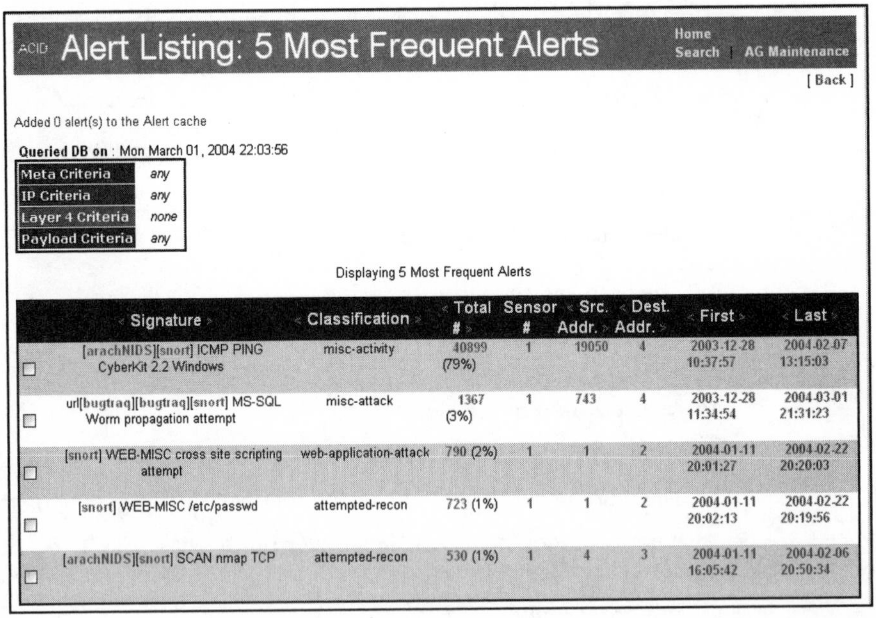

Figure 1-2:
ACID
prettifies
Snort's
output.

| ACID Alert Listing: 5 Most Frequent Alerts | | | | | | | |

Home
Search | AG Maintenance

[Back]

Added 0 alert(s) to the Alert cache

Queried DB on : Mon March 01 , 2004 22:03:56

Meta Criteria	any
IP Criteria	any
Layer 4 Criteria	none
Payload Criteria	any

Displaying 5 Most Frequent Alerts

Signature	Classification	Total #	Sensor #	Src. Addr.	Dest. Addr.	First	Last
[arachNIDS][snort] ICMP PING CyberKit 2.2 Windows	misc-activity	40899 (79%)	1	19050	4	2003-12-28 10:37:57	2004-02-07 13:15:03
url[bugtraq][bugtraq][snort] MS-SQL Worm propagation attempt	misc-attack	1367 (3%)	1	743	4	2003-12-28 11:34:54	2004-03-01 21:31:23
[snort] WEB-MISC cross site scripting attempt	web-application-attack	790 (2%)	1	1	2	2004-01-11 20:01:27	2004-02-22 20:20:03
[snort] WEB-MISC /etc/passwd	attempted-recon	723 (1%)	1	1	2	2004-01-11 20:02:13	2004-02-22 20:19:56
[arachNIDS][snort] SCAN nmap TCP	attempted-recon	530 (1%)	1	4	3	2004-01-11 16:05:42	2004-02-06 20:50:34

Getting to Know Snort's Buddies

Snort can do its job alone, but it can do its job better with a little help from some other applications. One of these fine pieces of software is Barnyard, a tool that offloads Snort's output processing. We cover installing and using Barnyard in Chapter 14. Other programs relate specifically to real-time alerting and attack mitigation, such as Syslog-NG, Swatch, and SnortSam. We cover all three of these real-time alerting and mitigation tools in Chapter 11. In Chapter 15, we tell you about ten more cool Snort tools for you to check out.

The busier Snort is, the more likely it's going to drop packets, and dropped packets are packets that don't get analyzed. Let Snort handle capturing and analyzing network traffic, and let other programs handle everything else when possible.

Chapter 2

Fitting In Snort

*T*hree factors determine the overall effectiveness of your Snort system: location, location, and location. With Snort, as in the world of real estate, where you are is just as important as what you do.

Before you start your Snort install, decide what you are protecting:

 ✔ A single server

 ✔ A group of systems

 ✔ An entire subnet

Once you know what part of your network you want to monitor, your decision on where to place your Snort monitor practically is made for you.

Network-Based IDS

Why run Snort on a single host? The following examples are perfectly good instances of when to run Snort on a single system, because both are examples of the smallest of networks: a single host.

If a single host is the limit of your network (or the piece of the network that you monitor for attacks), skip the rest of this chapter and go straight to Chapter 4 (if you're installing for Linux) or Chapter 5 (if you're installing for Windows):

✔ Your single host is a Web server locked up in a far-away cabinet in some-one else's data center. You might not want to pay the extra money for another couple units of rack-space just for a dedicated Snort system.

✔ You're a wireless java junkie with your own chair at the local Wi-Fi café. You might consider running Snort on your laptop to see when someone decides to — *ahem* — check your laptop for the latest system patch.

Once you start worrying about monitoring more than one host, you must decide whether you want to

✔ Run Snort on each of those hosts

✔ Run a single dedicated Snort system to watch an entire chunk of your network.

   With the amount of work involved in installing and maintaining Snort, you get more bang for your buck with a dedicated Snort sensor to watch entire sections of your network.

Snort isn't useless for monitoring a single host. But Snort only looks for attacks in network traffic. This puts Snort in the NIDS camp, regardless of whether you monitor a single host or an entire network with Snort.

Snort is a textbook definition of a Network IDS. It started its life as a juiced-up version of `tcpdump`, the ubiquitous packet capture agent that takes raw data straight off the wire, and was enhanced to compare that data to a list of known attack patterns, alerting you when traffic patterns match attack patterns. In a nutshell, that's what Snort does, and that's what it does best.

Exposing Snort to more of your network results in it watching more network traffic. The default setting in your snort.conf file is to define `var HOME_NET any`. This tells Snort to watch *any* traffic that whizzes past it and look for attacks, so getting Snort to monitor more of your network can be as simple as exposing it to more network traffic.

Finding a home for your Snort sensor

If you set up a Snort sensor as a dedicated NIDS, have it watch as much traffic as it can handle at one time. Why watch a single server, when you can moni-tor every host on your DMZ? Snort puts a network card in promiscuous mode, so it watches *all* network traffic that flies by. You can edit your snort.conf file to limit what you want Snort to react to, but the network card grabs every packet it can. The key to making Snort watch more of a network is letting it see more of that network.

Host-based IDS

In the world of intrusion detection systems (IDS), there are basically two flavors:

✔ Network-based IDS (NIDS): Snort is a NIDS. Snort puts a network card in promiscuous mode, looks at every packet that whizzes by (regardless of its ultimate destination), and alerts about packets that look like attacks.

✔ Host-based IDS (HIDS): A true HIDS watches events on the host itself (such as changes to important files and unsuccessful local logins) and decides whether these events indicate some shenanigans.

Snort can be run on a single host, configured to watch only the network traffic that is relevant to that host. This myopic monitoring does not make Snort a HIDS.

Imagine a Snort sensor that runs on the host it's meant to monitor; that sensor only sees network traffic for that particular host. Now imagine the following scenarios: One of your admins creates a privileged account for use after he turns in his letter of resignation; an unused account for a user on a lengthy sabbatical is suddenly active again; your company's top-secret plans for a submersible bicycle are copied to a floppy disk and taken off-site; or your login program is replaced with a keystroke logger. Snort can't detect any of these attacks while running on a single server because these attacks either happen at the console, or abuse existing privileges and don't occur over the network directed at network services. Snort would not see any traffic that indicates an attack.

When it comes time to choose the hardware for running Snort, and you're worried about Snort seeing enough of your network, pick a server that looks good. After all, the better you look, the more you see. Joking aside, we guide you in choosing the best hardware for a Snort sensor in Chapter 3.

Switches, repeaters, and hubs, oh, my!

For a Snort user, there's one important difference between hubs (or *repeaters)* and switches:

✔ Hubs repeat data to every port.

With hubs, a network card in *promiscuous mode* easily watches other people's network traffic (because everyone's packets already go to everyone else).

✔ Switches only send data to the port where that data's ultimate destination lies.

A switch knows which MAC address is on each port. It takes data that comes in on a port (or ports) and spits it back out on another port (or ports). A switch reduces the total traffic on the network by only sending data destined for a particular device's MAC address to the switch port that device is plugged in to.

A switch's ability to forward traffic only to devices that the traffic is destined for means that switches are much better performers and are more scalable than hubs. The other side of that coin, however, is that traffic not destined for a particular device is hidden from that device. Since your Snort box is just another device plugged into the switch, this presents a problem: If you want to monitor the entire network's conversations, you want to be able to listen to *all* of conversations at once. This is easy with a hub, but difficult with a switch.

Most modern switches can designate a specific port as a *monitoring port.* The monitoring port can watch all traffic between any port (or group of ports) on your switch. On some switches, such as Cisco switches, the monitoring port is called a SPAN port. Consult your switch's documentation to set up a monitoring or SPAN port.

Some switches can't be configured with a monitoring port. Those little eight-port switches that cost $100 a few years ago are a good example. If your switch can't designate a monitoring port, consider either

  ✔ Using a hub to repeat the traffic that you want to monitor

  ✔ Replacing your switch with one that allows you to designate a monitoring port

Location, location, location

What Snort monitors depends on where it is on your network. A diagram of a typical network is shown in Figure 2-1. Like most, this network uses a firewall to split Internet facing servers into a DMZ, and keeps end-user workstations and internal servers in a NAT network.

  ✔ A DMZ (De-Militarized Zone) network is a kind of limbo, a neither here nor there zone that has tight controls on what network traffic goes in and what comes out. Traditionally, it's a semi-trusted network where publicly facing Internet servers reside.

  ✔ NAT stands for Network Address Translation, a way to hide multiple machines using private IP space behind a much smaller chunk of public IP space. With NAT, your end-user workstations and internal file servers can initiate outgoing Internet connections, but other hosts on the Internet can't initiate connections the other way.

Keeping servers in a DMZ keeps your NAT network secure. If one of your Internet-facing servers in your DMZ is cracked, the damage should be limited because the hacker can't get out of the DMZ to your internal network.

Covering your assets

If your network is for a business or other organization that uses the Internet, network Internet access probably is critical to your business operating smoothly. Even e-mail can be vital to day-to-day operations, so keeping these servers safe is key. If you have publicly facing Internet servers in a DMZ, watch here for trouble: Internet access to your servers means that you can tell the entire world about www.yoursite.com, but the entire world can poke, prod, and tickle your servers, too.

Any place you have publicly facing Internet servers is a place for Snort.

If you use a separate DMZ network, you must do the following:

✔ Designate a port on your DMZ switch as a monitoring port.

✔ Tell your snort.conf file that you want to monitor this subnet.

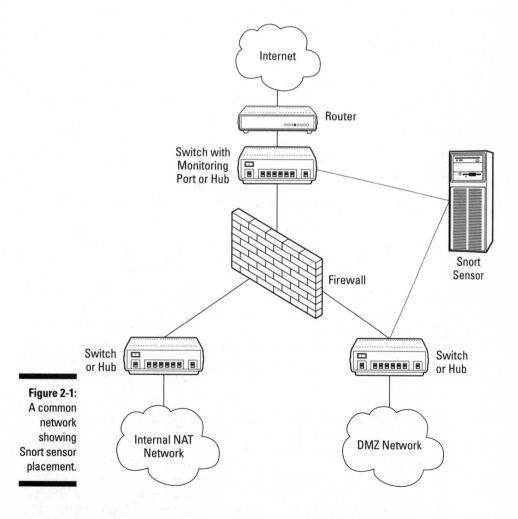

Figure 2-1: A common network showing Snort sensor placement.

After watching this traffic for a while, you start to see alerts for Web server attacks and attempts to squeeze your servers for network information. Keep an eye on Snort's alerts and start trimming your configuration to reduce false positives (we cover this in Chapter 9).

Monitoring your DMZ alerts you when someone attacks a server and tells you whether an already compromised server is attacking other servers in the DMZ. This information is critical to network forensics (covered in Chapter 10).

Seeing who isn't on the guest list

In almost every case, you should monitor *unfiltered Internet traffic*. This traffic is directed at your network, but hasn't had a chance to be rejected by your firewall. Though most bad traffic gets the boot from your firewall and never touches the protected parts of your network, it's nice to see that traffic is. If your boss ever wants stats on how well your firewall is doing its job, this is one great resource.

Figure 2-1 shows a switch in between the router and firewall. Although this isn't necessary, it's usually helpful to have unfiltered IP space for network troubleshooting. If there's a switch in front of your firewall, but you can't designate a monitoring port on it, throw a hub between your router and switch. This lets you plug your Snort sensor in front of the firewall; for many sites, it won't introduce any bottlenecks. (A T1 line is only 1.54 Mbps, and even the cheapest hub handles 10 Mbps.)

If you monitor unfiltered Internet traffic, you see *a lot* of alerts. You should see a slew of such attack alerts as

✔ Port scans that never make it past your firewall

✔ Random worm activity directed at hosts that don't exist

This data is proof that your firewall is doing its job.

Keeping tabs on the inside

Although it seems logical that you'd want to use Snort to monitor your internal NAT network filled with end-users and file servers, we don't recommend it until you've gained some experience scaling and tuning your Snort system for a couple of reasons:

✔ **Bandwidth:** Internal LANs typically run at 100 Mbps to ensure fast access to internal file servers or databases. Compare this to the size of the pipe from the Internet to your DMZ. If every host on your internal network has a 100 Mbps dedicated pipe (thanks to the magic of modern switches, this is now the norm), your Snort system must watch *a lot* of traffic at once. This is possible with Gigabit Ethernet interfaces and systems with *really fast* processors, but your super-fast Snort system may be pushed to its limits.

> ✔ **False positive alerts:** Snort has a built-in notion of us vs. them, which
> is most evident in the snort.conf settings var HOME_NET, and `var`
> `EXTERNAL_NET`. Snort has a very hard time correctly differentiating
> between legitimate internal network traffic and hostile attacks. You can
> get around this by setting both variables to `any`, but it doesn't change the
> fact that Snort is looking for attacks. Snorts default set of rules assumes
> that your `HOME_NET` needs to be protected from your `EXTERNAL_NET`.

If your system can handle watching the big bandwidth of a LAN, Snort is your
best friend for monitoring internal LAN traffic. Watching internal LAN traffic
can be a great way to make sure that your users are sticking to the network
policy if you have

> ✔ A high-performance Snort sensor with CPU cycles and RAM to spare

> ✔ A highly tuned rule set

> Your highly tuned rule set should include rules that you develop your-
> self. We cover writing your own rules in Chapter 8. You can write rules to
> alert you if you start seeing HTTP traffic coming from anything that isn't
> a sanctioned Web server. Or consider a rule to watch for spyware trying
> to phone home from your internal LAN.

Inviting More Pigs to the Party

So you want to monitor your network *everywhere;* you need Snort sensors in
front of your firewall, behind your firewall, next to your firewall, in your DMZ,
in your NAT network, under your desk, behind your chair, maybe even in the
office break room, you know, just in case. Sound paranoid? You bet! But no
two sites have the same monitoring requirements.

Fortunately, Snort is *modular* and *scalable.* It's relatively easy to deploy an
army of Snort sensors, though a small squad may be more appropriate.

You may be tempted to place a single Snort sensor on your network and put
an armful of different subnets in your `var HOME_NET` variable. If Snort can
see traffic on all of those subnets, it might be a good idea (if your system has
the CPU and RAM to keep up). But most network architectures are so complicated that seeing network traffic for different subnets requires a different
sensor for each subnet.

If you watch different subnets, you must use a different network interface to
listen to each subnet. This can mean either

> ✔ Running separate sensors for each subnet

> ✔ Putting multiple NICs in a single Snort host

A single, all-seeing Snort sensor

If you have more than one NIC (Network Interface Card) in a single Snort system, you can use the -i command line switch to control which interface to listen on. Versions of the libpcap library running on Linux kernels 2.2.x and higher let you listen to all interfaces at once using -i any. (In the old days, that required running a separate instance of Snort for each subnet you wanted to monitor.)

We don't recommend listening on all interfaces at once. Once you start running Snort, it needs some fine-tuning. Some rules may be appropriate for your DMZ network, and some may be more appropriate for watching unfiltered Internet traffic. You might even want to run some preprocessors on one network, but not another (preprocessors are covered in Chapter 9). Soon you realize that you want Snort custom-tailored for your network, but covering different subnets using the same configuration is more of a one-size-fits-all deployment. The Windows WinPcap library can't watch multiple interfaces at once, so running Snort on Windows with multiple network interfaces means running multiple instances of Snort.

Single processor host

If your single processor Snort system has enough CPU power, you can run multiple instances of Snort at once on the same CPU. Running multiple instances of Snort on your single-CPU system gives you the following benefits:

- ✔ Reducing the number of individual machines running Snort eases management.
- ✔ Multiple instances of the same running program are a cheap and dirty way to multi-thread.

Dual processor host

If you have a dual processor system, a different instance of Snort can run on each processor.

This can be a lifesaver: If one part of your network is under an unusually heavy load, it won't reduce the performance of the other Snort process. Figure 2-1 shows two instances of Snort watching two different subnets, all running on the same server.

Multiple Network Interface Cards

Monitoring multiple subnets means running Snort with multiple Network Interface Cards (NICs). Although Snort can monitor all NICs at once in some installations, we recommend running a different instance of Snort for each NIC so you can customize Snort's configuration for each subnet you monitor.

Adding more NICs to your Snort system shouldn't be hard if your Operating System supports the hardware; you'll be limited by the number of expansion cards your motherboard can handle. If you go hog-wild with your Snort install, and you run out of places to stick NICs, consider using a NIC with multiple interfaces on the card. Some PCI cards can have as many as four interfaces.

When using multiple NICs to monitor different subnets, make sure that these NICs don't have an IP address. If you run Snort on a *headless* server somewhere (headless means "no monitor", not "no cranium"), you need one IP address for access via SSH or log forwarding over syslog or MySQL. If you're *really* paranoid, you can run Snort on a system with a monitor and no IP address at all, although this severely limits Snort's scalability.

Eyes and ears everywhere

Although running a single Snort host with multiple NICs and multiple instances of Snort is a viable solution, your network may be expansive enough that this isn't feasible. This certainly is the case if your network has multiple physical locations. In this case, multiple Snort sensors with centralized logging are for you.

Adding Snort sensors to your network just entails setting up more hosts running Snort. For easier management, send the output from all of these sensors to the same place. This is done with the `output` module in your snort.conf file. Often, multiple sensors send their output to the same logging server or database server. Scaling your Snort installation across multiple hosts, multiple subnets, or multiple physical sites is covered in exquisite, gory detail in Chapter 13.

Figure 2-2 shows a typical network configuration where we see the following separation of duties within our Snort architecture:

✔ Separate Snort sensors watching different parts of a network. The dashed lines from Snort sensors to switches or hubs are un-addressed NICs that are monitoring traffic. Solid lines from Snort sensors to the NAT network are connections to addressed NICs for remote access.

✔ A separate database server (holding our Snort alerts) and Snort ACID console running on its own Web server.

Snort's scalability makes it easy to run each sensor, log database, or console on a dedicated machine. This N-tier architecture makes your Snort system more configurable, stable, and scalable as your network grows.

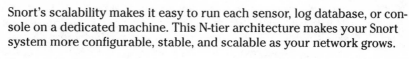

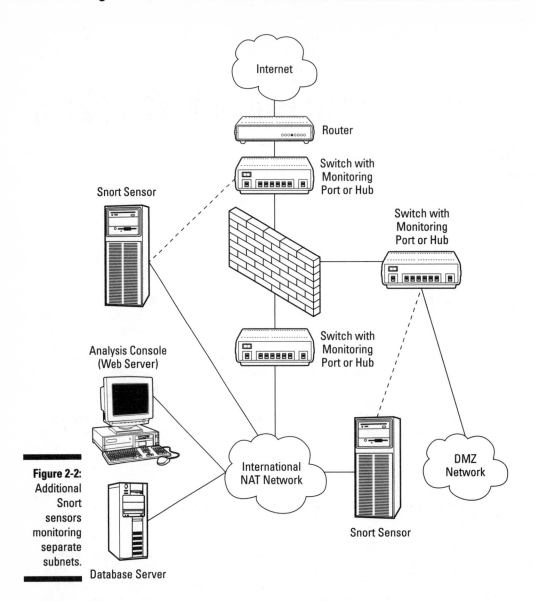

A *passive Ethernet tap* can hide your sensor completely from the rest of your network. You cut wires used for sending data, so you can monitor network traffic without alerting other systems of your presence. Pretty slick, eh? The wizards at snort.org offer a tutorial on constructing your own passive Ethernet tap. Take a spin over to `http://www.snort.org/docs/tap/` for the lowdown.

Chapter 3

Readying Your Preflight Checklist

*W*hen you start a construction project, it's good to know the tools you need and the type of foundation you're building on. The same applies to constructing your Snort Intrusion Detection System (affectionately known as "The Pig" because of its pig mascot). This chapter looks at both Linux and Windows as platforms for Snort, examines Snort's hardware requirements, and helps you make the right choices for your network.

If you already have a Snort IDS system up-and-running, then — first off — congratulations! Second, take a gander at this chapter anyway, because it's never too late to beef up that existing Snort sensor or start planning the next one.

Choosing Your Operating System

Snort is distributed both as source code (which you can compile yourself) and as binary files that are pre-compiled for you. The source code can be compiled for a number of platforms — including Linux, OpenBSD, FreeBSD, Solaris, Tru64, AIX, MacOS X and Windows. You read correctly: *Windows!* There are no known problems running Snort on any post-2000 version of Windows. Open-source tools such as Snort are not just the domain of Unix and Unix-ish operating systems anymore. Of course, actually compiling Snort on Windows is a daunting task — not recommended — but that's where the Snort executable binaries come in handy.

Pre-compiled binaries (for Linux and Windows only) are available from the `snort.org` Web site. The Linux binaries are distributed in the RPM package format, commonly used with RedHat Linux, the Fedora Project (a community-supported RedHat Linux spin-off), and Mandrake Linux. The Windows binaries are simply EXE files. For Linux, compiling from source is the recommended method of installation. For Windows, the binary is the best way to install.

Snort runs on various operating systems, each with its advantages and disadvantages. Table 3-1 offers a brief look at some of these OS choices — as well as what they have going for (and against) them.

Table 3-1	A Brief Overview of Snort's OS Choices	
Operating System	*Advantage*	*Disadvantage*
Linux	Flexibility	Almost *too* flexible (lots to figure out)
Windows	User-friendly	Bulky OS
IBM AIX	Scalability	Expensive RISC hardware
FreeBSD	Stability	Limited hardware choices
OpenBSD	Security	Limited hardware choices
Sun Solaris	Scalability	Expensive Sparc hardware
HP Tru64	Fast 64-bit platform	Expensive 64-bit hardware
MacOS X	User-friendly	Limited hardware choices

This book covers installing the Snort IDS for Linux and Windows. Sorry to leave all you BSD devils out of the fun, but the line had to be drawn somewhere. Linux and Windows were chosen for a couple of reasons:

- ✔ **Pre-compiled Snort binaries are available for both operating systems** at `http://www.snort.org/`.

- ✔ **Linux and Windows have a large combined market share.** They are also the fastest growing server operating systems on the market. IDC (a fancy IT-industry-analysis firm) reported in November 2003 that Linux server shipments grew by 50 percent — and Windows server shipments grew by 21 percent — from year to year. Servers using other Unix operating systems shipped only 4 percent more over the same period. We figured it's a safe bet that any given one of you has a Windows or Linux system in your organization.

If you choose *not* to run Linux or Windows, fear not! With the exception of the installation chapters, the majority of this book is devoted to Snort features that aren't specific to any platform. The day-to-day tasks of running a Snort IDS sensor are the same no matter what operating system you choose.

Running Linux: The pig digs the penguin

Small wonder that the Linux mascot is a penguin — the Linux operating system is an extremely cool platform for running Snort. We recommend you use a modern Linux distribution that uses version 2.4 or newer of the Linux *kernel* (the core of the Linux operating system). Linux Kernel version 2.4 gives you performance and security advantages over the older kernels. Linux Kernel 2.6, released in late December 2003, offers even better scalability, improved I/O performance, and support for high-end processors such as the AMD 64-bit Opteron.

Linux's advantages as a Snort IDS sensor can be summed up in four *P*s: performance, pruning, patching, and price.

The penguin is a top performer

The Linux TCP/IP stack (especially in the version 2.4 series and newer of Linux kernels) is excellent at handling the large amounts of data that pass through a Snort IDS network interface.

Most sysadmins (system administrators) seem to know intuitively that Linux is a much better performer as a Web server. For example, a study at IBM's Watson Research Center found that Linux could handle TCP/IP 21 percent faster than Windows 2000.

Pruning Windows versus pruning the penguin

The standard Windows installation brings with it (from Snort's point of view) some unneeded bells and whistles — chief amongst them the Explorer graphical user interface (GUI) and numerous GUI applications such as Notepad, WordPad, and HyperTerminal. Are any of these required for Snort's day-to-day functions? Nary a one. The GUI takes up memory and CPU cycles just to run (not to mention the hard-drive space it uses). Even though you can remove *some* of the built-in Windows applications, there's no way you're getting rid of the GUI (after all, that's what makes Windows *Windows*, right?)

With Linux you don't need to run — or even install — a GUI, and you can keep applications that aren't Snort-related down to a minimum. And Linux doesn't throw a tantrum if you take away some of its toys. You can run it as bare-bones as you wish, streamlining it into a fast, lean machine.

Why downtime is a big deal for a Snort IDS

Many a systems administrator is aware of the pain and suffering caused by downtime for upgrades: upset users, long hours, interrupted business, and — worse — the chance that the system won't come back up! Hence the reason most upgrades are scheduled during after-hours "maintenance windows" when business is least likely to be affected. The problem with a Snort IDS, however, is that intrusion attempts, network attacks, and worm infestations can occur at *any* time — day or night, weekday or weekend, workday or holiday. Your Snort IDS has to be "always on the job" to detect them. That fifteen minutes (or more) of upgrade downtime could be the window of opportunity an attacker needs to exploit a security hole and get by undetected. It is unrealistic to *never* expect any downtime for upgrades, but for security's sake, it's in your best interest to minimize it as much as possible.

Practically painless penguin patching

Because your Snort IDS is a critical part of your security infrastructure, you don't want it to be down very often — and when it is down, not for long.

There is what amounts to a holy war over which operating system is more secure, Linux or Windows. If you want drama, just check out Slashdot (http://www.slashdot.org/) on any given week for the latest Linux-versus-Windows rants. The truth of the matter is that an improperly configured or un-patched Linux system is just as insecure as an improperly configured or un-patched Windows system.

There is a definite difference, however, in the ways Windows and Linux systems are patched. Many Windows systems administrators know the pain of having to reboot their machine after each new Service Pack or Hotfix. This downtime means a bleary-eyed sysadmin has to perform this update during an after-hours "maintenance window" (usually in the wee hours of the morning or on a treasured kick-back-with-a-beer weekend). It also leaves you without your Snort system for several minutes (a computer eternity) while you shut the system down, wait for it to reboot, and make sure all services come back up unscathed. Now, with Microsoft taking the useful (if not always welcome) initiative of fixing security holes and releasing patches on a monthly basis, you're almost guaranteed the pleasure of rebooting at least once per month.

If you use Linux, unless there's a critical kernel patch (rare, but not unheard of), you never need to reboot after a patch. Hey, it *might* keep your weekends free for a few cold ones.

The penguin is worth more than its price

The final thing Linux has in its favor is its cost. It's free, just like Snort itself. Granted, you can purchase full-support distributions of Linux (such as Red Hat Advanced Server), but if you're willing to forgo commercial support, then plain old Red Hat Linux (or Fedora Linux, Red Hat's open-source, community-supported sister project) works perfectly well — as do various other Linux distributions. Large enterprises need multiple Snort sensors, which means multiple hardware and software deployments. In this case, using a free operating system can save you hundreds (or even thousands) of dollars — if you go about it right.

The pig jumps through Windows

The Snort IDS runs on Microsoft Windows 2000 Professional and Server, XP Professional, and 2003 Server. Because of the way Snort uses the network interface (it just listens and doesn't make connections), the Professional versions of 2000 and XP work fine (and save you hundreds of dollars in server-licensing costs).

Snort can run on Windows 95, 98, ME, NT, and XP Home — but we don't recommend it. These versions lack support for higher-end hardware, are less stable, and have poorer security than their newer counterparts. Plus, the Windows 95, 98, and NT versions have reached their end-of-life for both mainstream and extended support — if a security hole is found that affects those versions, you're out of luck if you want a Hotfix.

Using Windows as your Snort IDS platform is an advantage if Windows is the your organization's primary supported operating system. You already have the Windows gurus on staff, and have support agreements with Microsoft and other vendors in place. Your Snort IDS is supposed to give you peace of mind; a good comfort level with the operating system you're running it on contributes to that.

Another advantage to Windows is that easy-to-use Windows GUI. All Windows' system administration tasks — from partitioning hard drives to creating users — can be performed using point-and-click applications that are the same across Windows systems (though not always *exactly* the same across versions of Windows). Similar tasks under Linux either require command-line operations or GUI applications that vary depending on if you run the KDE desktop, Gnome desktop, or some other Linux desktop environment.

Which operating system is right for me?

If you're choosing on purely technical merit, we recommend that you run your Snort IDS on Linux. Linux systems are fast, typically have little downtime, and are very flexible and highly configurable. It's a reliable, Swiss-Army-knife OS with a whole slew of blade options — and you can remove the blades you don't need!

In the sometimes-Byzantine world of information technology, however, not all decisions are based on purely technical criteria. If you're more comfortable with Windows and you're not ready to jump into supporting a Linux system, then Windows is the most practical choice.

 If you choose to run your Snort IDS on Windows rather than on Linux, you're not at a *functional* disadvantage! Snort has the same features on both platforms, and we cover installing and configuring both. After all, this book isn't about Linux, and it's not about Windows: It's about Snort and other applications that help you use Snort to its fullest potential.

Sizing Up Your System

How big a computer system you need for your Snort IDS is the most difficult question to answer. It's never a one-size-fits-all situation. What you need for running Snort depends on some variables:

- ✔ The speed of your network (10 Mbps, 100 Mbps, 1000 Mbps, and so on). By and large, faster is better.

- ✔ The amount of data that passes through your network during its peak. The bigger the number, the faster the system you're likely to need.

- ✔ How long you want to keep your Snort logs and alerts. The longer you keep 'em, the more space you need to store 'em.

- ✔ What other services you want to run on the system (Web, PHP, MySQL, and so on). Services usually have an appetite for system resources.

- ✔ How much money you can spend on hardware, software, and associated support contracts. Shoestring budgets can really stunt system size.

  Yes, Snort itself is free, but you're not going to get through this without opening the wallet a little.

As you can see those variables can be quite . . . well, *variable* from network to network and organization to organization. That's why the Snort documentation and mailing lists are peppered with qualifying phrases about hardware requirements — "it depends," "more is better," and whatnot — even from Snort developers themselves. No cop-out, just practicality: It truly *does* depend on your particular needs, and more is definitely better — *if* you can get it. In the meantime, a few guidelines can help you choose the hardware that fits your current situation . . .

Keep the packets flowing

Snort's job is to listen to your TCP/IP network traffic and look for signatures in the data flow that might indicate a security threat to your network and your computer systems. It has to look at anywhere between 1 to 100 megabytes of traffic going across the network wire every second — which means that *anything* that slows down your computer system also thwarts Snort's ability to process the packets it sees.

If your hardware can't keep up with the flow of network data packets coming across your network interface, then Snort can't keep up. An overloaded system ends up dropping packets — and a packet dropped is a packet not analyzed for security threats — which means an attack might get in right under Snort's nose. Net effect: Your Snort IDS system might as well be completely down (for an elaboration on the perils of this situation, see the earlier sidebar "Why downtime is a big deal for a Snort IDS").

Looking at hardware options

To keep your Snort IDS from dropping network data packets, speed is the single most important factor. One approach is to unsnarl a number of hardware-related bottlenecks that can occur with a Snort IDS sensor. Choosing hardware that best fits your scenario helps to keep those bottlenecks to a minimum, and network data packets under control.

Processor requirements

Examining the traffic passing through your Snort sensor takes considerable processor (CPU) speed. Also, the more preprocessors (Snort modules that sort the packets before the Snort detection engine looks at them) you're running, the faster it needs to be.

Snort sensors that are looking at slow network speeds of 10 Mbps or less (such as a broadband or T1 connection) can get by with a budget CPU, such as a Celeron or Duron. Sensors that are looking at 100 Mbps networks need at least Pentium III or Athlon processors. A sensor watching a gigabit network needs at least a Pentium IV or Athlon XP. The next-generation 64-bit CPUs might also be worth looking at as operating systems, compilers, and applications are written to take advantage of these processors' capabilities. The two 64-bit CPUs on the market right now are Intel's Itanium and AMD's Opteron.

Adding an extra CPU can also help. Linux, Windows 2000 Professional and Server, Windows XP Professional, and Windows 2003 Server all have Symmetric Multi-Processing (SMP) capabilities, which means they can take advantage of systems having two or more CPUs. Snort can have a processor all to itself, and leaves the other chips for other applications. The newest Pentium IVs can also do something called Hyper-Threading, which makes a single processor behave like two processors to the OS. Windows XP, Windows 2003, and Linux Kernel 2.6 systems are especially good at taking advantage of Hyper-Threading. Hyper-Threading is a good way to get some of the advantages of a multi-processor system without the cost of adding an extra processor.

Also take into consideration what other applications you're running besides Snort. Running a Web server, MySQL database management system, PHP server-side scripting language, and the ACID Web-based reporting console for Snort adds some overhead — especially when you're running queries against the database to generate reports. This is a case where the dual-processor system helps. Barring that, beef up your system requirements to handle this extra load. For instance, where you may have been able to get by with a Celeron on a 10-Mbps network, the extra overhead from the additional software means you need at least a Pentium III.

Memory requirements

When we talk about memory requirements, we're talking about actual, physical RAM chips — not mere hard-drive storage. Although (at first glance) memory may not seem such a big deal for something input/output-intensive like Snort, where its job is to suck in the network traffic, analyze it, and then spit out alerts. In reality, however, the bulk of Snort's work is done in memory, where it buffers the network data while analyzing it. In short: The more (and faster) memory you have, the better.

Why is memory so important? Running out of RAM severely affects the performance of your Snort IDS and can cause it to drop network data packets. When a computer system runs out of physical RAM, it starts using storage space set aside on the hard drive that acts like virtual RAM. On Linux systems this is referred to as swap space (because it's swapping pages of memory between RAM and hard drive), and on Windows systems this is referred to as Virtual Memory (which you set via the System control-panel applet). Hard drive access is much slower than physical RAM access, so when a system starts "swapping" it slows down the entire computer, and Snort won't have a chance to pick up and analyze every network data packet that comes in.

For Linux systems, the minimum requirement for running a Snort IDS system is 128MB of RAM. If you're running Windows you're going to need more memory than a Linux system on an equivalent network to handle the over-head of the GUI. On a Windows system, start with no less than 256MB of RAM.

Fortunately, most new computers come with at least 128MB of RAM these days, and most new server-class systems come with at least 512MB of RAM. Memory prices fluctuate wildly over short periods of time, seemingly set in motion by the fluttering of butterfly wings in South America (as rational a take as any on the nature of commodity technology). The price can also vary depending on the speed of the RAM and demand for it (a new 512MB stick of RAM for an older computer might actually cost you more than a 512MB stick for a popular latest model).

Hard-drive storage and speed

Snort can require a lot of hard-drive space. A typical Linux installation requires 1 gigabyte of hard-drive space; a typical Windows installation requires 3 gigabytes of hard-drive space — and that's just for the operating system! Snort and MySQL requires another 60MB of hard drive space on top of that, just for the software itself.

What's going to chew up most of your disk space, however, is Snort's logs and alerts. The amount of hard drive space required is going to vary depend-ing on how much data you're keeping, how long you're keeping it, the amount of data coming into your network. A good place to start is 30GB of disk space for your database/logging partition, adding more as needed.

Another question is whether you should use IDE/ATA drives or SCSI drives. IDE/ATA drives are common on desktop computers, while SCSI drives are common on high-end servers. Gigabyte-to-gigabyte, IDE/ATA drives are much cheaper than SCSI drives. SCSI hard drive controller cards are also more expensive than IDE/ATA controllers (which these days are often simply built into motherboards).

The benefit of SCSI is in speed. You can get 10,000 and 15,000 revolutions per minute (RPMs) out of SCSI spindles, whereas IDE/ATA drives top out at 10,000 RPMs. The SCSI bus speed is also faster than IDE/ATA bus speed. In general, SCSI drives perform better than IDE/ATA drives in multi-drive and RAID sce-narios, whereas IDE/ATA drives perform better singly. A relatively new IDE/ATA standard called Serial ATA (SATA) closes some of this gap by offering 150MB/s transfer rates and hot-pluggable drives, while remaining software-compatible with the parallel IDE/ATA. SATA uses a new cabling standard, how-ever, so you need SATA-compatible controller cards and hard drives.

RAIDing your Snort IDS

RAID is an acronym for Redundant Array of Independent (or Inexpensive) Disks. It's a way to use several hard drives in conjunction (as an *array*) to increase performance or reliability. The industry defines eight RAID implementations (also called *RAID Levels*), labeled 0 through 7. We recommend the following when it comes to using RAID with your Snort IDS:

✔ Use a hardware-based RAID controller, such as an IDE or SCSI controller card that supports RAID. Although Windows and Linux can both support software-based RAID, the performance lost by saddling the OS with taking care of RAIDing isn't worth it on a Snort IDS sensor.

✔ Use RAID Level 0 when you want to maximize the amount of available hard-drive space. Level 0 writes data across several hard drives in stripes. This RAID level gives you the fastest performance out of your hard drives — but if one hard drive goes out, you lose all your data! Make sure you back up Level 0 implementations regularly.

✔ Use RAID Level 1 when you have two hard drives of the same size and want to mirror the data between them. That way, if one hard drive crashes, the other can be used as the primary hard drive until the first is replaced. RAID Level 1 does degrade performance somewhat on hard-drive writes, but hard-drive reads are faster than you get with many other RAID levels.

✔ Use RAID Level 5 when you need a high degree of fault tolerance and good performance. If one drive goes out, the system can keep running until it's replaced. One downside of RAID 5 is that it's slower in writing to the hard drive than are RAID Levels 0 and 1. Another downside is that one hard drive in your array is essentially unavailable to you for storage because of the amount of space needed to store the *parity information* that's used to rebuild a crashed hard drive. In other words, you lose $1/n$ of your overall storage space to parity information (where n is the number of hard drives in your RAID 5 array). For example, if you have three 120GB hard drives in your RAID 5 array, you really only have 240GB of storage space available. If you have eight 120GB hard drives, you only have 840GB of storage available.

RAID isn't a requirement for a Snort sensor, but it can help you increase the system's performance, or make sure it stays up.

If you can afford to spend the extra money for a system with SCSI hard drives, we recommend it. I/O is a big factor when it comes to your Snort IDS keeping up with the millions of packets flying by, and the SCSI speed gives you an advantage over an IDE system. Otherwise, try the new Serial ATA drives and controllers to get SCSI-comparable speeds at lower costs.

Network interface cards

It is best to have at least two *network interface cards* (NICs) in your Snort IDS sensor:

✔ One NIC for managing the system remotely (for example, using SSH or a remote desktop tool to get to the system)

✔ One or more NICs for network packet sniffing (which is Snort's job, after all)

The benefit of having two NICs is twofold:

✔ You can keep your management and sniffing tasks on separate NICs, so one task doesn't interfere with the other.

✔ You can put the management NIC on a *trusted* (secured, usually private) network and the sniffing NIC on an *untrusted* (unsecured, usually public) network. For instance, you can have the management NIC on a trusted internal network behind your firewall, and put the sniffing NIC outside your firewall (in what amounts to a hostile environment). The sniffing NIC isn't given its own IP address (it doesn't need one for sniffing), so it's safe from most network-based attacks.

A too-puny or otherwise mismatched NIC is an invitation to disaster. Use NICs on your Snort IDS sensor that fit the speed of your network. For instance, if you're running a 10-Mbps Ethernet network, use a 10-Mbps or 10/100-Mbps Ethernet NIC. If you're running a 100-Mbps Ethernet network, get a 100-Mbps Ethernet NIC. Lucky enough to have a *gigabit* Ethernet network? Then (you guessed it) use a gigabit Ethernet NIC. Not only does matching the NIC card speed to your network speed make good sense from the standpoint of ensuring Snort can snort enough data, but it might help you avoid speed auto-sensing troubles.

If you're in a high-performance network environment (especially a gigabit network or a 100-Mbps network that is highly utilized), we recommend using a server-class NIC instead of a desktop-class NIC. Server-class NICs can cost twice as much as desktop-class cards — but if the cash is available and your situation warrants the expense, they're worth considering. Server-class NICs are designed for high-performance applications that require a lot of network traffic, such as Snort. In addition, they include such features as encryption offloading and SNMP management — and those come in handy for managing your Snort IDS.

Giving Snort the fastest snoot

In some cases, you may want your Snort sensor to have a *faster* NIC than you typically run on your network. For example, say you have a switch that has mostly 100-Mbps Ethernet ports, but also a couple of gigabit Ethernet ports. Even if you're primarily using the 100-Mbps ports for your systems, connecting your Snort IDS sensor to a gigabit port gives Snort a bigger straw to suck on while sniffing the network.

Chapter 4

Makin' Bacon: Installing Snort for Linux

....

In This Chapter

▶ Starting with a secure system

▶ Installing and configuring Snort

▶ Installing and configuring MySQL for Snort

....

*W*hen you first see the list of prerequisite software, installing Snort for Linux may seem like a daunting prospect, especially if you're new to Linux and its eccentricities. But don't panic! In this chapter, we walk you through setting up Snort itself, and the MySQL database to hold your logs and alerts, all while keeping the geek-speak to a minimum (where possible).

If you're already an accomplished Linux admin, this chapter not only serves as a no-nonsense guide to installing Snort, but points out several Linux-admin tips and tricks along the way, so read on!

Staying Safe

If you're going through the trouble of installing an Intrusion Detection System, you're obviously concerned about network security. Naturally, you want to make sure that your freshly minted Snort box is adding to the overall security of your network, not detracting from it. How embarrassing would it be for your IDS itself to be cracked in to? Or used as a mail relay to spew spam? Or for your Snort logs to be available for all the world to see over the Internet? Don't laugh, it could happen. But not to you, because you know better, right? Good. If not, don't worry: We help you get there.

Starting with a clean slate

If at all possible, you want to install Snort on a dedicated system with a fresh installation of your favorite Linux distribution. Most software ages about as well as cheese; some about as well as fish. The older your initial Linux install is, the more likely there are going to be software bugs, security vulnerabilities, or leftover garbage that's just going to clutter things up. So make sure you know what you're getting yourself into, and start with a fresh Linux installation.

Once you've got Linux installed and running, it's time to lock it down. Linux is well-known as a secure and stable operating system, but it's just as easy to run an insecure Linux server as it is to run an insecure Windows server. Most modern Linux distributions come with almost everything you could possibly need to run a server or workstation. But when it comes to running a secure Snort server, these optional extras are unnecessary, and can open your server up to attacks if left untended.

Keeping a low profile

The more network services you leave running on your server, the easier time an attacker is going to have cracking in. If all you want to do is monitor network traffic, and later report on it, you don't need to run network services like a DNS server, or mail server, and you certainly don't want to be running a file server. But how do you find out what network services are running and what aren't?

Throughout the book (and this chapter especially), you'll see the pound sign (#) and the dollar sign ($) at the beginning of a Linux command. These are basic command-line prompts, much like the C:\> prompt that Windows command-line users are accustomed to seeing. The difference here is that the dollar-sign prompt indicates that you are logged in as a regular user, while the pound-sign prompt means that you are the all powerful root user. When you see that pound-sign prompt, feel the power — but use it carefully.

To check the network status of your system, run the command netstat (Network Status, Net-Stat, clever, eh?). If you're logged in as root (and if you're going to be mucking around with network services, you'd better be) you can run netstat as follows to see what ports are open on your system, and what program has them open:

```
netstat -anp
```

-a shows all network connections

-n lists addresses as IP addresses, not host and domain names

-p lists the program that's using the network

If you just ran that command, you'll notice you got ample output. To read it before it screams off the top of your terminal, pipe the netstat command to more.

```
netstat -anp | more
```

This is a little more manageable. See the following sample output. You're really concerned with the services that are listed as LISTENING. These are network services, ready to be used and abused by anyone on the Internet, and after a default Linux install, all kinds of services are running that you don't want or need.

```
# netstat -anp
Active Internet connections (servers and established)
Proto Recv-Q Send-Q Local Address      Foreign Address     State       PID/Program name
tcp     0      0     0.0.0.0:32768      0.0.0.0:*           LISTEN      1560/
tcp     0      0     127.0.0.1:32769 0.0.0.0:*              LISTEN      1682/xinetd
tcp     0      0     0.0.0.0:111        0.0.0.0:*           LISTEN      1541/
tcp     0      0     0.0.0.0:22         0.0.0.0:*           LISTEN      1668/sshd
tcp     0      0     127.0.0.1:631      0.0.0.0:*           LISTEN      1741/cupsd
tcp     0      0     127.0.0.1:25       0.0.0.0:*           LISTEN      1702/
tcp     0     240    192.168.2.29:22 192.168.2.27:33093 ESTABLISHED 1908/sshd
udp     0      0     0.0.0.0:32768      0.0.0.0:*                       1560/
udp     0      0     0.0.0.0:111        0.0.0.0:*                       1541/
udp     0      0     0.0.0.0:631        0.0.0.0:*                       1741/cupsd
udp     0      0     0.0.0.0:888        0.0.0.0:*                       1560/
Active UNIX domain sockets (servers and established)
Proto RefCnt Flags     Type     State      I-Node PID/Program name  Path
unix  2      [ ACC ]   STREAM   LISTENING  2069   1721/gpm          /dev/gpmctl
unix  9      [ ]       DGRAM               1685   1519/syslogd      /dev/log
unix  2      [ ]       DGRAM               2178   1782/anacron
unix  2      [ ]       DGRAM               2087   1730/crond
unix  2      [ ]       DGRAM               2052   1711/
unix  2      [ ]       DGRAM               2038   1702/
unix  2      [ ]       DGRAM               1980   1682/xinetd
unix  2      [ ]       DGRAM               1746   1560/
unix  2      [ ]       DGRAM               1693   1523/klogd
```

The last column shows the PID (process ID) and program name that's using that particular network resource. To stop the process right away, run kill -TERM 999 where 999 is the particular PID you want to stop. If kill -TERM won't stop it, kill -9 will. (For more options, see the man page for kill.)

That's great for stopping the service immediately, but chances are, it'll start back up the next time the server is rebooted. Of course you're thinking, *But this is a Linux box! I'll never have to reboot it!* Accidents happen, hardware fails, power lines snap, coffee is spilled. Be prepared.

To keep these services from starting up again, you have two choices: Remove or modify the initialization script that starts the service, or remove the entire software package.

To toy with the initialization scripts, look in the /etc/init.d/ directory. Each file in this directory is a script that stops, starts, or restarts a corresponding network service. The following output gives an example of some standard initializations scripts on a RedHat Linux system. What you see on your Linux system may be slightly different depending on your distribution and what software packages you chose at install-time.

```
# ls /etc/init.d/
anacron*    functions*   kdcrotate*   network*   random*      rwhod*      xfs*
apmd*       gpm*         keytable*    nfs*       rawdevices*  sendmail*   xinetd*
arpwatch*   halt*        killall*     nfslock*   rhnsd*       single*     ypbind*
atd*        identd*      kudzu*       nscd*      rstatd*      snmpd*      yppasswdd*
autofs*     ipchains*    lpd*         portmap*   rusersd*     sshd*       ypserv*
crond*      iptables*    netfs*       pppoe*     rwalld*      syslog*
```

The cheap-and-dirty way to stop these services from starting up is to make a new directory, and move the unwanted script to the new directory. This is like making mashed potatoes with a sledgehammer: effective but messy. The next time your server restarts, it will complain loudly about not being able to find the corresponding initialization script. Although, since it can't find the script, the service will not start.

A more elegant method exists, but is usually different depending on which distribution of Linux you're running.

Disabling services in Red Hat Linux

On Red Hat Linux, and most other distributions that are RPM-based (such as SuSE and Mandrake), you can use the chkconfig command to modify when these scripts are kicked off.

For example, to disable sendmail on your server, follow these steps:

1. Check to see when sendmail is called on to start and stop:

```
[root@redhatbox init.d]# chkconfig --list sendmail
sendmail        0:off   1:off   2:on    3:on    4:on    5:on    6:off
```

The numbers listed are run levels; you're really only concerned with the default run level (which is what's running right now, unless you did something non-default when you booted the system).

2. Check to see what run level you're in, using the runlevel command:

```
[root@redhatbox init.d]# runlevel
N 3
```

Hey, who says Linux isn't intuitive? Looks like we're in run level 3 (the default for Red Hat, unless you're running a GUI), and sendmail is set to run by default. Aha!

3. **Disable** `sendmail` **for run levels 2, 3, 4 and 5:**

```
[root@redhatbox init.d]# chkconfig --level 2345 sendmail off
```

4. **Check to make sure your command actually worked:**

```
[root@redhatbox init.d]# chkconfig --list sendmail
sendmail        0:off   1:off   2:off   3:off   4:off   5:off   6:off
```

Success!

This process is a little less severe than removing the software package entirely, and `sendmail` is a good thing to keep around, especially if you want to actually *send mail* someday.

Disabling services in Debian GNU/Linux

Debian Linux uses a different command, but it follows a similar idea. The command is `update-rc.d`, and it gives you two general options:

✔ You can tinker with the command syntax, and remove the service from specific run levels.

✔ To be sure you get the job done right, you can remove the service from *every* run level, and here (again) you have two options:

   • The usual way to do so is to remove the `init` script from the `/etc/init.d/` directory, and then let `update-rc.d` do the rest.

   • If you want to terminate the service gracefully, shut it down using the `init` script first, and then remove the `init` script.

In this section, as a classic example, we prevent `sendmail` from starting on our Debian system. The steps look like this:

1. **Verify that the** `sendmail` **initialization script exists.**

   To do so, change to the `/etc/init.d` directory and have a look at what's listed there.

2. **Create a directory to hold the initialization scripts you plan to remove:**

```
# cd /etc/init.d
# ls sendmail
sendmail
# mkdir removed_init_scripts
```

3. **Stop any running instances of** `sendmail`:

```
# ./sendmail stop
Stopping Mail Transport Agent: sendmail.
```

4. **Move the** `sendmail` **initialization script to the** `removed_init_scripts` **directory.**

```
# mv sendmail removed_init_scripts/
```

5. **After the initialization script is removed, run** `update-rc.d` **like this:**

```
# update-rc.d sendmail remove
 Removing any system startup links for /etc/init.d/sendmail ...
   /etc/rc0.d/K20sendmail
   /etc/rc1.d/K20sendmail
   /etc/rc2.d/S20sendmail
   /etc/rc3.d/S20sendmail
   /etc/rc4.d/S20sendmail
   /etc/rc5.d/S20sendmail
   /etc/rc6.d/K20sendmail
```

Voilà! No more `sendmail`.

Disabling services in Gentoo Linux

Gentoo Linux (more formally known as Linux, The Next Generation) also has a script to ease the pain of manually enabling and disabling network services. Look at `/sbin/rc-update`.

The following syntax removes the service (replace `default` with the run level your system booted into):

```
/sbin/rc-update -d yourservice default
```

Here's what it looks like in action:

```
# cd /etc/init.d
# ls sendmail
sendmail
# rc-update -d sendmail default
 * sendmail removed from the following run levels: default
 * Caching service dependencies...                    [ ok ]
 * rc-update complete.
```

Now that you know how to disable network services and other daemons, repeat the process for each network service that's listening for connections until you have nothing but SSH left. To confirm, run `netstat -anp` again. Only `sshd` should be left listening.

Compile from source code or install a binary?

Throughout this book, we'll come across extra software that has to be installed to make your Snort box everything it wants to be. Since Snort is an open-source software project, its dependencies and prerequisite software pieces are also open-source. One blessing of this situation is that when you download the software, you're getting a copy of the human-readable source code: the stuff that some caffeinated *coder* (a hip term for a computer-programmer geek) diligently banged out on the keyboard using a text editor. This is wonderful for coders, but bad for machines (which prefer to read their instructions in the binary language of zeros and ones). To placate those gimme-binary-only machines, you run your code through a *compiler,* a piece of software that turns the human-readable stuff into instructions that are specific to *your machine.* This is a kind of tailor-fit; the resulting machine code (often just called *binary code*) is optimized for your particular system. Sound good? It is.

Popping in the binary

But what about pre-compiled binaries? You may find the software we discuss available as .rpm files, .deb files, or .pkg files. These are *pre-compiled binary* packages: a package of files where the source-code has already been compiled for a particular architecture (i386, IA64, Sparc, whatever) and packaged with the necessary configuration files, man pages, and directions on where to put all of this stuff. You simply tell your system to install the package, and it moves the files around accordingly. Most of the time, your package-management software also checks for software dependencies and warns you accordingly, sometimes even downloading and installing the prerequisites for you. Sound cushy? It is, but that convenience can cost you. We favor compiling from source code instead. Read on . . .

Using the source

For the purposes of this book, we'll be telling you to download the source code and compile it yourself. Why? Well, let us count the ways . . .

- ✔ **Universal application.** Compiling from source code is the same across all Linux distributions; a single set of instructions can guide you.

- ✔ **Open-source software is updated regularly.** Getting the latest version can greatly enhance your peace of mind.

- ✔ **Each update is released as source code, not as a pre-compiled binary.** Usually it's up to someone who works for a company that markets a Linux-based product — or otherwise supports some distribution of Linux — to compile the source code to fit a specific architecture. This extra step alone often ensures that pre-compiled binary packages are a bit behind the freshly released source code — a few days at best, or several major revisions at worst. In one case, the binary package for Snort itself is so out of date that even installing it becomes a security risk. (We won't mention which distribution by name, but you apt-get users know who you are.)

✔ **Compiling it yourself tailors the code to your system.** Do yourself a favor — *use the source, Luke!* You'll get the latest version of the software, compiled *for your machine and your processor,* not some faceless beige box.

✔ **Everybody needs a hobby, right?** (Insert innocent grin here.) If you get involved in the software deeply enough, you'll love having the source code available to dig through (or possibly even modify).

If you're not familiar with compiling software from source, just take a deep breath and take it slow. The directions we include will get you there, and all the software we list comes with ample documentation should you find yourself lost in the woods.

Securing the SSH Daemon

A *daemon* (pronounced either as *day*-mon or *dee*-mon) is just another name for a program that usually starts automatically, and runs constantly in the background.

Okay, assume you've turned off all extraneous network services and kept 'em off. There's one remaining service to look at: the SSH daemon. Unless you like sitting at a terminal in front of your Snort box every time you need to check on it, leave the SSH daemon running so you can access your Snort system remotely.

OpenSSH is the *de facto* standard in modern Linux distributions because it's open-source and free. SSH stands for *Secure SH*ell, but how secure is it? If you're running an older version of SSH, chances are good that your system is a far cry from being secure. To see just how secure or insecure your version is, check out http://www.openssh.org/security.html for a brief history of security vulnerabilities in OpenSSH. We recommend starting with the latest (therefore most secure) version.

If you're running the SSH daemon that shipped with your Linux distribution, you're probably running its precompiled SSH binary package. Not a problem — exactly — except some Linux vendors (most notably Red Hat) release patched versions of their software without changing the revision number for that software package. For example, if you're running kewlserver-3.14 and a security vulnerability is discovered, the maintainers of kewlserver normally release a software patch, and then re-release the patched software as kewlserver-3.15. Your Linux vendor may only fix the security vulnerability and not the revision number. Thus, if you install the updated .rpm (or .deb or .pkg) package, your kewlserver may no longer have a security vulnerability — but it may still report itself as kewlserver-3.14.

The moral of this story is that if you're running software from a package, check with the maintainer of that package to make sure it's a secure version of the software.

To upgrade your version of OpenSSH, either

- ✔ Check for updated packages for your particular Linux distribution.
- ✔ Grab the latest source code and start compiling.

PGP and hashing: accept no substitutes

When you download source code from the Internet, how can you be sure that what you're downloading is exactly what the author wrote? How can you be sure that someone hasn't tampered with the code? Even if you're download-ing the source code from some crew of self-proclaimed security gurus, how do you know someone else hasn't already cracked their server and replaced the original code with something far more nefarious? The answer is to check the software for either a PGP signature or an MD5 hash.

PGP signature

To guarantee a file's integrity, the software author uses his or her own PGP (Pretty Good Privacy) encryption key to "sign" the software. This process creates a string of characters indicating that the author — and only the author — declares that the software has not been tampered with.

GnuPG is a free, open-source program that uses the OpenPGP standards and comes with most Linux distributions (if you don't have it, you can get it at http://www.gnupg.org/). If you're not up to speed on public-key encryp-tion, check out the International PGP home page at http://www.pgpi.org, where you'll find oodles of documentation and FAQs. The following demon-stration uses the GnuPG command gpgv for signature verification.

Chances are, you don't already have the software author's public key on your PGP keyring, so the following session also shows how to grab it and use it.

Traditional encryption systems relied on a single secret key to encrypt and decrypt data. This worked well, but it meant that both the sending and receiving parties had to know the secret key. Public key encryption uses two different keys that are mathematically related to each other; one is a secret key available only to its owner, and the other is a *public key* available to (you guessed it) the public at large. This encryption scheme means you can send an encrypted message to someone you've never met before, using his or her public key, and you can be sure that person is the only one who can decrypt it (since that person is the only one who has access to that private key).

```
$ wget -q
          ftp://ftp.openbsd.org/pub/OpenBSD/OpenSSH/portable
          /openssh-3.7.1p2.tar.gz
$ wget -q
          ftp://ftp.openbsd.org/pub/OpenBSD/OpenSSH/portable
          /openssh-3.7.1p2.tar.gz.sig
$ gpgv openssh-3.7.1p2.tar.gz.sig
gpgv: /home/snortfd/.gnupg/trustedkeys.gpg: keyring created
gpgv: Signature made Tue Sep 23 04:56:21 2003 CDT using DSA
          key ID 86FF9C48
gpgv: Can't check signature: public key not found
$ gpg --keyserver pgp.mit.edu --recv-keys 86FF9C48
gpg: /home/snortfd/.gnupg/secring.gpg: keyring created
gpg: /home/snortfd/.gnupg/pubring.gpg: keyring created
gpg: requesting key 86FF9C48 from pgp.mit.edu ...
gpg: key 86FF9C48: public key imported
gpg: /home/snortfd/.gnupg/trustdb.gpg: trustdb created
gpg: Total number processed: 1
gpg:                    imported: 1
$ gpgv openssh-3.7.1p2.tar.gz.sig
gpgv: Signature made Tue Sep 23 04:56:21 2003 CDT using DSA
          key ID 86FF9C48
gpgv: Can't check signature: public key not found
$ gpgv --keyring ~/.gnupg/pubring.gpg openssh-
          3.7.1p2.tar.gz.sig
gpgv: Signature made Tue Sep 23 04:56:21 2003 CDT using DSA
          key ID 86FF9C48
gpgv: Good signature from "Damien Miller (Personal Key)
          <djm@mindrot.org>"
```

MD5 hash

An MD5 hash is a type of encryption code generated when the encryption
software examines a file and uses a mathematical "hashing" process to generate a single line of text *based on the entire contents of the software file*. If you
change a single character in the file, the MD5 hash code is no longer the
same.

The following transcript shows the author downloading the latest version of
Apache for Linux and checking its MD5 sum.

```
$ wget -q http://apache.webmeta.com/httpd/httpd-2.0.48.tar.gz
$ wget -q http://apache.webmeta.com/httpd/httpd-
          2.0.48.tar.gz.md5
$ cat httpd-2.0.48.tar.gz.md5
466c63bb71b710d20a5c353df8c1a19c  httpd-2.0.48.tar.gz
$ md5sum httpd-2.0.48.tar.gz
466c63bb71b710d20a5c353df8c1a19c  httpd-2.0.48.tar.gz
```

As you can see in the transcript, the MD5 sum that was published by Apache
jives with the output from our own md5sum command, so we know that the
software we just downloaded hasn't been tampered with.

Compiling the code

The instructions for compiling software are generic and should work across the majority of Linux distributions without modifications. If you suspect that your installation is significantly different from a generic installation, or if you're curious to see what kind of options are available, you can run `./configure --help` (which makes the `configure` script list all options) at compile time.

OpenSSH depends on OpenSSL, which is available at `http://www.openssl.org/`. OpenSSL has had its share of security vulnerabilities as well, so make sure you run the most recent version.

Here's the royal road to compiling and installing OpenSSL and OpenSSH:

1. **Download the source code from** `http://www.openssl.org/` **and put it somewhere convenient on your system.**

A good place for source code is in `/usr/local/src/`. A good place to put downloaded software as a compressed *tarball* (Unix slang for a bunch of files stuck together in file with a `.tar`, `.tar.Z`, `tar.gz`, or `.tgz` extension) would be a directory such as `/usr/local/src/tarballs/`. You can delete the tarball and the source directory later. If (like us) you like working with a bit of a safety net, keep the tarball and source around until you're sure you don't need 'em anymore (say, after the next version is released).

Downloading, compiling, and installing `openssl` looks like this:

```
# cd /usr/local/src/tarballs/
# wget http://www.openssl.org/source/openssl-0.9.7c.tar.gz
# wget http://www.openssl.org/source/openssl-0.9.7c.tar.gz.asc
# gpgv openssl-0.9.7c.tar.gz.asc
gpgv: Signature made Wed Mar 17 06:09:54 2004 CST using RSA key ID 49A563D9
gpgv: Can't check signature: public key not found
# gpg --keyserver pgp.mit.edu --recv-keys 49a563d9
gpg: requesting key 49A563D9 from pgp.mit.edu ...
gpg: key 49A563D9: public key imported
gpg: Total number processed: 1
gpg:               imported: 1  (RSA: 1)
# gpgv --keyring ~/.gnupg/pubring.gpg openssl-0.9.7d.tar.gz.asc
gpgv: Signature made Wed Mar 17 06:09:54 2004 CST using RSA key ID 49A563D9
gpgv: Good signature from "Mark Cox <mjc@redhat.com>"
gpgv:               aka "Mark Cox <mjc@apache.org>"
# cd ../
# tar -xvzf tarballs/openssl-0.9.7c.tar.gz
# cd openssl-0.9.7c/
# script ~/openssl.install.notes
# ./config shared
# make
```

```
# make test
# make install
# echo "/usr/local/ssl/lib" >>/etc/ld.so.conf
# ldconfig
# exit
```

OpenSSL installs without a hitch (well, we can hope, right?). And every good OpenSSL needs an OpenSSH, so . . .

2. **As a preparation for installing OpenSSH, set up the** `script` **command to keep a log of what's going on.**

See the "Let your script do the watching . . ." sidebar in this chapter for details.

The code that tells `script` what to watch for looks like this:

```
# cd /usr/local/src/tarballs/
# wget ftp://ftp.openbsd.org/pub/OpenBSD/OpenSSH/portable/openssh-
        3.7.1p2.tar
# cd ../
# tar -xvzf tarballs/openssh-3.7.1p2.tar.gz
# cd openssh-3.7.1p2/
# script ~/openssh.install.notes
# ./configure --with-pam
# make
# make install
# exit
```

If your Linux distribution uses Pluggable Authentication Modules (PAM) (most, including RedHat), you'll want to read the documentation distributed with the OpenSSH software and run `configure` with the `--enable-pam` switch. Otherwise you'll quickly find yourself locked out of your own box!

Let your script do the watching . . .

The Unix command `script` watches all visible input/output through the terminal and logs it to a text file somewhere. If you're on a fast enough system, you're going to have a hard time keeping up with the text as it flashes skyward on your terminal. The `script` command is invaluable when looking for configure warnings or other errors that may not kill the configure script, but will cause headaches down the road. The syntax is `script somefile` where *somefile* is the file to capture the terminal session; `script -a somefile` will append to your log file, instead of overwriting it. To exit a `script` session, just type `exit` when you're done, and the program stops logging your terminal session.

Bringing OpenSSH into port

Although unorthodox settings may head off a little unauthorized fumbling by users, any network-security geeks worth their weight in bits will tell you: Security-through-obscurity isn't a recommended strategy. Even so, sometimes a "creative" departure from the default has its place. For example, why bother running the latest version of SSH on the default port (22)? Why let every one in the world bang on your SSH server when you'll only be allowing a small handful of people (maybe only yourself) access to the machine? Here's a chance to do yourself another favor, and run the SSH daemon on a non-standard port. Pick a port that's not already in use, and one you can remember. You have 65535 ports to choose from, so choose wisely.

If you're changing the default port that the SSH daemon listens to, you can make another couple of changes while you're at it. Specifically, you want to allow *only* SSH traffic that uses SSH protocol version 2, since it is more secure than version 1. This can cause problems with some older SSH clients though, since some only support version 1 of the protocol. Check your client before making this change. Also, it's a good practice to deny root logins that use SSH, and not to allow folks to connect using empty passwords.

3. **To ensure that the SSH daemon starts when your machine does, make sure you have an initialization (`init`) script in** `/etc/init.d/`.

    The initialization script that was there originally may not work anymore, especially if the version of SSH that came with your system lives at `/usr/sbin/sshd` and the one you just installed lives in `/usr/local/sbin/sshd`. Various handy, fresh `init` scripts are distributed with OpenSSH; you can find them in subdirectories of the `$openssh_source/contrib/` directory.

4. **Choose a port for the SSH daemon.**

    Yes, you can choose the default port (22), but check out the "Bringing OpenSSH into port" sidebar in this chapter for an alternative — a little cyber-hot-rodding that makes good practical sense.

5. **Specify a port for the SSH daemon by editing the appropriate lines in your** `sshd config` **file.**

    Most likely your configuration file is `/etc/ssh/sshd_config` if you're using the version that came with your Linux distribution. It should be `/usr/local/etc/sshd_config` if you compiled from source using the default values. Those default values have pound signs (#) in front of them to indicate that what follows is a comment, and is safe to ignore. If you don't want to use the default values, make sure you change them, and remove the pound sign. When you're done, the following lines (not necessarily in this order) in your `sshd_config` file should look like this:

```
Port 65432
Protocol 2
PermitEmptyPasswords no
PermitRootLogin no
```

That's it. You've got OpenSSL and OpenSSH installed and ready to rock.

Physical security

When your system is secure from a cyber-world perspective, it's time to make sure it's secure from a real-world perspective.

The principal component of physical security is restricting physical access to the system. If you've already got a server-closet/systems-room/data-center environment for your servers, chances are you only allow certain folks in there. That's great, but it's just a start. Try to stay practical if you impose any additional physical-security measures. Start (maybe stop?) with the obvious:

✔ Restrict access to the power switch.

✔ Restrict access to specific CD-ROM or floppy drives by using a server case that has a locking faceplate. Keep the key in a safe place.

Some other suggestions you may hear — such as using a BIOS password are overkill. Remember, you want the system to restart *without intervention* in case of a power outage. If you're super-paranoid about physical access, check out the man page for your LILO or Grub, depending on which you're using. Additional lock-down methods are available.

One of the most effective security measures for physically securing your server is also one of the easiest: Unplug the keyboard. It sounds trivial, but it's vital, especially if your server is on a switch box, sharing keyboard, video, and mouse (KVM) with other systems. We have had Linux servers spontaneously rebooted by slap-happy Windows administrators giving a three-finger salute (simultaneously pressing the Ctrl+Alt+Del keys) to every blank screen on a KVM switch when looking to log on to their Windows server. While Ctrl+Alt+Del will give you a login prompt in Windows, unless you've changed this default behavior, it will reboot a Linux box.

Loose ends

When you have a secure system, take a minute and look things over. Reboot your system to make sure everything starts up as expected. Is sshd running? What port is it running on? Anything else running? Use netstat -anp to make sure. Is root allowed to log in using SSH?

If everything looks good to you, take a breather. You're ready to install Snort and MySQL, and you'll need your wits about you for this one.

Installing MySQL for Linux

MySQL touts itself as the world's most popular open-source database, and with good reason. With more than 4 million active installations, many of the world's largest organizations — including Yahoo!, The Associated Press, and even those rocket scientists at NASA — are running MySQL. And you can too, if you aren't already.

Getting the code

This is one place where we deviate from our "Use the Source" mantra, and say it's okay to use MySQL from pre-compiled binaries. In fact, the MySQL Web site recommends it.

Installing MySQL goodies from the Linux package

Since practically every version of Linux includes MySQL, you probably already have it installed. If so, you've got a few matters to look at:

- **Make sure you have both the client and server pieces installed.** If you do, you can skip ahead to the Installing Snort section. If not, ask yourself whether you want to

    - Compile from source

    - Install binaries from MySQL.org

    - Install a binary package from your Linux distribution

- **If you install precompiled binary packages from your Linux distribution, make sure you get all the included MySQL packages.** Typically, there are separate packages for

    - The client

    - The server

    - Documentation

    - A collection of "common files" needed by both client and server

- **If you're not sure about what you need, or you're having a hard time figuring it out, try compiling from source code.** (You *knew* we were going to say that.) There's not too much hassle involved, but be prepared to give your compiler some time to work. This is a complex software package, and you may have time to catch a cup of coffee before the whole installation is finished. While we're on the subject . . .

Installing MySQL from source code

MySQL is available from `http://www.mysql.com/downloads/index.html`. Make sure you check its note regarding licensing costs. MySQL is covered under the GPL (GNU Public License, available in the back of this book), and unless you want support, a warranty, or you have plans to distribute MySQL code as part of your non-open-source software, you don't need a commercial license.

There are two ways you can download MySQL:

- ✔ **As actual source code:** You can compile it for your system.
- ✔ **As a glob of binary files:** These have already been compiled for your system by the fine folks at MySQL. This is different than the binary package put out by your Linux vendor, in that these binaries are not specific to a certain distribution of Linux, but are released for a specific architecture, (such as i386 or IA64).

True to form, we detail (next) how to install using the source code. That's because it should be the same regardless of which version of Linux you use.

Preparing your system for MySQL

Before installing the software on your system, save yourself some hassle: Get it ready for a MySQL installation. First item of business is to check your system to see whether it already has a MySQL user account and group in place. Here's what the process looks like:

1. **Check for a MySQL user account by issuing this command:**

   ```
   cat /etc/passwd | grep -i mysql
   ```

   If the command doesn't produce any output, then you don't have a MySQL user account.

2. **Look for a MySQL group in the** `/etc/group` **file (you need one there too), using this command:**

   ```
   cat /etc/group | grep -i mysql
   ```

   If you do get output from this command (or the one in Step 1), chances are you already have MySQL installed on your system. Here's what the output looks like on a system that already has MySQL installed:

   ```
   # cat /etc/passwd | grep -i mysql
   mysql:x:27:27:MySQL Server:/var/lib/mysql:/bin/bash
   ```

3. **Make sure that the** `root` **user account can execute MySQL commands.**

   To do so, check the `root` account's `$PATH` variable to see whether the MySQL executable path (`/usr/local/mysql/bin`) is in there. If it's not there, edit `/root/.bash_profile` (sometimes installed as `/root/.profile`) to put `/usr/local/mysql/bin` into the `PATH` statement for `root`. For example, here's what `/root/.profile` looked like on our system before editing:

   ```
   # ~/.profile: executed by Bourne-compatible login shells.

   if [ -f ~/.bashrc ]; then
     . ~/.bashrc
   fi


   PATH=/usr/local/sbin:/usr/local/bin:/usr/sbin:/usr/bin:/sbin:/bin:/usr/bin/
             X11
   export PATH

   mesg n
   ```

   Here is the same file after editing:

   ```
   # ~/.profile: executed by Bourne-compatible login shells.
   if [ -f ~/.bashrc ]; then
     . ~/.bashrc
   fi
   PATH=/usr/local/sbin:/usr/local/bin:/usr/sbin:/usr/bin:/sbin:/bin:/usr/bin/
             X11:/usr/local/mysql/bin
   export PATH
   mesg n
   ```

   When your `root` user account's `~.profile` resembles this one, its MySQL executable path is in place. To take advantage of this change, you'll either have to log out and then log back in, or type

   ```
   # source ~/.profile
   ```

   The profile is only read at login, so this step forces your system to re-read your profile and apply any changes you may have made.

4. **Make sure your files and permissions are set up correctly to accommodate MySQL.**

   With the MySQL executable path in place and your permissions set correctly, you're ready to compile MySQL.

Compiling and installing MySQL

Compiling the MySQL from source code (rather than installing binaries) requires a little attention to detail. For example, make sure you grabbed the right software package before you install what's in there (remember there are different packages for the client, server, common files, and documentation). The command `tar -tvzf mysql-package.tar.gz` is a handy way to check, since it will tell you what files are in a tarball without actually extracting them. Assuming you downloaded the right tarball to `/usr/local/src/tarballs/`, you're ready to proceed with the installation.

Doing the installation and configuration

Here's the drill for installing MySQL:

1. **Change to the directory from which you want to unpack your MySQL source code:**

   ```
   # cd /usr/local/src
   ```

2. **Check the MD5 sum or PGP signature on your downloaded source code and compare it to the signature on the** `mysql.com` **Web site at**

   ```
   # md5sum mysql.tar.gz
   ```

3. **Using the** `tar` **command, un-gzip and un-tar the source code:**

   ```
   # tar -xvzf /usr/local/src/tarballs/mysql.tar.gz
   ```

4. **Change to the** `mysql` **directory that was created in your source directory.**

5. **Run the** `configure` **program like this:**

   ```
   # cd mysql/
   # ./configure --prefix=/usr/local/mysql
   ```

   The `--prefix` flag identifies the directory where you want to install MySQL (we recommend `/usr/local/mysql`). Don't worry if this directory doesn't yet exist; the installation creates it.

6. **Build and install MySQL with the** `make` **and** `make install` **commands:**

   ```
   # make
   # make install
   ```

   You're ready to tell your Linux system how to find the MySQL shared libraries (which Snort needs to access).

7. **Run the** `echo` **and** `ldconfig` **commands as follows:**

   ```
   # echo "/usr/local/mysql/lib/mysql" >>/etc/ld.so.conf
   # cat /etc/ld.so.conf
   # ldconfig
   ```

   Here `echo` adds a line to your library configuration file, `ld.so.conf`. The `ldconfig` command reloads that configuration file. Some distributions (notably Gentoo) automatically generate this file; check your distribution's documentation if you're unsure.

Not just any old password for root

If the root password is cracked, it's like giving anyone the keys to the city *and* the treasure vault. When you set a password, make it tough to crack but possible for you to remember. Avoid writing it down; if you absolutely must write it down, put it somewhere seriously secure. You never know when you'll need it again, and it's not easy to reset the root password if you've forgotten it, so make it stick. In our example, we use new password, but only (need we say it?) a "dummy" would use that as an actual password. Make yours something obscure to anyone but you. Using a combination of letters, numbers, and punctuation can help make it more secure, as does avoiding dictionary words, phone numbers, names, and dates.

8. **Run the** script **command as follows:**

```
# scripts/mysql_install_db
```

This command sets up the initial mysql database that MySQL uses for its internal configuration.

9. **Run the** mysqladmin **program to set a** root **password for your MySQL server.**

You don't want to leave your databases wide open for anyone to administer! Behold and heed our admonitory sidebar — and for maximum safety, run the mysqladmin program as shown here:

```
# /usr/local/mysql/bin/mysqladmin -u root -h localhost
          password 'new-password'
```

10. **Change the permissions on the newly created directories, and run** ldconfig **against** /usr/local/lib/, **as follows:**

```
# chown -R root /usr/local/mysql/
# chown -R mysql /usr/local/mysql/var
# chgrp -R mysql /usr/local/mysql
# cp support-files/my-medium.cnf /etc/my.cnf
# cat /etc/ld.so.conf
# echo "/usr/local/lib" >>/etc/ld.so.conf
# ldconfig -v
```

Checking the installation

We could say something profound at this point about second-guessing Murphy's Law, but simple is best: Check to make sure all this stuff worked. Here's how:

1. **Type the following at a command prompt:**

   ```
   /usr/local/mysql/bin/mysqld_safe --user=mysql &
   ```

   If you get no error messages, you should see the MySQL server listing in the process list:

   ```
   ps -ef | grep -i msyql
   ```

2. **Check the process list for the following bunch of entries:**

   ```
   root    7754  0.0  0.1  2056  976 ?        S   Dec23   0:00 /bin/sh
           /usr/local/mysql/bin/mysqld_safe --datadir=/usr/local/mysql/var
           --pid-file=/usr/local/mysql/var/boris.pid
   mysql   7782  0.0  2.1 54148 12648 ?       S   Dec23   0:00
           /usr/local/mysql/libexec/mysqld --basedir=/usr/local/mysql --
           datadir=/usr/local/mysql/var --user=mysql --pid-
           file=/usr/local/mysql/var/boris.pid --skip-locking --port=3306 -
           -socket=/tmp/mysql.sock
   mysql   7784  0.0  2.1 54148 12648 ?       S   Dec23   0:00
           /usr/local/mysql/libexec/mysqld --basedir=/usr/local/mysql --
           datadir=/usr/local/mysql/var --user=mysql --pid-
           file=/usr/local/mysql/var/boris.pid --skip-locking --port=3306 -
           -socket=/tmp/mysql.sock
   mysql   7785  0.0  2.1 54148 12648 ?       S   Dec23   0:00
           /usr/local/mysql/libexec/mysqld --basedir=/usr/local/mysql --
           datadir=/usr/local/mysql/var --user=mysql --pid-
           file=/usr/local/mysql/var/boris.pid --skip-locking --port=3306 -
           -socket=/tmp/mysql.sock
   ```

   If you see ten or twelve of these lines, don't panic; this is normal. If you don't see any of these lines, check the log files in /usr/local/mysql/var/ for errors.

3. **If your MySQL server is running, make sure the MySQL daemon starts and stops when your server (respectively) boots up and shuts down.**

   If your MySQL source is in /usr/local/src/mysql, look for the following file and copy it to /etc/init.d directory:

   ```
   /usr/local/src/mysql/support-files/mysql.server
   ```

MySQL — at your service

Starting and stopping the MySQL daemon at startup and shutdown works especially well when you enable MySQL as a service. You can do so by using the tools and scripts listed in the "Disabling Services" section of this chapter, or you can do so manually by creating links to the initialization script from the appropriate rc.d directory.

4. **To start and stop the MySQL daemon when the system enters or exits the default run levels, use the commands in the "Disabling Services" section of this chapter, or issue the following commands:**

```
# cd /etc/rc3.d
# ln -s ../init.d/mysql.server S85mysql
# ln -s ../init.d/mysql.server K85mysql
# cd ../rc2.d
# ln -s ../init.d/mysql.server S85mysql
# ln -s ../init.d/mysql.server K85mysql
# cd ../rc5.d
# ln -s ../init.d/mysql.server S85mysql
# ln -s ../init.d/mysql.server K85mysql
# cd ../init.d/
# chmod 755 mysql.server
```

5. **Reboot your server to check the effectiveness of your initialization scripts.**

   No time like the present. After all, Snort's not installed yet, the machine isn't in production, and there'll be plenty of time for accumulating uptime soon.

Installing Snort for Linux

Installing a base Snort system is actually pretty easy, if you don't want any fancy frills. This chapter details how to install and configure Snort and how to configure the MySQL databases for logging all of Snort's output. Other databases are available for Snort's logging, but MySQL is by far the most popular with Snort, and it's got the greatest amount of support out there, so that's what we've detailed.

Advanced logging concepts are covered in Chapter 6 and putting a pretty picture on the pig through reporting and visualizations is covered in Chapter 7.

But wait, there's more

Snort won't run on its own, and requires some underlying software to run. Here's a lineup of the usual suspects . . .

Setting up libpcap

One required piece of software for Snort is libpcap, a packet-capture library. It's available at http://www.tcpdump.org/release/ and installs easily. Don't forget to check the digital signature! Assuming you've downloaded the source to /usr/local/src/tarballs and you wish to untar it to /usr/local/src/ like this:

```
# cd /usr/local/src/tarballs
# gpgv libpcap-0.7.2.tar.gz.asc
gpgv: Signature made Wed Feb 26 01:36:50 2003 CST using DSA
        key ID 89E917F3
gpgv: Can't check signature: public key not found
# gpg --keyserver pgp.mit.edu --recv-keys 89E917F3
gpg: requesting key 89E917F3 from pgp.mit.edu ...
gpg: key 89E917F3: public key imported
gpg: Total number processed: 1
gpg:                 imported: 1
# gpgv --keyring=~/.gnupg/pubring.gpg libpcap-
        0.7.2.tar.gz.asc
gpgv: Signature made Wed Feb 26 01:36:50 2003 CST using DSA
        key ID 89E917F3
gpgv: Good signature from "tcpdump.org (SIGNING KEY)
        <tcpdump-workers@tcpdump.org>"
# cd ../
# tar -xvzf ../tarballs/libpcap-3.7.2.tar.gz
# cd libpcap-3.7.2/
# script ~/libpcap.install
# ./configure
# make
# make install
# exit
```

Setting up PCRE

Snort requires PCRE to build. PCRE (no, it *isn't* pronounced "peccary," as far
as we know) stands for Perl-Compatible Regular Expressions, and Snort now
lets you write rules using this powerful text-matching syntax. PCRE is gaining
popularity every day, and by the time you read this, you may already have it
installed on your system. We didn't, so here's how to get and install it:

```
# cd /usr/local/src/tarballs
# wget -q ftp://ftp.csx.cam.ac.uk/pub/software/programming/
        pcre/pcre-4.5.tar.gz
# wget -q ftp://ftp.csx.cam.ac.uk/pub/software/programming/
        pcre/pcre-4.5.tar.gz.sig
# wget -q ftp://ftp.csx.cam.ac.uk/pub/software/programming/
        pcre/Public-Key
# gpg --import Public-Key
gpg: key FB0F43D8: public key imported
gpg: Total number processed: 1
gpg:                 imported: 1  (RSA: 1)
# gpgv --keyring ~/.gnupg/pubring.gpg pcre-4.5.tar.gz.sig
gpgv: Signature made Wed Dec 10 10:45:53 2003 CST using RSA
        key ID FB0F43D8
```

```
gpgv: Good signature from "Philip Hazel <ph10@cam.ac.uk>"
gpgv:                   aka "Philip Hazel <ph10@cus.cam.ac.uk>"
# tar -xvzf tarballs/pcre-4.5.tar.gz
# cd pcre-4.5/
# script ~/notes/pcre.install
Script started, file is /root/notes/pcre.install
# ./configure
# make
# make install
```

Adding the /usr/local/lib line

Make sure your /etc/ld.so.conf file has a /usr/local/lib line in it, which it should if you installed MySQL as shown in the "Compiling and installing MySQL" section of this chapter. If not, add it in, and run ldconfig as root.

We haven't typed exit yet, so we're including this step in the script output for the record.

```
# echo "/usr/local/lib" >>/etc/ld.so.conf
# ldconfig -v
# exit
Script done, file is /root/notes/pcre.install
```

Downloading and compiling Snort

The latest version of the Snort source code is available from http://www.snort.org. The Snort home page will list what the latest stable version available for download is.

Check for new source code early and often. Updates from developers are frequent.

Subscribing to the various Snort mailing lists is an easy way to keep up to date with the latest Snort news. The Snort-Announcements list is very low volume, typically limited to new software announcements. You can find a link to the mailing lists on the snort.org Web site.

Software updates typically mean new software features, so check in on the Snort Users mailing list occasionally to see what's new, and what other people are having trouble with; chances are you might be having the same problem.

Preparing your system for Snort

Snort can run under its own user account in its own group. This arrangement allows you to run some very powerful software as someone other than `root`, which is always nice when you consider the fact that the software is designed to indiscriminately read and parse wild packets from the Internet.

Adding the Snort user account and group

After all that build-up installing Snort's prerequisites, you might find the actual steps for installing Snort disappointingly simple.

1. **Run the following commands as `root` to add the Snort user and group:**

   ```
   # groupadd snortgroup
   # useradd -g snortgroup snortuser
   ```

2. **Make a directory for your Snort configuration file.**

   You can put it anywhere. We use `/usr/local/snort/etc` (the `-p` switch will create the *parent* directory `/usr/local/snort` as well as the `etc` directory underneath it).

3. **Create a directory for Snort's log file.**

   `/var/log/snort` sounds good to us.

   ```
   # mkdir -p /usr/local/snort/etc
   # mkdir /var/log/snort
   ```

Downloading Snort

It's time to download Snort, if you haven't already. Don't forget to check the PGP signature, or at least the MD5 sum. We didn't already have the public key for the Snort.org release team — and chances are, you won't either — so we've included the step to download the public key, after which you should recheck the digital signature on the tarball.

```
# wget -q http://www.snort.org/dl/snort-2.1.0.tar.gz
# wget -q http://www.snort.org/dl/snort-2.1.0.tar.gz.asc
# gpgv snort-2.1.0.tar.gz.asc
gpgv: Signature made Thu Dec 18 11:16:50 2003 CST using DSA key ID 1946E4A1
gpgv: Can't check signature: public key not found
# gpg --recv-keys --keyserver pgp.mit.edu 1946E4A1
gpg: requesting key 1946E4A1 from pgp.mit.edu ...
gpg: key 1946E4A1: public key imported
gpg: Total number processed: 1
gpg:               imported: 1
# gpgv snort-2.1.0.tar.gz.asc
gpgv: Signature made Thu Dec 18 11:16:50 2003 CST using DSA key ID 1946E4A1
gpgv: Can't check signature: public key not found
# gpgv --keyring ~/.gnupg/pubring.gpg snort-2.1.0.tar.gz.asc
gpgv: Signature made Thu Dec 18 11:16:50 2003 CST using DSA key ID 1946E4A1
gpgv: Good signature from "Snort.org releases <releases@snort.org>"
```

Opening the Snort tarball

So you've got the goods, and you know they're . . . well, *good*, right? Let's un-tar this pig and get compiling.

1. **We're going to work out of** /usr/local/src/snort-*version*/ **so we move up a directory to run** tar.

```
# cd /usr/local/src
# tar -xvzf tarballs/snort-2.1.0.tar.gz
```

2. **Run the** configure **script, which will make several determinations about the best way to compile the software for your system.**

We've listed some of the more popular configuration options in our text, but others may be right for you. Run the configure script with the help option ./configure —help to see what other options are available, and whether they make sense for you to use; pipe the output to more or less for easier reading, or redirect it to a file to peruse later.

3. **Since we just went through all the trouble of installing MySQL, you definitely want to specify the** —with-mysql **option.**

We list the MySQL directory that resulted from installing from source code. If you installed a vendor-supplied package, your MySQL files may be in a different directory. You can find the MySQL directory by typing the following:

```
find / -name "mysql"
```

4. **If the** configure **script bails on you with an error message about not being able to find your** libpcap **files, you may need to specify their location as well.**

Look for libpcap by using this command:

```
find / -name "libpcap.a"
```

Before you start to configure and compile the software, run the script command to capture the terminal output to a file. You'll want to read it later if there are errors, and it will come in handy the next time you want to install the software.

Compiling Snort

Other than specifying an option or two, compiling Snort is disappointingly mundane:

```
# script ~/notes/snort.install
Script started, file is /root/notes/snort.install
# ./configure --with-mysql=/usr/local/mysql
# make
# make check
# make install
# exit
```

When you've got a working Snort binary, you need to create a place for the Snort rules to live, and start hacking on your `snort.conf` file. We've already made the `/usr/local/snort/etc` directory, and we recommend putting the Snort rules in their own directory `/usr/local/snort/rules`. There are a couple of other configuration files that need to move too, so don't forget those (listed in the following instructions):

- `reference.config` is a collection of URLs for references found in the Snort rules.
- `classification.config` file helps in classifying and prioritizing alerts.

You should still be in the `/usr/local/src/snort-version` directory that's holding all of the Snort source code.

```
# mkdir /usr/local/snort/rules
# cp rules/* /usr/local/snort/rules/
# cp etc/snort.conf /usr/local/snort/etc/
# cp etc/reference.config /usr/local/snort/etc/
# cp etc/classification.config /usr/local/snort/etc/
# cp etc/unicode.map /usr/local/snort/etc/
# cp etc/threshold.conf /usr/local/snort/etc/
```

The rules in `/usr/local/snort/rules` are rules that were included when your particular version of Snort was released. Snort rules change, and new ones are released regularly — sometimes daily — just as new threats to the Internet emerge daily. (Chapter 12 explores how to keep your rules updated automatically, and even how to write your own. Right now, we're making sure that we can get Snort running at all, so we won't bother tinkering with the rules just yet.)

When you've got the necessary files moved, you're ready to configure Snort for your network.

Configuring Snort

Snort is a very flexible piece of software — detailing all its configuration options (and the best ways to take advantage of them) is something we do with much more gusto in Parts II and III of this book. The steps given here get you going with a good set of generic options — which you set in the `snort.conf` configuration file in `/usr/local/snort/etc`. Go ahead and open it up with your favorite Unix text editor (`vi`, `emacs`, or `pico -w` are good choices). You can also download the configuration file to another system and open it; just make sure you use a text editor that won't mangle it. The `snort.conf` file is heavily commented, with useful hints at every turn.

$HOME_NET sweet $HOME_NET

If you're only interested in watching DNS traffic that's sent to your DNS servers, or SMTP traffic that's sent to an SMTP server, then you can specify which host on your network sends and receives which kind of traffic. Although such a setup can conserve the resources of your Snort box, it's also a good way to miss important network traffic — or even a potential attack. If you manage a large enough network, chances are good that you have different people managing different network services, and they might not consult you when they bring up a new DNS, SQL, SMTP, or (even) Web server. And you can bet they won't consult you if they're bringing up a new server "just for testing." If all your Snort server variables are set to $HOME_NET, you've got those new critters covered.

Defining network variables

The first step in configuring Snort is telling it which network(s) to monitor:

1. **Set the** `var HOME_NET` **variable to the slice of network you want to monitor.**

   You can monitor a single host, a whole network, or anything in between. The configuration file uses `var HOME_NET any` as a default; whatever network it sits on becomes its "home network" to monitor (not a bad default value). If your Snort box has multiple network interfaces and sits on multiple network segments, check out Chapter 13 to see how to scale Snort for multiple networks.

2. **Tell Snort which network you consider the "external" network.**

   The file uses `var EXTERNAL_NET any`, and this is a good default value.

3. **Set all server variables to** `$HOME_NET`.

   Even if you're the only person managing your network, you should realize that given enough time, your servers aren't going to be where they were when you installed Snort, and your `snort.conf` file will need editing. So unless your network configuration is truly set in stone, leaving all server variables set to `$HOME_NET` means Snort always knows where to look. (See the "$HOME_NET sweet $HOME_NET" sidebar in this chapter.)

Defining other operating variables

The next variable to define is where your Snort rules live. We moved our rules to `/usr/local/snort/rules`, like this:

```
var RULE_PATH /usr/local/snort/rules
```

Make sure your `snort.conf` file reads accordingly:

- ✔ If you have a low-powered (or near-maxed-out) machine as your Snort box, you may want to uncomment the `config detection: search-method lowmem` line to make the most of your available resources.

- ✔ By and large, the default settings for the Snort decoder and the detection engine can stay as-is. Tweaking the decoder is best done after you've already logged some network traffic — if you're trying to lower the network noise level, having a sample to work with is a great help.

- ✔ Some network traffic on the logs is also good before you try configuring the preprocessor (a bit of fine-tuning that we address in Chapter 9). For now, the default values are fine.

Configuring the system for Snort logs

Now that Snort knows what to watch for, you need to tell it where to send its alerts when it sees something alert-worthy. Snort lets you specify multiple output plugins. For example, you can send its output to any combination of

- ✔ the `syslog` facility
- ✔ an external database
- ✔ a binary `tcpdump` file

This little section sets up basic logging — including logging to `syslog` and to a MySQL database. Nifty output tricks such as unified logging are covered in Chapter 5.

Logging Snort using syslog

Logging to two different destinations may seem repetitively redundant (boy, you can say *that* again), but it can also be very handy, especially when troubleshooting problems. If you're like us, and you find reading a flat text file easier than pulling data from a database, you'll be glad to have Snort logging its own status through the Unix `syslog` facility. Here's how to point Snort's snout in the right direction:

1. **Uncomment and edit one of the output `alert_syslog` lines to read like this:**

   ```
   output alert_syslog: LOG_LOCAL3
   ```

   You can pick any local `syslog` facility from 0 to 7. Just make sure it's not already in use.

2. **Edit your `/etc/syslog.conf` file to make sure the log facility you just specified isn't already in use, and tell `syslog` which file to write the Snort logs to.**

   For example, consider this `syslog.conf` file from a Red Hat system:

```
# Log all kernel messages to the console.
# Logging much else clutters up the screen.
#kern.*                                          /dev/console

# Log anything (except mail) of level info or higher.
# Don't log private authentication messages!
*.info;mail.none;authpriv.none;cron.none;local3.none
            /var/log/messages

# The authpriv file has restricted access.
authpriv.*                                       /var/log/secure

# Log all the mail messages in one place.
mail.*                                           /var/log/maillog

# Log cron stuff
cron.*                                           /var/log/cron

# Everybody gets emergency messages
*.emerg                                                 *

# Save news errors of level crit and higher in a special file.
uucp,news.crit                                   /var/log/spooler

# Save boot messages also to boot.log
local7.*                                         /var/log/boot.log
local3.*                                 /var/log/snort/snort.log
```

The last line indicates that *any* logs received from the `local3 syslog` facility should be written to `/var/log/snort/snort.log`. A `syslog.conf` file that works like this tells `syslog` where to put your Snort logs.

3. **Confirm that the log file is actually there.**

   Try changing to `/var/log/snort` to see whether the log file exists. If it doesn't, create it in Step 4.

4. **If the `snort.log` file doesn't exist, create it by using the `touch` command, and then use `chown` to make sure the `snortuser` you created can write to the file:**

```
# cd /var/log
# touch snort/snort.log
# chown -R snortuser.snortgroup snort/
```

   These commands establish that the file is present and is owned by `snortuser`.

5. **Restart the `syslog` daemon to ensure that your changes take effect.**

More `syslog` tips and tricks, including details on `syslog-ng` (the next generation of `syslog`), are in Chapter 6.

Tell syslog where to go and Snort to shut up

Some Linux systems will write all log entries of a certain priority to the same file. In the Step 2 example given here, the Red Hat server logs anything with the priority of `info` to `/var/log/messages` (a familiar file to all you Red Hat admins). Snort can be very chatty at times, sometimes more than you want. To keep Snort log entries from popping up in your `/var/log/messages` file, specify that *no* `local3` log entries go to that file. In the `syslog.conf` file shown in Step 2, the `local3.none` entry in the first uncommented line takes care of exactly that chore.

Configuring Snort to log to a MySQL database

For faster access to your Snort logs by other programs, like ACID, the Analysis Center for Intrusion Detection (see Chapter 7), you should configure Snort to log to a database. And since you just installed and configured MySQL, that's where you'll be sending Snort's output.

1. **In the** `snort.conf` **file, find the following line:**

   ```
   # output database: log, mysql, user=root password=test
             dbname=db host=localhost
   ```

2. **Change the line so it contains the correct values for your Snort/ MySQL installation.**

   Some of these values haven't been set yet, although some have been. For example, we already added a `snort` user, so you can change the `user=root` section to read `user=snortuser` or whatever you named your `snort` user (Ralph? Brunhilde?) when you added him or her in the previous section.

3. **Create a name for the database you've designated to hold your Snort logs.**

   You'll be creating the database to go with this name soon, along with a password. (We use the placeholder *snortdb* as the database name in Step 5.)

4. **Specify a host server.**

   At this point, we assume that the MySQL server you're logging in to is the same box you're running Snort on. (Logging in to a separate database server is covered in Chapter 13.) Your host here is `127.0.0.1` or `localhost`.

5. Edit your output-database line so it resembles this one:

```
output database: log, mysql, user=snortuser password=h4wg dbname=snortdb
        host=localhost
```

The new unified-output plug-in allows even faster log processing, and it is truly the wave of the future. And by "the future" we mean Chapter 6, the logging chapter, where unified logging is addressed in detail. For now, leave the unified logging lines commented out.

The next section covers which rule sets to enable. (We cover Snort rules in greater detail in Chapter 8.) From a practical standpoint, you want to have already captured some data before you decide which rules just aren't for you.

Preparing the MySQL database for Snort

After you've configured Snort to log to a MySQL database, make sure that database is prepared to accept Snort's logs. Here's how it looks:

1. Using the `mysql` client, you can:

- Create every database you want Snort to use for logging

- Grant appropriate permissions on these databases to the Snort user account

For example, here's a transcript of setting up the Snort databases on our server:

```
hawg:/# mysql -u root -p
Enter password:
Welcome to the MySQL monitor. Commands end with ; or \g.
Your MySQL connection id is 7 to server version: 3.23.49-log

Type 'help;' or '\h' for help. Type '\c' to clear the buffer.

mysql> create database snortdb;
Query OK, 1 row affected (0.02 sec)

mysql> grant INSERT,SELECT on snortdb.* to snortuser@localhost;
Query OK, 0 rows affected (0.00 sec)
mysql> SET PASSWORD FOR snortuser@localhost=PASSWORD('h4wg');
Query OK, 0 rows affected (0.00 sec)
mysql> grant CREATE,INSERT,SELECT,DELETE,UPDATE on snortdb.* to
        snortuser@localhost;
Query OK, 0 rows affected (0.00 sec)
mysql> flush privileges
mysql> exit
Bye
hawg:/#
```

When this process is complete, the databases exist, and `snortuser` has the appropriate permissions on them.

2. **Build the database structure for each database Snort will use.**

   This is easy to do, thanks to the scripts included in the `contrib` directory where your Snort source code resides. Here's how you get to them:

   ```
   # cd /usr/local/src/snort-2.1.0/
   # mysql -u root -p <./contrib/create_mysql snortdb
   Enter password:
   #
   ```

3. **Make sure your Snort databases are set up and ready for action.**

   This transcript shows us doing just that:

   ```
   # mysql -u root -p
   Enter password:
   Welcome to the MySQL monitor. Commands end with ; or \g.
   Your MySQL connection id is 10 to server version: 3.23.49-log

   Type 'help;' or '\h' for help. Type '\c' to clear the buffer.

   mysql> SHOW DATABASES;
   +----------+
   | Database |
   +----------+
   | mysql    |
   | snortdb  |
   | test     |
   +----------+
   3 rows in set (0.00 sec)

   mysql> use snortdb
   Database changed
   mysql> SHOW TABLES;
   +------------------+
   | Tables_in_snortdb |
   +------------------+
   | data             |
   | detail           |
   | encoding         |
   | event            |
   | icmphdr          |
   | iphdr            |
   | opt              |
   | reference        |
   | reference_system |
   | schema           |
   | sensor           |
   | sig_class        |
   | sig_reference    |
   | signature        |
   ```

```
| tcphdr           |
| udphdr           |
+------------------+
16 rows in set (0.00 sec)

mysql> exit;
Bye
#
```

Huzzah! Snort is ready to keep an eye (nose?) on your MySQL databases.

So now you've got Snort's prerequisite software installed and compiled, the MySQL server installed and configured, the Snort databases set up, and Snort itself configured and ready to run. Take a moment and take a deep breath — now you're ready to make sure all this stuff actually works!

Is this thing on?

This is the moment when you find out whether all this hard work is going to pay off. Before you go any farther, take a moment; savor the anticipation.

Okay. Now you're ready to test your Snort installation. Conveniently, Snort includes a switch you can use to start it up in test mode — where it checks your configuration file, your rules, your database, everything. Here's a typical test scenario:

1. **To start testing, use `-T` and watch the output.**

   Chances are you're going to see errors. Don't panic, just read the error message(s), fix the problem(s), and try again.

2. **Make sure Snort knows where to find its configuration file.**

   Remember, when you start Snort, you have to specify where that file is — and we're running the Snort user account as `snortuser`, not as `root` — so specify that too with `-u snortuser`, as follows:

   ```
   hawg:/# /usr/local/bin/snort -T -u snortuser -c
            /usr/local/snort/etc/snort.conf
   ```

3. **Success? Huzzah! Not yet? Rats. Read the error message carefully and consider these common pitfalls:**

   • Check for typos in your `config` file.

   • Make sure a necessary file didn't get moved.

   • If your problem starts looking big, take a tour of the Snort users' mailing-list archives.

Open-source is as much a community as it is a set of programs. Somebody somewhere has probably run into the same problem. You'll feel better knowing that someone else has had the same trouble, and you'll feel a whole lot better once you get it resolved and your server is running.

Starting up Snort at boot time

When you've got Snort up and running, sniffing packets and logging data . . . congratulations! The last step is to get Snort to shut down cleanly and start up automatically when your system shuts down or boots up.

Thankfully, the kind developers at Snort.org have already written an initialization script to handle this. Might as well dig it out (root it out?) and set it up:

1. **Look in the** `contrib/` **directory of your Snort source for a handy shell script called** `S99Snort`.

2. **Copy the** `S99Snort` **script into your** `/etc/init.d` **directory.**

3. **Rename the script as** `snort` **and make sure it's executable.**

   It becomes your new initialization script for Snort. Here's the code that does the trick:

   ```
   # cp /usr/local/src/snort-version/contrib/S99snort /etc/init.d/snort
   # chmod 755 /etc/init.d/snort
   ```

4. **Read your new snort initialization script and edit it appropriately.**

   Be sure to edit the `CONFIG`, `IFACE`, `SNORT_GID`, as well as the `OPTIONS` parameter. You don't want Snort to run under the all-powerful `root` account, but rather under the `snortuser` account just created. For our installation, the parameters are

   ```
   SNORT_PATH=/usr/local/bin
   CONFIG=/usr/local/snort/etc/snort.conf
   IFACE=eth1
   SNORT_GID=snortgroup
   OPTIONS="-D -u snortuser"
   ```

   Make sure the initialization script for your system is edited the way you want it before you move on to Step 5.

5. **Make sure the initialization script is called at boot time.**

   You can do so in one of these ways:

- Use the scripts we mention in this chapter (in the "Keeping a low profile" section) for disabling/enabling services.

  or

- Link the snort initialization script to the runlevel directories.

  Here's what linking the init.d/snort script looks like:

```
# cd ../rc2.d/
# ln -s ../init.d/snort S99snort
# ln -s ../init.d/snort K99snort
# cd ../rc3.d/
# ln -s ../init.d/snort K99snort
# ln -s ../init.d/snort S99snort
# cd ../rc5.d/
# ln -s ../init.d/snort S99snort
# ln -s ../init.d/snort K99snort
```

  Voilà!

6. **Test the new arrangement by rebooting your server.**

  You should have a working Snort installation that starts automatically for you.

It's in the (network) cards . . .

It's a good idea to have multiple network cards in your Snort box — at least two: one for managing the system itself, and one just for sniffing packets. The packet-sniffing interface should not be given an IP address, but it should be brought up at boot time. The easiest way to do this is just to give the ifconfig command for the interface, but not to specify an IP address: # /sbin/ifconfig eth1 up. For more about using multiple network cards, see Chapter 3.

Chapter 5

Installing Snort and MySQL for Windows

*F*or an average Windows user, installing Snort is a little more of a headache than for your average Linux user. This is because Snort was developed initially for open-source Unix-like platforms such as Linux, and if you are at all familiar with Linux, you know what that means: command-line options and text-based configuration files. For a Windows user who's used to point-and-click configuration, command-line is a little intimidating. Add to that the fact that there's little supporting documentation for the Windows platform on Snort's Web site or the rest of the Internet, and you have all the makings of a bumpy ride.

Never fear: This chapter gives you step-by-step installation instructions for getting your Snort IDS up and running on Windows.

The Windows Snort IDS Box

These are the minimum requirements for a Windows Snort box:

- A PC running Windows NT 4.0, Windows 95, Windows 98, Windows 2000 (Server or Professional), Windows XP (Home or Professional), Windows 2003 Server

- A packet-capture driver for Windows (WinPcap is really your only choice)

- One or more network interface cards (NICs) and a network connection

- Snort

The preceding requirements are definitely the *minimum* requirements for running Snort on a Windows box: You can get Snort up and running with that configuration. You can also drive a front-wheel-drive car with just the two front wheels, but you're not going to get very far, your tail-end will spew a lot of sparks, and you might explode along the way. The point is that the minimum requirements are not necessarily the best configuration. In the following sections we go over specific recommendations for the Windows OS, logging database, and system resources.

Choosing your Windows OS

Just because Snort can run on practically any 32-bit version of Windows, doesn't mean you should run Snort on just any version of Windows. We recommend running Snort on either Windows 2000 Professional or Windows XP Professional for the following reasons:

✔ Windows 2000 and XP Professional are more secure and stable than the "home user" Windows systems, such as Windows 98, Windows ME, or Windows XP Home Edition. This is due to features such as the NTFS filesystem, better multitasking, and better memory management in 2000 and XP Professional.

✔ The "home user" Windows systems, such as Windows 98, Windows ME, or Windows XP Home Edition are not suitable for running a Web server such as Internet Information Services (IIS). A Web server is required for the ACID visualization console we cover in Chapter 7.

✔ The "home user" editions of Windows only support a single processor, whereas Windows 2000 and XP Professional support dual processors.

✔ Windows 2000 and XP Professional are still supported by Microsoft, unlike Windows NT 4.0 (or earlier versions of NT).

✔ Windows 2000 and XP Professional are cheaper alternatives than Windows 2000 Server or Windows 2003 Server.

In some high-performance environments the server-class versions of Windows 2000 and 2003 might make more sense, such as when you want to take advantage of systems that have more than two CPUs.

The minimum configuration only gets you text-based logging and alerts, which can be hard to manage. In the long run, we want to be able to classify alerts and use reporting and visualization tools such as the ACID console we cover in Chapter 7. In order to do this, we need to run an RDBMS (Relational Database Management System, a fancy name for a database program).

MySQL, your SQL

The RDBMS we chose is MySQL. MySQL is a free database that works on a number of platforms, including Windows. As a Windows user you might already be familiar with some of the Microsoft database products, such as MS SQL and Access, and are wondering why we aren't using those. MySQL has a number of things going for it as a backend database for Snort:

✔ Snort can log directly to MySQL natively, as the alerts come in. Snort can't currently log in real-time to Access databases.

✔ Snort's unified logging output can be converted directly to MySQL using the Barnyard utility (covered in Chapter 14). Barnyard cannot currently convert Snort's unified logging output directly to Access formats.

✔ MySQL is supported by many extra Snort tools, including the ACID visualization console we cover in Chapter 7. ACID currently does not support Access databases.

✔ Did we mention that MySQL is free? MS SQL and Access licenses aren't free, which can increase the cost of your Snort IDS if you don't already own those licenses.

If you've never used MySQL or any other RDMS before, don't worry. You don't need to be a database guru or even understand SQL queries to get Snort up and running with MySQL. We provide instructions to get Snort logging to MySQL under Windows.

Two resource hogs: Windows and Snort

All Windows-based operating systems have high base hardware requirements relative to other operating systems, even with as much unnecessary stuff removed as possible. When it comes to recommended hardware, for Snort, the faster and more the better. Snort needs as much processor speed and memory you can throw at it, relative to the activity on your network:

✔ If Snort runs out of resources, it drops packets; it won't analyze all of the network packets that come under its nose. With Snort dropping packets, the entire purpose of an IDS is defeated; an attack on your network or hosts can come at any time. (Murphy's Law says the attack will probably come when your IDS is overloaded.)

✔ If you plan to run MySQL (or another database system), IIS (or another Web server), and ACID (and all its dependencies) on the same computer as Snort, consider fielding a *very* fast system.

For high-traffic production networks, you'll get the best performance from Snort by running the database, Web server, and sensor on different computers. Look at your network traffic and the requirements for the OS you select before setting up a Snort system. Chapter 3 should give you a better idea about how to size your Snort system to your particular environment.

Program storage requirements

With MySQL and support programs, the full Snort complement could fill as much as 60MB of hard drive space. That's not a huge amount of space by today's I-need-hundreds-of-gigs-just-for-my-downloaded-music standards, but that figure is only for the software itself, not the data you're going to collect using it. The Snort executable takes a measly 400KB of disk space. The entire Snort package takes 5.8MB on initial install.

Data storage

Your data storage requirements depend on what you do with the data:

- ✔ If you're capturing all packets on your network and storing them with Snort (not something you'd normally keep around forever, though) your storage needs will grow exponentially, daily.

- ✔ If you are running a single sensor and looking for only a few alerts or using a small rule base, you don't need much disk storage space.

In our testing environment, we captured alerts off of the basic Snort rules, and these alerts average about 5KB per alert in the text alert format. Though the size of the alert may be pretty standard, how many are generated on your network and how many are captured are up to you. Chapter 8 gives more detailed guidelines on rules and how to use them to maximize your Snort system.

Partition configuration

When installing your Windows operating system, set up at least two partitions on the hard drive:

- ✔ A small partition sized for the OS and applications running on your computer. By "small" we mean large enough to hold the Windows operating system, which can take as much as 3GB of disk space. We recommend making this partition at least 6GB in size.

- ✔ A larger partition for data depending on the amount of data you plan for Snort to capture. This is where your Snort logs and alerts go, so the amount of space varies depending on your network. It's a good idea to make it as large as you can.

Separate OS and data partitions keep the partitions from corrupting each other in case one fills up, and makes it much easier to back up to the partitions individually on separate schedules.

For extra security on your Web server we recommend having your IIS document root on its own partition, too.

Keeping Your Windows Locked

Before installing Snort and any other components, it's important to lock down your Windows system. After all, what good is a Snort IDS that's been compromised by an attacker? No good at all.

Hardening any Windows OS has become more difficult over the past few years, as more and more applications are integrated with the base operating system. Even so, following the guidelines and recommendations set forth in this section will help you secure your Windows-based Snort system.

Limit physical access

Physically secure the system in the following ways:

- ✔ Locate your Snort sensor in a secure area, accessible only to people who need physical access to the machine.

- ✔ Configure the system to boot only from the hard drive. You don't want someone bypassing Windows' security controls simply by booting off a floppy disk or CD-ROM, or even a keychain-sized USB drive!

- ✔ Consider using a system with a locking front panel that prevents an unauthorized person from booting from a floppy disk or CD-ROM.

Nobody should have access to the console of the Snort IDS sensor but you!

Tighten OS access control

Limiting the users who can log on to your system and having a good password policy are imperative. Here are a few suggestions for keeping your accounts secure:

✔ Set up a strong password policy on the system.

- Always use a complex password that uses a combination of upper and lower case letters, numbers, and special characters (*!#$).

- Use passwords of eight characters or more.

- Enable logging of login attempts, failures, and successes.

✔ You need one user on this system: the Administrator.

- Immediately change the Administrator account name.

- Rename and disable the Guest account (you can't remove it).

- Remove all other accounts.

Nothing makes a hacker's job easier than choosing a simple word or name for your password, or allowing guest access to your system. So, don't make a hacker's day: Follow the preceding account lockdown suggestions.

Harden the OS

Hardening an OS means to take measures to increase security and reduce vulnerabilities that go beyond the default installation of the OS. Since Windows is a general-purpose OS designed for user-friendliness, there are many features turned on by default that aren't required on a Snort system. Here are a few suggestions for hardening a Windows Snort IDS box:

✔ Install only components that are absolutely necessary to run the OS.

Windows operating systems install many programs that you don't need for a Snort IDS. Most notable are such applications as Windows Media Player and Outlook Express. Install *nothing* extra and add what programs you need, later.

When given the option, *just say no.*

✔ After installing Windows, turn off all unneeded services.

Windows runs a plethora of services in the background that aren't needed for every implementation of the OS. Figure out what you need and turn off the rest.

✔ Disable unneeded network protocols. All you need is TCP/IP. That's it. Everything else: *out the window!*

Use `netstat` from the command line on your Windows box to list the network services that are listening (or connected) at any given time. To use `netstat` to list all the listening ports by protocol, open a command window and type

---

Patch, patch, and patch again

We can't emphasize enough the importance of patching on Internet-facing Windows systems! All the infamous destructive Windows worms of 2003 — Slammer, Blaster, Nachi — used known holes for which patches already existed.

If you're concerned about patching a production Snort IDS, set up a second Windows Snort box as a test bed. Set up that box to automatically use Windows Update to detect and download the latest critical patches, and test it first. If everything continues to work perfectly after patching, do it on the production system. Same goes if you're in an enterprise environment and use Microsoft's Systems Management Server (SMS) or Software Update Services (SUS) for patching: Test, then deploy.

Just do it, and plan to do it regularly (Microsoft is currently releasing patches once a month, so this makes it much easier to plan). The comfort zone between the discovery of a vulnerability and the release of a worm is rapidly shrinking.

```
netstat -an
```

- ✔ Conduct all remote communications to and from the sensor with secure protocols and applications, such as IPSec, SSL, and ssh.

- ✔ Apply all security updates, patches, and service packs.

    Maintenance is imperative. Regularly check for new security updates, patches and service packs. New Windows-specific exploits hit the wire all too frequently.

There are reams of information available on the Internet for securing Windows systems. Here are a few of our favorite Windows security resources:

- ✔ The security wizards at SANS list the Top 20 critical security vulnerabilities for Windows (at http://www.sans.org/).

- ✔ The Center for Internet Security (a group that includes SANS, government agencies, and private industry) has a security benchmarking tool at http://www.cisecurity.org/.

- ✔ Microsoft's Baseline Security Analyzer and IIS Lockdown Tool is available at its Web site, http://www.microsoft.com/. Always get the latest versions.

Hardening your Windows Snort IDS is an ongoing process.

Installing the Base Snort System

Installing the base Snort system requires two components: the WinPcap packet capture library, and the Snort IDS program itself. In the following sections we configure and install both WinPcap and Snort.

WinPcap

WinPcap (Windows Packet Capture Library) is a *packet-capture driver*. Functionally, this means that WinPcap grabs packets from the network wire and pitches them to Snort.

WinPcap is a Windows version of `libpcap`, which is used for running Snort with Linux. For more on `libpcap`, see Chapter 4.

Functions

The WinPcap driver performs these functions for Snort:

- ✔ Obtains a list of operational network adapters and retrieves information about the adapters.
- ✔ Sniffs packets using one of the adapters that you select.
- ✔ Saves packets to the hard drive (or more importantly for us, pitches them to Snort).

Installation

The installation and configuration of WinPcap is dead easy, with almost no intervention by you:

1. **Download the latest installation file from**

   `http://winpcap.polito.it/install/default.htm`

   The installation file is generally called something like WinPcap_3_0.exe.

2. **Double-click the executable installation file and follow the prompts.**

   WinPcap installs itself where it belongs.

Snort calls WinPcap directly on any of the functions to grab and analyze network packets. If the driver did not install properly, Snort does not function.

Accept no substitutes for Windows

These tools verify that the programs you download from the Internet haven't been tampered with by a miscreant (this process is called "integrity checking"). We highly recommend that you use them.

✔ A Windows equivalent for md5sum is MD5summer. MD5Summer is free and has

an easy-to-use GUI interface for generating MD5 checksums. It can be found at http://www.md5summer.org/.

✔ A Windows binary for GnuPG can be found at http://www.gnupg.org/(en)/download/index.html.

Time for a Snort

Snort.org distributes a convenient install package for Windows available at its Web site:

http://www.snort.org/dl/binaries/win32/

Download this package (generally called snort-2_1_0.exe) and perform the following steps to install Snort:

1. **Double-click the executable installation file.**

   The GNU Public License appears.

2. **Click the I Agree button.**

   Installation Options window appears.

3. **In the Installation Options dialog box, click the appropriate boxes to select from among these options:**

   • **I do not plan to log to a database, or I am planning to log to one of the databases listed above.** Choose this option if you are not using a database or if you are using MySQL or ODBC databases. Snort has built-in support for these databases, and for our example, we chose this option.

   • **I need support for logging to Microsoft SQL Server.** Only click this radio button if you already have SQL Server client software installed on this computer, and you plan to use MSSQL as your logging database.

   • **I need support for logging to Oracle.** Only choose this option if you have the Oracle client software installed on this computer, and you plan to use Oracle as your logging database server.

4. **Click the Next button.**

   The Choose Components window appears.

5. **In the Choose Components window, select the components you want to install and then click the Next button.**

   We recommend selecting all of the components. The Snort option is the snort executable, the Documentation option gives you a few documents on using Snort and the Contrib option installs the contrib directory containing goodies such as scripts for building database tables in the MySQL, MSSQL, PostGres, and Oracle database systems.

   The Install Location window appears.

6. **Choose a directory to install to.**

   We chose to keep all of our Snort-related applications in the same root directory on our D:\ drive (the data partition we mentioned). The path to our Snort installation is: D:\snortapps\snort, but you can install it anywhere on your drive.

7. **Click the Install button.**

8. **When the installation is complete, click the Close button.**

   An information window appears.

9. **Click the OK button.**

   You're done! Now it's time to move on to configuring your Snort system.

Bending Snort to Your Will

A new Snort installation requires a few configuration points. Conveniently, one file has all the configuration settings required (*Snortpath* is the path to your Snort installation):

```
Snortpath/etc/snort.conf
```

When you're ready to configure Snort, open snort.conf in a text editor. Figure 5-1 shows snort.conf in WordPad, but you can use:

- ✔ Edit (from the command line)
- ✔ Notepad
- ✔ Any other text editor that won't corrupt the text with crazy formatting characters the way some fully featured word processors will.

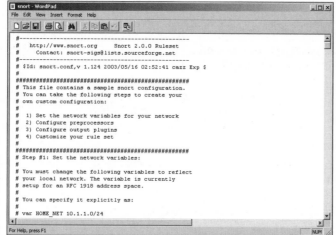

Figure 5-1:
snort.conf is
best viewed
while firmly
seated.

This configuration isn't a series of handy questions, button clicks, and good feelings. You're parsing through a flat text file and entering the proper settings by hand.

Double-check *everything* you type in to the snort.conf file. If entries aren't exactly correct, Snort doesn't work. Guaranteed.

The following configuration options in the snort.conf file are essential to a properly functioning Snort installation:

- ✔ Network settings
- ✔ Rules settings
- ✔ Output settings
- ✔ Include settings

Network settings

The network settings allow you to set Snort to monitor any range of network IP addresses, from a single IP address, several IP addresses in groups or individually, and entire IP subnets. You can configure the IP address range and the subnet.

The placement of the Snort sensor depends on both the configuration file and how much "pipe" it can suck from. In a switched environment, when using prodigious VLANs, additional network configuration may be required to give Snort the best possible sample of network traffic. Chapter 2 provides all the detail you need to set up Snort in any network environment.

You can control the network range that Snort monitors by changing the `var HOME_NET` setting in snort.conf. Your options are:

Entire network

By default, snort.conf contains the following line, which monitors the entire local network:

```
var HOME_NET any
```

If you don't change this setting, Snort monitors the entire network segment the Snort system is attached to.

Single IP address

To monitor a single IP or computer insert the IP address range and the subnet of the network or host into snort.conf. To do this, replace the existing var HOME_NET configuration line with this form:

```
var HOME_NET IPAddressRange/Subnet
```

The IPAddressRange/Subnet notation may not be something you're familiar with; it's not normally used to configure a network interface on Windows systems. This particular type of IP address notation is called CIDR notation, and we give you the run-down on it in Chapter 1, in the sidebar "Understanding CIDR notation."

The following examples monitor a Class C network with an IP address range of 192.168.10.0 – 192.168.10.255 and a subnet of 255.255.255.0:

✔ This line monitors the entire Class C network:

```
var HOME_NET 192.168.10.0/24
```

✔ This line monitors a single host on the Class C network:

```
var HOME_NET 192.168.10.2/32
```

Multiple hosts

You can specify a number of hosts within the network space you are monitoring by listing them in the `var HOME_NET` configuration statement. The line takes this form:

```
var HOME_NET IPAddressRange/Subnet,IPAddressRange/Subnet,...
```

Separate each IP address in the `var HOME_NET` configuration statement by a comma *without* spaces. If there are any blank spaces in the list of IP addresses and subnets, then Snort fails to start.

The following example monitors three hosts on a typical class C network:

```
var HOME_NET 192.168.10.2/32,192.168.10.3/32,192.168.10.6/32
```

Rules, rules, rules

So Snort can detect attacks and alert you when attacks occur, Snort needs to know where its rulebase is (and you need to know it if you want to write new rules).

By default, the rulebase is in *Snortpath*\rules (*Snortpath* is the location of the Snort install).

To set the rules path in the snort.conf file, replace the existing `var RULE_PATH` line with this form (*Snortpath* is the location of the Snort install):

```
var RULE_PATH SnortPath\rules
```

Figure 5-2 shows an example of a properly configured `var RULE_PATH` line in the snort.conf file.

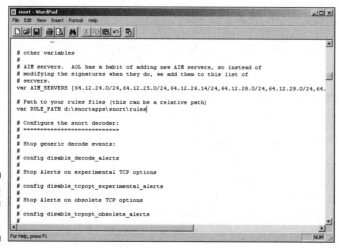

Figure 5-2:
The Tao of
Snort Rules.

Output settings

Output settings are very important in Snort, for they define how Snort's information will be presented to you. We go into output settings in-depth in Chapter 6, but for now we're concerned with configuring Snort to output to an alert text file and a database.

Alert output

The alert output setting is added to the snort.conf configuration file. The snort.conf file will also come in handy when we port that information into our MySQL database. Follow these steps:

1. **Find the output line that appears by default as:**

   ```
   # output log_tcpdump: tcpdump.log
   ```

   Because the default line begins with the comment character (#), Snort ignores it.

2. **Change the preceding default output line to this:**

   ```
   output alert_fast: alert.ids
   ```

   This setting creates a flat text file in the 'log' directory where Snort appends each alert created when one of its rules fires on incoming network packets.

Delete the comment character (#) from the beginning of the changed line so Snort doesn't ignore it when processing the configuration file.

Database outputs

These configuration settings configure Snort to push information to MySQL, the Windows database we recommend.

Even if MySQL hasn't been installed yet, this is the right time to get everything ready for MySQL on the Snort side of the house.

Collecting database information

Before configuring the database output settings, you must decide on the following information. Unless you're working with an existing database, these four settings are totally up to you.

Feel free to write your information in the following blanks, but guard it carefully or destroy it unless you want some wily social-engineering "3l33t haxor" to get all your database information.

✔ User: _____

This is the MySQL user for the database where Snort stores its data. We like 'elvis' (who doesn't?), but it can be anything you want.

✔ Password: _____

This is the password for the MySQL database user.

✔ dbname (for logs and alerts): _____

This is the database name where Snort will store its alerts and logs.

✔ YOURHOSTNAME _____

This is the hostname of your database server. If you are running your database on the same system as your Snort sensor, then it is the same name.

If you don't know your computer's hostname, you can find it by typing hostname at the command prompt. The prompt returns the hostname of your machine.

Don't use default users, database names, and passwords unless you want your box hacked.

Editing the output settings in snort.conf

When you have the database information ready, you can configure the output settings in `snort.conf`.

The following steps show how to edit `snort.conf` to log alerts to a MySQL database for your system. There are examples for our own test system, which has a MySQL database called `snorty` as the user `elvis` with a password of `3l33th@x0R` on the local IP address (127.0.0.1) at port 3306 with a sensor name of `elvisisdead`.

If you plan to install your database on a separate server, put the correct IP address where the database resides. For this demonstration, the database is running on the same server as Snort.

Follow these steps to configure the output settings in the snort.conf file:

1. **Find the following default output line in the** `snort.conf` **file:**

```
# output database: log, mysql, user=root password=test
        dbname=db host=localhost
```

2. **Configure the logs. Using your own database information, change that default output line to something like this:**

```
output database: log, mysql, user=User password=Password
        dbname=dbname host=YOURHOSTNAME port=portnumber
        sensor_name=thesensorname
```

Delete # from the beginning of the changed line so Snort doesn't ignore the line.

For example, we changed the default to this line:

```
output database: log, mysql, user=elvis
        password=3l33th@x0R dbname=snorty host=127.0.0.1
        port=3306 sensor_name=elvisisdead
```

3. **Configure the alerts. Using your own database information, add a new output line like this:**

```
output database: alert, mysql, user=User
        password=Password dbname=dbname host=YOURHOSTNAME
        port=portnumber sensor_name=thesensorname
```

For example, we added this output line:

```
output database: alert, mysql, user=elvis
        password=3l33th@x0R dbname=snorty host=127.0.0.1
        port=3306 sensor_name=elvisisdead
```

Include configuration

Two standard Snort configuration files must be referenced for Snort to properly classify and provide references to the alerts it generates: classification.config and reference.config.

classification.config

classification.config holds alert levels for the rules that Snort monitors against network traffic.

To set the classification.config file in the snort.conf configuration file, follow these steps:

1. **Find this default line in the** `snort.conf` **file:**

```
Include classfication.config
```

2. **Insert the actual path for the** `classification.config` **file into the preceding** `Include` **line, like this:**

```
Include SnortPath\etc\classification.config
```

For example, the actual snort.conf file on our test system has this line:

```
Include D:\snortapps\Snort\etc\classification.config
```

reference.config

reference.config contains URLs referenced in the rules that provide more information about the alert event.

To set the `reference.config` file in the `snort.conf` file, follow these steps:

1. **Find this default line in the** `snort.conf` **file:**

   ```
   Include reference.config
   ```

2. **Insert the actual path for the** `reference.config` **file into the preceding** `Include` **line, like this:**

   ```
   Include SnortPath\etc\reference.config
   ```

   For example, the actual snort.conf file on our test system has this line:

   ```
   Include D:\snortapps\Snort\etc\reference.config
   ```

Testing the Installation

Snort runs in three different modes: Sniffer, Packet Logger, and Network Intrusion modes.

Sniffer mode

Sniffer mode is the simplest iteration of Snort. To run it, follow these steps:

1. **From the command line (within the** `SnortPath\bin` **directory) type**

   ```
   snort -v
   ```

   This command runs Snort as a packet sniffer with the `verbose` switch, outputting TCP/IP packet headers to the screen (see Figure 5-3). As you know if you're a coffee-guzzling network engineer, Snort is working at its most basic level. But don't panic . . .

Figure 5-3:
Aagh!
What's that?

2. Press Ctrl+C keys together to stop the output.

Snort/WinPcap summarizes its activities, as shown in Figure 5-4.

Figure 5-4:
A summary
of *Aagh!*
What's
that?

```
C:\WINNT\System32\cmd.exe                                         _|□|×
================================================================================
Snort analyzed 388 out of 388 packets, dropping 0(0.000%) packets

Breakdown by protocol:              Action Stats:
     TCP: 362        (93.299%)      ALERTS: 0
     UDP: 0          (0.000%)       LOGGED: 0
    ICMP: 16         (4.124%)       PASSED: 0
     ARP: 10         (2.577%)
   EAPOL: 0          (0.000%)
    IPv6: 0          (0.000%)
     IPX: 0          (0.000%)
   OTHER: 0          (0.000%)
 DISCARD: 0          (0.000%)
================================================================================
Wireless Stats:
Breakdown by type:
   Management Packets: 0            (0.000%)
   Control Packets:    0            (0.000%)
   Data Packets:       0            (0.000%)
================================================================================
Fragmentation Stats:
Fragmented IP Packets: 0            (0.000%)
   Fragment Trackers: 0
   Rebuilt IP Packets: 0
   Frag elements used: 0
 Discarded(incomplete): 0
   Discarded(timeout): 0
   Frag2 memory faults: 0
================================================================================
TCP Stream Reassembly Stats:
   TCP Packets Used: 0              (0.000%)
   Stream Trackers: 0
   Stream flushes: 0
   Segments used: 0
 Stream4 Memory Faults: 0
================================================================================
pcap_loop: read error: PacketReceivePacket failed
Run time for packet processing was 78.433000 seconds

C:\snortapps\snort\bin>
```

3. To receive a more detailed capture of packets on the wire, type

```
snort -vd
```

This command provides the TCP/IP headers and packet information (descriptive).

4. Type snort **at the command line for a full list of all the switches.**

If you're getting TCP headers, you know that so far you're right on track.

5. If you have more than one network card in your Snort IDS system, type

```
snort -W
```

This command determines how WinPcap has these adapters numbered, and is only available in the Win32 version of Snort.

6. If you're running Snort from the command line with two network adapters, specify which adapter to monitor:

```
snort -v -i#
```

is the number of the applicable adapters (as shown on the output of the snort -W command).

You must use this -i switch whenever you run the snort program on the command line.

Packet Logger

You can test Snort's logging abilities with the -1 (log) switch, by typing:

```
snort -dev -l SnortPath\log
```

This runs Snort in descriptive verbose mode and logs all its findings to the directory called log under the Snort install directory. The individual packets are filed in hierarchical directories based on the IP address from where the packet was received, as seen in Figure 5-5.

Figure 5-5:
Pretty cool-looking, but not a very useful way to do it.

Several command-line switches are specific to logging and output, including the ability to log all packets to a single binary file. Play around with those as needed. Chapter 6 goes over a few of your options.

Setting Up MySQL for Snort

While MySQL isn't required with Snort, it is required for a front-end console such as ACID. If you set up MySQL or another database system, you can see the alerts without the front-end console, but you really don't need that kind of pain.

Installing MySQL

Before you install MySQL, you have to get hold of it. MySQL can be downloaded from http://www.mysql.com/downloads/index.html.

Get the *latest* production version of MySQL for your Windows operating system.

When you've downloaded, perform these steps to install MySQL:

1. **Uncompress the MySQL ZIP file into a temporary directory.**

   This file is ZIP file usually called something like `mysql-4.0.17-win.zip`. You need a compression utility (such as WinZip or WinRAR) to uncompress it on a Windows 2000 platform, but Windows XP has built-in transparent access to compressed archives with extensions such as `zip`, `gzip` and `tar`.

2. **Where you uncompressed the file, double-click** `setup.exe`.

   The Welcome window appears.

3. **Click Next, read the information, and click Next again.**

   The Information window appears. If you install MySQL in a directory other than `C:\mysql`, you must create an initialization file; the Information window describes this process.

4. **At the Destination Location window, click Next if you want to install it to the default directory (**`c:\mysql`**).**

5. **Choose the Typical install and click Next.**

   MySQL installs itself.

6. **When the installation is finished, click the Finished button.**

   You're all installed now.

To finish the initial configuration of MySQL, perform these steps:

1. **Open a command window and navigate to**

   `$SQLPATH\bin`

   `$SQLPATH` is the path to the directory in which you've installed `mysql` (ours is `C:\mysql\`).

2. **In the *SQLPath*\bin directory, type the following command:**

   `winmysqladmin`

   The MySQL administration console window appears and prompts you for a login.

Whoa, red light!

If the MySQL Admin traffic light is Red, MySQL can't start. It probably can't read its `.cnf` and `.ini` files. MySQL first reads the `my.ini` file (usually located in the `C:\Winnt` directory). If it can't read that, it reads the `my.cnf` file, usually located in the root directory (`C:\`). Check both of those files with a text editor (WordPad or Notepad) and ensure that lines like these appear (carefully check the slashes):

```
basedir=SQLPath
datadir=SQLPath/data
[WinMySQLadmin]
Server=SQLPath/bin/mysqld-
    nt.exe
user=USER
password=PASS
```

For the preceding lines, the variables in your files should have these values:

✔ SQLPath: the path to where you installed MySQL (that is, the `root` MySQL directory path)

✔ USER: the MySQL account's username

✔ PASS: the MySQL account's password

The resulting configuration file looks something like this:

```
basedir=C:/mysql
datadir=C:/mysql/data
[WinMySQLadmin]
Server=C:/mysql/bin/mysqld-
    nt.exe
user=root
password=Fry4tat3rZ
```

Carefully check the orientation of the slashes (/). They are Unix-like forward slashes, not the backslashes you typically use with the Windows filesystem. If these aren't right, MySQL won't start.

3. **Use any login name and password you want.**

   This sets the `root` password for MySQL. Ours looked like this:

   ```
   login: root
   password: Fry4tat3rZ
   ```

4. **Click the OK button, and MySQL starts up as a service.**

   A traffic light appears in your system tray, showing a green light.

   If the light is red, MySQL can't start. The "Whoa, red light!" sidebar in this chapter can help you diagnose the problem.

Configuring MySQL for Snort

When MySQL is up and running, you're ready to configure it to take data from Snort. To check that everything is A-OK, right-click the traffic-light icon in the system tray and click Show Me. Click the Start Check tab. The `my.ini` line should show a `yes`, and all other lines should show `OK`, as in Figure 5-6.

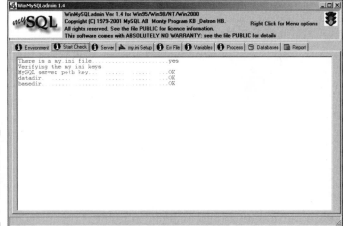

Figure 5-6:
Everything
is A-OK
with
MySQL.

Setting up the my.ini file

You can set up the my.ini file from the Admin console (`winmysqladmin`) or with a text editor. We prefer the Admin console; you can edit the `my.ini` file directly from the Setup tab of the `winmysqladmin` console. To set up the `my.ini` file using the Admin console, perform the following steps:

1. **Run** `winmysqladmin` **from a command prompt.**

2. **Bind MySQL to this system's localhost IP address.**

   In this case, it's `127.0.0.1`.

3. **Set the communication port.**

   For a typical MySQL installation, it's 3306.

4. **Set the** `key_buffer` **setting for Snort data.**

   (We chose to keep no more than 64MB in the Snort buffer.) When you're finished, the text in the `my.ini` Setup tab should look like the following code snippet (with the exception of the password line, which should contain your password):

```
#This File was made using the WinMySQLAdmin 1.4 Tool

#Uncomment or Add only the keys that you know how works.
#Read the MySQL Manual for instructions

[mysqld]
basedir=C:/mysql
bind-address=127.0.0.1
datadir=C:/mysql/data
#language=C:/mysql/share/your language directory
#slow query log#=
#tmpdir#=
```

```
port=3306
set-variable=key_buffer=64M
[WinMySQLadmin]
Server=C:/mysql/bin/mysqld-nt.exe
user=root
password=YOURPASSWORD
```

Any text that follows a pound (#) symbol is a comment and ignored by MySQL. If your code looks the way it should, then your my.ini file is set.

5. **Click the Save Modifications button (in the lower-left corner).**

   MySQL prompts you to confirm the changes.

6. **Click the Yes button.**

   MySQL alerts you that the changes have been made and confirmed.

7. **Click the OK button.**

   The changes are accepted.

8. **Right-click anywhere on the window, and then click the Hide Me menu option to close the console.**

Digging in SQL guts

Once MySQL is configured properly, clean up MySQL, configure it for Snort, and secure it. All this essential stuff is done from the command line.

In the MySQL command interface, every command must end in a semicolon (;).

The first order of business is to clean up some chaff by deleting the default databases.

1. **In the** *SQLPath*\bin **directory, log in to** mysql **from the Windows command prompt, type the following command, and press Enter:**

   ```
   mysql -u root -p
   ```

   You're asked for your MySQL root password.

2. **Enter the** root **password and press Enter.**

   A welcome message reminds you that commands must end with a semicolon. Your prompt changes to

   ```
   mysql>
   ```

3. **At the prompt, type the following and then press the Enter key:**

   ```
   use mysql;
   ```

   This command puts you in the database called mysql.

4. **Get rid of any** host **entries, like this:**

```
delete from user where host = "%";
```

5. **Delete other user accounts, like this:**

```
delete from user where user = "";
```

6. **Make sure the** root **account is the only user account here, like this:**

```
select * from user;
```

This command displays user information. You should only see root as a user.

7. **Delete the** test **database by typing the following:**

```
drop database test;
```

8. **Ensure that only the** mysql **database exists by typing this command:**

```
show databases;
```

The following should appear:

```
+----------+
| Database |
+----------+
| mysql    |
+----------+
1 row in set (0.00 sec)
```

If you get that, you're ready to create your Snort databases.

Create the Snort databases

At the mysql> prompt, type the following commands and press the Enter key after each one:

```
create database snort;
create database archive;
```

When you execute a show databases; command now, you should see this:

```
+----------+
| Database |
+----------+
| mysql    |
| snort    |
| archive  |
+----------+
1 row in set (0.00 sec)
```

Creating Snort's user accounts

With the Snort databases in place, set up the user accounts that Snort is to use when it logs in to add data to its databases. As an example, the following steps walk through setting up the `elvis` user account.

1. **At the** `mysql>` **prompt, type the following and press Enter after each line:**

   ```
   grant INSERT,SELECT,UPDATE on snort.* to elvis@localhost
            identified by "3l33th@x0R";
   ```

   Refer to Chapter 7 for more about user setup.

2. **Verify the** `elvis` **user's permissions type:**

   ```
   show grants for elvis@localhost;
   ```

   MySQL displays the `elvis` user's permissions, which should match those you gave the `elvis` user account when you created it.

3. **If you made a mistake, go back and redo the** `snort` **user account's permission.**

   The `snort` user account must be allowed to do its business, otherwise nothing will work.

Is this thing on?

After configuring the user accounts, make sure everything's working:

1. **Open the MySQL console by issuing the following command:**

   ```
   winmysqladmin
   ```

2. **Click the** `my.ini` **Setup tab, and then click the Create ShortCut on Start Menu button.**

   This creates a shortcut in the Windows Startup folder so MySQL starts automatically when your Windows 2000 box starts.

3. **Check the Windows Task Manager (right-click the Windows toolbar and select Task Manager).**

   In Windows 2000 and XP, you can press Ctrl+Shift+Esc instead.

   Here's where you make sure that both `snort.exe` and `mysqld-nt. exe` are running in the Process list. If you are still running the console, `winmysqladmin.exe` also appears in the process list.

Locking MySQL and throwing away the key

Choose a strong password for your `root` user and make sure you remember it, since it's your only admin interface to MySQL. *Don't* duplicate our example (Fry4tat3rZ) — but you knew that. Choose a password that includes numbers, upper- and lowercase letters, and special characters. To change the password for the `root` user, type the following at the `mysql>` prompt and press the Enter key:

```
set password for  = password ("YOURPASSWORDHERE");
```

You should get a confirmation. Then you can type `quit;` and press the Enter key to exit.

Configuring Snort as a Service

To run Snort as a background service on Windows 2000, XP, or 2003, you must know

- Where your rules directory is
- Where you want Snort to create its log file

When we added the database output configuration to the `snort.conf` file, we made Snort rely on MySQL. If we try to run Snort as a service without having MySQL installed and configured, the Snort service fails because it's looking for MySQL databases. Keep this in mind if you configured Snort for MySQL support, but skipped the section on installing and configuring MySQL.

The following examples are a generic configuration. Your configuration may vary slightly.

Windows 2000, XP, and 2003 service commands

The general procedures for installing and uninstalling services on a Windows 2000 system are pretty straightforward:

- To install a program as a service on Windows 2000, XP, or 2003, execute the following command at the command line (replace *Program* with the executable you want to install as a service):

```
Program /SERVICE /INSTALL
```

✔ To Uninstall a program from the Services, execute this command (replace *Program* with the executable you want to uninstall from the Services):

```
Program /SERVICE /UNINSTALL
```

Installing Snort as a service

To install Snort as a service, follow these steps:

1. **Specify your Snort path by typing the following command at the command line (in the /bin directory of your Snort installation) and then pressing Enter:**

```
snort /SERVICE /INSTALL -de -c SnortPath\etc\snort.conf
        -l SnortPath\log -i#
```

For the preceding command:

- snort is the name of the Snort executable.

- /SERVICE is the Windows command to access the Services commands.

- /INSTALL is the Services command that installs the program as a Windows service.

- -de is a pair of switches: the -d switch tells Snort to dump Application-Layer network information; the -e switch displays Second-Layer header information.

- -c $SnortPath\etc\snort.conf is where the -c switch tells Snort to use the configuration file specified by $SnortPath\etc\snort.conf.

- -l $SnortPath\log is where the -l switch (that's a lowercased *L*) tells Snort to log to the path: $SnortPath\log.

- -i# tells the -i switch tells Snort to capture log data on the network interface specified, and # is the number of the interface you want Snort to monitor.

  (If you're unsure which network adapter you want Snort to monitor, type snort -W to list available interfaces — and then choose one. Note that the switch is case-sensitive.)

- *SnortPath* is the path to your root installation of Snort. (For example, ours is D:\snortapps\snort.) The # sign after the -i switch represents the actual network interface that you want Snort to monitor.

2. **Specify the** -i **switch by typing the following command at the command line and then pressing Enter:**

```
snort -W
```

Using WinpCap, Snort outputs the names of your network adapters (probably just one) to the screen, preceding each one by a number. This number is the one you want for the -i switch.

If the service fails to start or if you get an error after executing this command, make sure that you

- Typed the command correctly

- Properly configured the snort.conf file (as discussed in the preceding sections)

In some situations, you won't receive a specific failure message for Snort. In these cases, check the Event Viewer in the Windows Control Panel for details about the error. Usually, there are problems with either your snort.conf file or your MySQL (or other database system) installation.

Part II
Administering Your Snort Box

The 5th Wave   By Rich Tennant

"Someone want to look at this manuscript I received on email called, 'The Embedded Virus That Destroyed the Publisher's Servers When the Manuscript was Rejected.'?"

In this part . . .

This part covers the day-to-day tasks of running your Snort IDS. It starts by showing you how to use Snort's primary output: logs and alerts. Once you have that down, it takes you through installing the ACID console for getting visuals. Snort's intrusion detection rules are at the core of its operation, so it shows you how to create new rules and tweak them to reduce alerts that don't pertain to you. Finally, it shows you how to deal with an actual attack against your computer systems!

Chapter 6

Snorting through Logs and Alerts

Your Snort box is up and running and packets are whizzing around your network at light speed. Are these the packets of productive netizens surfing the Web, transferring files, or playing online games? Or are these pernicious packets packed with peril? Who knows? Your Snort box knows! But will it tell you? If so, how much will it tell you? And will what it tells you make sense, or will it be a jumble of pig-Latin?

If you've ever tried to teach a pig to talk, you know that meaningful communication doesn't come easy. We promise that getting this pig to squeal is much easier, and much more rewarding.

Snort's Basic Output

Snort can log its output in a variety of formats. You can choose your format based on your need for speed, ease post-processing, machine readability, or human readability. Snort can do it all.

tcpdump binary

tcpdump binary is the ultimate in speed and flexible post-processing. This nearly universal method doesn't require the processor-intensive conversion to text. When tcpdump-style logging is used, Snort easily keeps up with very busy networks without dropping packets.

Binary data is great for machines, but tough for people. There are 10 kinds of people in this world: those who understand binary data, and those who don't.

ASCII logging

If you have a hard time interpreting a language made solely of ones and zeros, then consider ASCII logging options.

This chews more CPU cycles than binary logging, but the results are a lot easier for us humans to interpret.

Logging to a database

Logging directly to a database is one of the most useful options for reporting your Snort data and sharing it with others. Although database tables aren't easy to read without a software client, software clients are abundant, and programs to translate the cold hard world of database entries into the warm, fuzzy, and colorful world of Web pages are also plentiful.

Chapter 7 delivers the scoop on how to install and configure ACID: the Analysis Console for Intrusion Detection, a top-notch reporting tool for Snort.

Snort's output facilities

Snort basically has two ways to spit out data. The Snort developers identify these with the technical sounding term *output facilities* instead of the more colloquial *data spitters*. You can tell Snort to

✔ Alert you when an attack is happening, complete with information on
- What kind of attack it is
- Where it's coming from
- Where it's going
- Where to find more information about the attack

✔ Log the actual packets of the attack, showing
- MAC addresses
- IP addresses
- Packet payload
- Timestamp
- TCP flags

Usually, Snort can simultaneously send alerts and log data.

The alert facility

The alert facility is used by Snort to *tell you* when the network traffic matches the criteria defined in a rule. Well, okay, it won't grab you by the ears and yell, "You're getting hacked!" But here's an example of what it might say (all names and IP addresses have been changed to protect the innocent, not to mention the less-than-innocent):

```
01/20-22:34:35.218093  [**] [1:469:1] ICMP PING NMAP [**] [Classification:
            Attempted Information Leak] [Priority: 2] {ICMP} 192.168.1.68 ->
            172.16.34.18
```

This is your Snort box telling you that someone out there is using nmap, a network-security scanning tool, to ping your system — a sure sign that a port scan will shortly follow!

The preceding code says more than "You're getting pinged." In addition to a few jazzy asterisks, it includes

- ✔ Date and time (including the microsecond appended to the second itself)
- ✔ The SID (Snort ID), an identifier indicating which rule was tripped. This is written in the following format:

```
[sig_generator:sig_id:sig_revision]
```

   - *sig_generator* indicates which part of Snort generated the alert
   - *sig_id* is the Snort signature ID, which indicates which rule was tripped
   - *sig_revision* is the revision number of this rule
- ✔ A brief text message
- ✔ Classification and priority of the attack
- ✔ The protocol of the packet that tripped the rule
- ✔ Source and destination IP addresses involved

Whew, that's a lot! And that's just for the alert_fast output module, which prints a minimum of information. Other modules will print the MAC addresses, TCP flags, or even the packet payload in ASCII or hex. The options aren't limitless, but Snort can print enough detail to satisfy even the most hardcore wire head.

The log facility

The log facility doesn't sound any alarms. It quietly logs all of the packet information relevant to this particular attack. There are times when you may want to log attack data without generating alerts. For example, running Snort as a souped-up packet sniffer. Here's the same Nmap ping logged by the logging facility. It shows the details of the port scan to port 80 as well:

```
01/14-19:42:03.114656 0:10:67:0:B2:50 -> 0:A0:CC:D2:10:31 type:0x800 len:0x3C
192.168.1.68 -> 172.16.34.18 ICMP TTL:37 TOS:0x0 ID:44936 IpLen:20 DgmLen:28
Type:8  Code:0  ID:13988   Seq:7720  ECHO

=+=+=+=+=+=+=+=+=+=+=+=+=+=+=+=+=+=+=+=+=+=+=+=+=+=+=+=+=+=+=+=+=+=+=+=+

01/14-19:42:03.114717 0:A0:CC:D2:10:31 -> 0:10:67:0:B2:50 type:0x800 len:0x2A
172.16.34.18 -> 192.168.1.68 ICMP TTL:255 TOS:0x0 ID:2734 IpLen:20 DgmLen:28
Type:0  Code:0  ID:13988  Seq:7720  ECHO REPLY

=+=+=+=+=+=+=+=+=+=+=+=+=+=+=+=+=+=+=+=+=+=+=+=+=+=+=+=+=+=+=+=+=+=+=+=+

01/14-19:42:03.115157 0:10:67:0:B2:50 -> 0:A0:CC:D2:10:31 type:0x800 len:0x3C
192.168.1.68:50488 -> 172.16.34.18:80 TCP TTL:36 TOS:0x0 ID:3836 IpLen:20
            DgmLen:40
***A**** Seq: 0x3C4A079E  Ack: 0x498A079E  Win: 0x800  TcpLen: 20

=+=+=+=+=+=+=+=+=+=+=+=+=+=+=+=+=+=+=+=+=+=+=+=+=+=+=+=+=+=+=+=+=+=+=+=+

01/14-19:42:03.115194 0:A0:CC:D2:10:31 -> 0:10:67:0:B2:50 type:0x800 len:0x36
172.16.34.18:80 -> 192.168.1.68:50488 TCP TTL:255 TOS:0x0 ID:0 IpLen:20
            DgmLen:40 DF
*****R** Seq: 0x498A079E  Ack: 0x0  Win: 0x0  TcpLen: 20

=+=+=+=+=+=+=+=+=+=+=+=+=+=+=+=+=+=+=+=+=+=+=+=+=+=+=+=+=+=+=+=+=+=+=+=+

01/14-19:42:03.420876 0:10:67:0:B2:50 -> 0:A0:CC:D2:10:31 type:0x800 len:0x3C
192.168.1.68:50468 -> 172.16.34.18:80 TCP TTL:41 TOS:0x0 ID:64826 IpLen:20
            DgmLen:40
******S* Seq: 0x6E30F501  Ack: 0x0  Win: 0xC00  TcpLen: 20

=+=+=+=+=+=+=+=+=+=+=+=+=+=+=+=+=+=+=+=+=+=+=+=+=+=+=+=+=+=+=+=+=+=+=+=+

01/14-19:42:03.420964 0:A0:CC:D2:10:31 -> 0:10:67:0:B2:50 type:0x800 len:0x3A
172.16.34.18:80 -> 192.168.1.68:50468 TCP TTL:64 TOS:0x0 ID:0 IpLen:20 DgmLen:44
            DF
***A**S* Seq: 0xAC878D4E  Ack: 0x6E30F502  Win: 0x16D0  TcpLen: 24
TCP Options (1) => MSS: 1460

=+=+=+=+=+=+=+=+=+=+=+=+=+=+=+=+=+=+=+=+=+=+=+=+=+=+=+=+=+=+=+=+=+=+=+=+

01/14-19:42:03.459314 0:10:67:0:B2:50 -> 0:A0:CC:D2:10:31 type:0x800 len:0x3C
192.168.1.68:50468 -> 172.16.34.18:80 TCP TTL:47 TOS:0x0 ID:0 IpLen:20 DgmLen:40
            DF
*****R** Seq: 0x6E30F502  Ack: 0x0  Win: 0x0  TcpLen: 20

=+=+=+=+=+=+=+=+=+=+=+=+=+=+=+=+=+=+=+=+=+=+=+=+=+=+=+=+=+=+=+=+=+=+=+=+
```

If you'll run Snort as an Intrusion Detection System, you need to generate alerts. Most of the time you'll want to log relevant packet information as well so you can trace the steps of an attack packet by packet.

Snort's Output Modules

As of version 1.6, Snort uses output modules, or output plug-ins, to write the data sent by the logging and alerting output facilities.

Snort's alerting and logging facilities don't actually write the data. They send data to the appropriate output module, which handles the formatting and writing of the logs. Anyone can write their own output module for handling Snort's output in specific ways, and multiple output modules can be combined for custom logging.

Snort can be run in a few ways.

- ✔ As a daemon, constantly running as a background process monitoring the network for intrusion attempts
- ✔ From the command line as a packet sniffer (much like its forefather tcp-dump)
- ✔ As a kind of super packet sniffer that captures data, then compares it to known attack signatures on the fly

Some of Snort's output modules are better suited for daemon mode and some for packet-sniffing mode. They can all be combined with one another, and used effectively no matter how you run Snort.

As we'll see, each output module is called with a slightly different syntax depending on whether you call it from the command line, or the configuration file. By default the output modules send their data to /var/log/snort, but of course, a different directory can be specified to suit your tastes.

A different log directory can be specified on the command line by using the -l switch. All ASCII (plain text) packet logs and alerts will go to this directory. If the -l switch isn't used, logs will go to /var/log/snort by default.

Any option that's specified on the command line will silently override that same option in the snort.conf file. For instance, if you have output alert_fast: snort.log in your snort.conf file, but you call snort on the command line with the -A full switch, Snort will run with full alerts, and your snort.log file will contain the fully decoded packet header as well as the alert itself. (We cover the fast and full alerting options themselves in more detail in the following section, "Alerting modules.")

Alerting modules

Snort's got a couple of different ways to generate alert data depending on how much detail you want in your alerts, and where you want to send them. We start with some of the more basic options, and work our way up in complexity.

Configuration of output modules is done within the snort.conf configuration file. (From our Linux installation in Chapter 4, the configuration file is `/usr/local/snort/etc/snort.conf`. In the Windows installation in Chapter 5, the location is `D:\snortapps\Snort\etc\snort.conf`.) Open snort.conf and find the output plug-ins section. In the default snort.conf, this section is labeled with the comment "Step #3: Configure output plug-ins." Find the section either by searching for Step #3, or by searching for the word "output." All of the following output module configuration is done within this section.

alert_fast

This is a straightforward, no nonsense way for you to get Snort alerts. The alert_fast module will print alerts in a one line format to whatever file you specify. It's fast because Snort doesn't burn CPU cycles converting packet headers to ASCII or writing them to the output file.

The syntax to use in your snort.conf file to specify the `alert_fast` output module is:

```
output alert_fast: snort.log
```

To use fast alerts when calling Snort on the command line, use the `-A fast` option.

Fast alerts show the flavor of attack, its classification, source, destination, and a timestamp. Not much else gets logged using the `alert_fast` output module, which is one of the reasons it's so fast.

```
01/16-22:57:23.872383  [**] [1:1122:4] WEB-MISC /etc/passwd [**]
          [Classification: Attempted Information Leak] [Priority: 2] {TCP}
          192.168.1.68:44258 -> 172.16.34.18:80
01/16-22:57:24.668612  [**] [1:1113:4] WEB-MISC http directory traversal [**]
          [Classification: Attempted Information Leak] [Priority: 2] {TCP}
          192.168.1.68:44266 -> 172.16.34.18:80
01/16-22:57:24.668612  [**] [119:2:1] (http_inspect) DOUBLE DECODING ATTACK [**]
          {TCP} 192.168.1.68:44266 -> 172.16.34.18:80
01/16-22:57:24.767891  [**] [1:1113:4] WEB-MISC http directory traversal [**]
          [Classification: Attempted Information Leak] [Priority: 2] {TCP}
          192.168.1.68:44267 -> 172.16.34.18:80
01/16-22:57:24.767891  [**] [119:2:1] (http_inspect) DOUBLE DECODING ATTACK [**]
          {TCP} 192.168.1.68:44267 -> 172.16.34.18:80
01/16-22:57:24.867426  [**] [1:988:6] WEB-IIS SAM Attempt [**] [Classification:
          Web Application Attack] [Priority: 1] {TCP} 192.168.1.68:44268 ->
          172.16.34.18:80
```

Wow, that *was* fast! Remember, this data gets logged to `/var/log/snort/alert` by default.

alert_full

The `alert_fast` output module will print Snort alerts with the full packet headers decoded into plain text. This gives you significantly more information about an attack, but it comes at the price of significantly decreased performance, and shouldn't really be used unless your Snort box is on a lightly trafficked network. Use this option on a network with a lot of traffic, and Snort *will* drop packets. Not only that, but you'll be writing gobs of data to your hard drive, reducing free space and causing an I/O bottleneck on your system.

To generate full alerts, edit your `snort.conf` file to specify the following output module configuration:

```
output alert_full: alert.full
```

Here we see the logs written to `/var/log/snort/alert.full`, as specified in the preceding output module configuration:

```
[**] [1:1668:5] WEB-CGI /cgi-bin/ access [**]
[Classification: Web Application Attack] [Priority: 1]
01/16-23:06:11.675382 0:10:67:0:B2:50 -> 0:A0:CC:D2:10:31 type:0x800 len:0xDD
192.168.1.68:44561 -> 172.16.34.18:80 TCP TTL:47 TOS:0x0 ID:53932 IpLen:20
          DgmLen:207 DF
***AP*** Seq: 0xD5349716  Ack: 0x2B34D8BB  Win: 0x16D0  TcpLen: 32
TCP Options (3) => NOP NOP TS: 322913730 135653681

[**] [1:1201:7] ATTACK-RESPONSES 403 Forbidden [**]
[Classification: Attempted Information Leak] [Priority: 2]
01/16-23:06:11.675864 0:A0:CC:D2:10:31 -> 0:10:67:0:B2:50 type:0x800 len:0x268
172.16.34.18:80 -> 192.168.1.68:44561 TCP TTL:64 TOS:0x0 ID:12687 IpLen:20
          DgmLen:602 DF
***AP*** Seq: 0x2B34D8BB  Ack: 0xD53497B1  Win: 0x16A0  TcpLen: 32
TCP Options (3) => NOP NOP TS: 135653685 322913730

[**] [1:1852:3] WEB-MISC robots.txt access [**]
[Classification: access to a potentially vulnerable Web application] [Priority:
          2]
01/16-23:06:13.035036 0:10:67:0:B2:50 -> 0:A0:CC:D2:10:31 type:0x800 len:0xDF
192.168.1.68:44572 -> 172.16.34.18:80 TCP TTL:47 TOS:0x0 ID:27543 IpLen:20
          DgmLen:209 DF
***AP*** Seq: 0xD5D72DD3  Ack: 0x2BD8E79A  Win: 0x16D0  TcpLen: 32
TCP Options (3) => NOP NOP TS: 322913866 135653817
[Xref => http://cgi.nessus.org/plugins/dump.php3?id=10302]

[**] [1:1145:6] WEB-MISC /~root access [**]
[Classification: Attempted Information Leak] [Priority: 2]
01/16-23:06:13.233595 0:10:67:0:B2:50 -> 0:A0:CC:D2:10:31 type:0x800 len:0xDA
192.168.1.68:44574 -> 172.16.34.18:80 TCP TTL:47 TOS:0x0 ID:5770 IpLen:20
          DgmLen:204 DF
```

```
***AP*** Seq: 0xD55950D4  Ack: 0x2B16C39E  Win: 0x16D0  TcpLen: 32
TCP Options (3) => NOP NOP TS: 322913886 135653837

[**] [1:1156:4] WEB-MISC apache DOS attempt [**]
[Classification: Attempted Denial of Service] [Priority: 2]
01/16-23:06:13.542489 0:10:67:0:B2:50 -> 0:A0:CC:D2:10:31 type:0x800 len:0x1D5
192.168.1.68:44577 -> 172.16.34.18:80 TCP TTL:47 TOS:0x0 ID:62470 IpLen:20
          DgmLen:455 DF
***AP*** Seq: 0xD62EB27E  Ack: 0x2B97F12D  Win: 0x16D0  TcpLen: 32
TCP Options (3) => NOP NOP TS: 322913917 135653868
```

Full alerts can also be specified on the command line using the -A full switch. But unless you're doing some network debugging or you're on a network segment with light traffic, this option isn't recommended.

alert_syslog

Sending alerts to a log file is great, but the methods we just mentioned lack a bit of flexibility. What if you want to send the alert data to a remote logging server? Or what if your Snort sensor is on a lightly trafficked network, and you want alerts sent to the same log file as other security alerts, like invalid logins, or attempts by users to "su" to root? To add a bit of flexibility to your logging, use the alert_syslog option to send your alerts to the Unix syslog facility.

Alert_syslog basically does the same thing as alert_fast: It formats Snort alerts as a single line showing what kind of attack is happening, the classification, source, and destination of the attack. Alert_syslog shines by taking advantage of the syslog daemon's features.

One of the nicest features of syslog is the ability to send logs to a remote log server. If a computer system has been compromised, it's wise not to trust the log files on that system, since most attackers will concentrate on covering their tracks after getting in almost as much as they concentrate on cracking the system in the first place. With remote logging, the attacker will have a much harder time covering their tracks, since they must compromise both your remote logging server and the one they just broke into.

Configuring Snort for syslog logging is as easy as specifying the following in your snort.conf file:

```
alert_syslog: <facility> <priority>
```

You can use any one of the following facilities:

```
LOG_AUTH
LOG_AUTHPRIV
LOG_DAEMON
```

```
LOG_LOCAL0
LOG_LOCAL1
LOG_LOCAL2
LOG_LOCAL3
LOG_LOCAL4
LOG_LOCAL5
LOG_LOCAL6
LOG_LOCAL7
LOG_USER
```

and any of the following priorities:

```
LOG_EMERG
LOG_ALERT
LOG_CRIT
LOG_ERR
LOG_WARNING
LOG_NOTICE
LOG_INFO
LOG_DEBUG
```

The preceding options give you lots of possibilities, but if you simply want to get Snort logging to the local syslog log file and move on, enter the following in your snort.conf configuration file:

```
output alert_syslog: LOG_AUTH LOG_ALERT
```

Snort doesn't care which syslog priority you specify as much as syslog does. That is to say that if you specify the LOG_ALERT priority, Snort will spit out the same data as if you specified the LOG_DEBUG priority. The difference matters when it comes to telling syslog where to send the data. For example, if you have the following lines in your snort.conf file (remember, you can specify multiple outputs):

```
output alert_syslog: LOG_LOCAL3 LOG_ALERT
output alert_syslog: LOG_LOCAL3 LOG_DEBUG
```

and you've got this in your syslog.conf file:

```
local3.debug                    /var/log/snort.debug
local3.alert                    /var/log/snort.alert
```

after running Snort for a while, both /var/log/snort.debug and /var/log/snort.alert will be identical. Of course, you could do the same thing by using one alert_syslog module and one alert_fast module, both pointed at different files:

```
output alert_syslog: LOG_LOCAL3 LOG_ALERT
output alert_fast: /var/log/snort/snort.alert
```

So why specify different priorities? Mainly because syslog wants to see *some kind* of priority attached to a log entry. It also comes in handy if you intend to send the same data to two different locations. If you're really paranoid about system security, you might want to keep one copy of your snort logs on your snort system, and another identical copy on your remote logging server. This way, if your log files ever differ between the two systems, you can reasonably suspect that shenanigans are afoot, and someone's been tampering with your logs!

Logging to a remote syslog server

So how do we configure syslog for remote logging? Thankfully, it's not nearly as hard as you might think. There is no difference in your snort.conf file if you're using local syslog logging or remote logging, in both cases you simply specify which facility and priority to use. The changes need to be made in the syslog.conf file on your Snort system, as well as the initialization script that starts the syslog daemon (syslogd on Linux systems) on the remote logging server.

To send syslog entries to a remote server instead of a local file, simply specify an @ sign and the server's IP address instead of a local file. For example, to send all local3 facility logs to 192.168.1.51, your syslog.conf file should include the following line:

```
local3.*   @192.168.1.51
```

To keep one copy of your logs locally, and one copy on a remote syslog server, you could include the following in your snort.conf file:

```
output alert_syslog: LOG_LOCAL3 LOG_ALERT
output alert_syslog: LOG_LOCAL3 LOG_DEBUG
```

and this in your syslog.conf file:

```
local3.debug                    /var/log/snort.debug
local3.alert                    @192.168.1.51
```

Naturally, you need to configure your remote logging server to accept this data, as well as tell it where to write the data. In this case, we're sending data with the local3 facility, and telling the remote syslog server where to write the data is no different than if it originated locally:

```
local3.*                 /var/log/snort.log
```

To tell the syslog daemon to accept log data from remote sources, syslogd must be started with the -r switch. If you're running Red Hat Linux or SuSe Linux, check /etc/sysconfig/syslog file.

On Red Hat, change the line that reads:

```
SYSLOGD_OPTIONS="-m 0"
```

to

```
SYSLOGD_OPTIONS="-r -m 0"
```

And on SuSE, add a -r to your `SYSLOGD_PARAMS=""` line, so it reads:

```
SYSLOGD_PARAMS="-r"
```

If you're running Debian GNU/Linux, look at `/etc/init.d/sysklogd`. About a dozen lines down in the file, change the line:

```
SYSLOGD=""
```

to:

```
SYSLOGD="-r"
```

Once you've edited the appropriate file and changed the way syslogd starts up, don't forget to restart it so your changes take effect!

Now if you look at the `/var/log/snort.log` file on your remote log server, you should see your alerts:

```
Jan 15 16:12:59 yoursnortbox.yourdomain.com snort: [1:483:2] ICMP PING CyberKit
          2.2 Windows [Classification: Misc activity] [Priority: 3]: {ICMP}
          192.168.200.50 -> 172.16.34.18
Jan 15 16:15:41 yoursnortbox.yourdomain.com snort: [1:483:2] ICMP PING CyberKit
          2.2 Windows [Classification: Misc activity] [Priority: 3]: {ICMP}
          10.64.229.250 -> 172.16.34.18
Jan 15 16:16:23 yoursnortbox.yourdomain.com snort: [1:2003:2] MS-SQL Worm
          propagation attempt [Classification: Misc Attack] [Priority: 2]:
          {UDP} 10.77.29.69:1282 -> 172.16.34.18:1434
Jan 15 16:17:37 yoursnortbox.yourdomain.com snort: [1:483:2] ICMP PING CyberKit
          2.2 Windows [Classification: Misc activity] [Priority: 3]: {ICMP}
          64.123.246.211 -> 172.16.34.18
```

Notice how the hostname of your Snort box is appended at the beginning of each line? You'll be glad this information is there if you're running a centralized log server with multiple machines logging to it.

Replacing syslog with syslog-ng

`syslog` is a wonderful tool that's been in the Unix world for a long time. So long, in fact, that it's starting to look a little long in the tooth. Enter `syslog-ng` — the Next Generation of `syslog` — a drop-in replacement that includes better remote logging and log forwarding, built-in message filtering, and logging over TCP as well as UDP protocols. (The older `syslog` only handles the less-secure UDP protocol.) On the drawing board for future versions of `syslog-ng` is message integrity and encryption.

Why should you consider `syslog-ng`? If our glowing description of its features hasn't enticed you enough, imagine having the capability to easily split your Snort alerts out to different files *depending on the nature of the attack.* (While this is technically possible with traditional `syslog` and some hacking of your `snort.conf` and `local.rules` files, `syslog-ng` makes the process much easier.) What about real-time file monitoring of all your `syslog` files? Or the capability to launch specific programs based on the content of incoming log entries? Add-on software such as Swatch can help handle these tasks when you're using the traditional `syslog` program, but why rely on external software when you can do it all from `syslog-ng`? Even if you install `syslog-ng` solely for use with Snort right now, once you've become familiar with its power and flexibility, you'll be amazed at what you can do.

Some distributions of Linux are starting to ship with `syslog-ng` as an install-time option, and others have syslog-ng available as a precompiled binary. If your favorite distribution lacks a `syslog-ng` package, you can grab the source code and compile it for yourself (not a bad idea anyway, even if there's a binary package available for you).

`syslog-ng` lives at `http://www.bala bit.com/products/syslog_ng/` where you can find links to the source code, documentation, and mailing lists. If you're going to install syslog-ng, it's a good idea to subscribe to the mailing list, or at least peruse the archives a bit. You'll find more up-to-date information this way than by reading the Web site or even the documentation included in the syslog-ng source code.

`syslog-ng` depends on libol, a support library that's also available from the syslog-ng Web site. Once you've got both packages downloaded, installation is relatively painless. Assuming you've downloaded the source tarballs to `/usr/local/src/tarballs`, installation is as follows (the version numbers of libol and `syslog-ng` will have most likely changed by the time you read this):

```
# cd /usr/local/src
# tar -xvzf tarballs/libol-
   0.3.2.12.tar.gz
# tar -xvzf tarballs/syslog-ng-
   1.6.1.tar.gz
# cd libol-0.3.12/
# ./configure
# make
# make install
# ldconfig
# cd ../syslog-ng-1.6.1/
# ./configure
# make
# make install
```

Once you've got syslog-ng compiled, it's time to build a syslog-ng.conf file. This can be an overwhelming task if you must start from scratch, but most folks won't, since there are already sample configuration files included in the doc/ and contrib/ subdirectories of the syslog-ng source code. If you've already got a custom tailored syslog.conf file that you're very proud of, and you sneer at the notion of someone's default configuration file fitting your needs, you can relax; there's a shell script that will generate a syslog-ng.conf file from your existing syslog.conf file.

Since we've already customized our syslog.conf file, let's use the script to generate an appropriate syslog-ng.conf file. Before running the script, make sure you've got an /etc/syslog-ng directory. We're going to run the script, and redirect the output to this directory, creating our new configuration file in one fell swoop.

```
# mkdir /etc/syslog-ng
# cd /usr/local/src/syslog-ng-
    1.6.1/contrib
# cat /etc/syslog.conf |
    ./syslog2ng > /etc/syslog-
    ng/syslog-ng.conf
```

Swoop! You've got a configuration file! Pull it up in your favorite text editor and give it a gander.

You'll notice that the script has kept each line from your original syslog.conf file in the new file, but the line is commented out, so syslog-ng ignores it when initialized.

Once you've got your configuration file set up, you'll want to make sure you've got an initialization script in place so syslog-ng starts up at boot time. There are many sample initialization scripts in the contrib/ directory; find one that matches your system, and place it in your /etc/init.d directory (or wherever your initialization scripts go for your flavor of Linux). For more information on setting up initialization scripts, see the section titled "Keeping a low profile" in Chapter 4. Once syslog-ng is set to start at boot time, disable the old syslog script so syslog won't start at boot time.

To see some of the neat tricks you can do with syslog-ng and how they can apply to your Snort installation, check out Chapter 11.

If you're running Snort on a Windows platform, you don't have a native syslog daemon, and the differences between the alert_syslog output module and the alert_fast output module may be so small as to not be worth your worry. If you decide that remote logging is just so cool that you've got to try it in Windows, grab a patch from by Frank Knobbe that lets you use syslog-style remote logging from the command line, without clobbering the rest of your logging settings in your snort.conf file. The patch is available from the Snort.org Web site at: http://www.snort.org/dl/contrib/patches/win32syslog/.

If you decide that syslog by itself is such a cool idea that you've got to have a syslog daemon for Windows, check out the Kiwi Syslog Daemon, from Kiwi Enterprises at http://www.kiwisyslog.com. Kiwi Syslog Daemon comes in two versions: A freeware version that you can download and use without paying anything, and a licensed version that comes with extra features (such as database logging and better performance) for around $99.

alert_CSV

CSV stands for Comma Separated Values, a nearly universal intermediate format for importing data into databases or spreadsheets. If you want to process your Snort alerts in a database that's not natively supported by

Snort, like MS Access, or import them into a spreadsheet such as Excel, or run them through your own home-brewed analysis program, the alert_CSV output module is for you. To specify it in your snort.conf file, use the following format:

```
output alert_CSV: <destination file> <format>
```

Where `<destination file>` is the file where you want your CSV-formatted data to land, and `<format>` is a comma separated list of alert data to write. If you want to log everything, you can specify `default` as the format to use. Table 6-1 lists all of the CSV fields you can write. If you use the default format, the fields will be written in the order listed in Table 6-1, top to bottom.

Table 6-1	CSV Fields Used by the alert_CSV Output Module
Module Syntax	*What You're Actually Capturing*
timestamp	The date and time of the attack
msg	Alert message, telling you what kind of attack it is
proto	Protocol of the packet that caused the alert
src	Source IP address of the packet that caused the alert
srcport	Source port of the attack packet
dst	Destination IP address of the attack packet
dstport	Destination port of the packet
ethsrc	Ethernet source (MAC address)
ethdst	Ethernet destination (MAC address)
ethlen	Ethernet frame size
tcpflag	Any TCP flags associated with the attack packet
tcpseq	TCP sequence number
tcplen	TCP packet length
tcpwindow	TCP window size
ttl	Time to live
tos	Type of service
id	Identification
dgmlen	Datagram length
iplen	IP length

Module Syntax	What You're Actually Capturing
icmptype	ICMP type
icmpcode	ICMP code
icmpid	ICMP ID
icmpseq	ICMP sequence number

So to just start logging all format information to a CSV file called alert.csv, add the following entry to the snort.conf configuration file:

```
output alert_CSV: /var/log/snort/alert.csv default
```

Here's a snippet of the alert.csv log file showing some ICMP (ping) probe activity, using the default format we specified in the preceding alert_CSV configuration:

```
01/15-21:39:00.801134 ,ICMP PING CyberKit 2.2
         Windows,ICMP,67.95.155.138,,172.16.34.18,,0:10:67:
         0:B2:50,0:A0:CC:D2:10:31,0x6A,,,,,,111,0,40019,92,
         20,8,0,,
01/15-21:43:07.555566 ,ICMP PING CyberKit 2.2
         Windows,ICMP,213.86.221.179,,172.16.34.19,,0:10:67
         :0:B2:50,0:C0:F0:2B:E5:F8,0x6A,,,,,,107,0,25381,92
         ,20,8,0,,
01/15-21:45:35.047068 ,ICMP PING CyberKit 2.2
         Windows,ICMP,213.249.229.182,,172.16.34.18,,0:10:6
         7:0:B2:50,0:A0:CC:D2:10:31,0x6A,,,,,,105,0,17518,9
         2,20,8,0,,
```

Too much information? You can simplify it by telling the alert_CSV module to log only what you want. Maybe you're only interested in the timestamp, alert message, source IP address, and destination IP address. Use this line in your snort.conf file:

```
output alert_CSV: /var/log/snort/alert.csv timestamp,msg,src,dst
```

It will generate much more succinct data, such as this entry showing many Web-based attacks against a Web server:

```
01/16-20:33:08.978678 ,ATTACK-RESPONSES 403 Forbidden,172.16.34.18,192.168.1.68
01/16-20:33:10.250312 ,WEB-MISC robots.txt access,192.168.1.68,172.16.34.18
01/16-20:33:10.490020 ,WEB-MISC /~root access,192.168.1.68,172.16.34.18
01/16-20:33:10.792501 ,WEB-MISC apache DOS attempt,192.168.1.68,172.16.34.18
01/16-20:33:11.614642 ,WEB-MISC .DS_Store access,192.168.1.68,172.16.34.18
01/16-20:33:11.709005 ,WEB-MISC .FBCIndex access,192.168.1.68,172.16.34.18
01/16-20:33:12.792244 ,WEB-CGI printenv access,192.168.1.68,172.16.34.18
```

This looks a little easier to handle. With Snort, as with all things in life, make sure you know what you need, and don't be concerned with what you don't need.

Logging modules

Logging modules are used to log packet information. Sounds simple enough, right? Logging modules are typically called by alert modules in order to log packet information relevant to a particular alert, but they can also be called by some of the preprocessors, or called independently from the command line.

Confused? Follow along in Figure 6-1. For IDS mode, in a nutshell: Snort captures network traffic and applies a preprocessor on it that normalizes the traffic into a recognizable format. If the preprocessor deems the traffic noteworthy, it can call an output module to send an alert, or log the packet, or do both (depending on how the preprocessor is written). Snort then compares the normalized network traffic to a list of rules. If the packet matches a particular rule, then Snort generates an alert using the appropriate alert module (specified in snort.conf or on the command line). When the alert is generated, Snort *also* calls the appropriate logging module to log details of the network packets that matched the rule. Now when you see the alert in your logs, you can go back and examine the packet information responsible for generating the alert.

Default logging in ASCII format using -l

Snort can be used to log network traffic without generating alerts. In fact, Snort started life as a hopped-up version of tcpdump, the ubiquitous packet capture program used by network geeks everywhere. The simplest way to generate logging (not alerting) is to call Snort from the command line and tell it to log packet data somewhere using the -l switch which specifies a logging directory.

The -l switch is available and useful from the command line only. If you are running Snort with the -D switch for daemon mode, and you're specifying a snort.conf file with the -c switch, you're not going to get much use out of using the -l switch for logging packet information.

Create a test logging directory, then tell snort to send its log data there. At a command prompt under Linux, do the following:

```
# mkdir /var/log/snort/test_logging
# /usr/local/bin/snort -l /var/log/snort/test_logging/
```

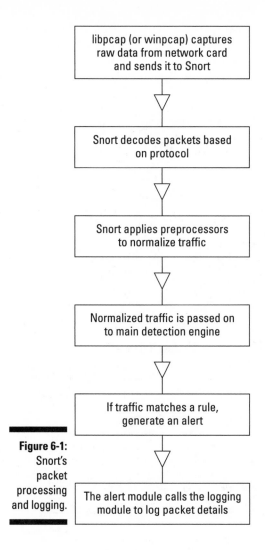

libpcap (or winpcap) captures
raw data from network card
and sends it to Snort

Snort decodes packets based
on protocol

Snort applies preprocessors
to normalize traffic

Normalized traffic is passed on
to main detection engine

If traffic matches a rule,
generate an alert

The alert module calls the logging
module to log packet details

Figure 6-1:
Snort's
packet
processing
and logging.

In Windows:

```
C:\snort\bin>mkdir c:\snort\logs
C:\snort\bin>snort -l c:\snort\logs
```

Let this run for a minute or so, then kill it by hitting Ctrl+C. Now take a look at
the /var/log/snort/test_logging directory. You'll see a set of subdirectories, one for each IP address that's been sending packets to and from your
network. If you look at the files in these subdirectories, you'll find a bunch of
files, named for the protocol, source port, and destination port of each
packet. Here's someone poking at my Web server (the nerve!):

```
# cd /var/log/snort/test_logging/
# ls
192.168.1.68  10.100.11.17  ARP
# cd 192.168.1.68/
# ls
TCP:45955-80  TCP:45961-80  TCP:45967-80  TCP:45973-80  TCP:45979-80
# less TCP:45991-80
01/16-23:34:11.865655 192.168.1.68:45991 -> 172.16.34.18:80
TCP TTL:47 TOS:0x0 ID:44483 IpLen:20 DgmLen:60 DF
******S* Seq: 0x3ED87B82  Ack: 0x0  Win: 0x16D0  TcpLen: 40
TCP Options (5) => MSS: 1460 SackOK TS: 323081793 0 NOP WS: 0
=+=+=+=+=+=+=+=+=+=+=+=+=+=+=+=+=+=+=+=+=+=+=+=+=+=+=+=+=+=+=+=+

01/16-23:34:11.865697 172.16.34.18:80 -> 192.168.1.68:45991
TCP TTL:64 TOS:0x0 ID:0 IpLen:20 DgmLen:60 DF
***A**S* Seq: 0x933AEFD2  Ack: 0x3ED87B83  Win: 0x16A0  TcpLen: 40
TCP Options (5) => MSS: 1460 SackOK TS: 135821704 323081793 NOP
TCP Options => WS: 0
=+=+=+=+=+=+=+=+=+=+=+=+=+=+=+=+=+=+=+=+=+=+=+=+=+=+=+=+=+=+=+=+

01/16-23:34:11.901372 192.168.1.68:45991 -> 172.16.34.18:80
TCP TTL:47 TOS:0x0 ID:44484 IpLen:20 DgmLen:52 DF
***A**** Seq: 0x3ED87B83  Ack: 0x933AEFD3  Win: 0x16D0  TcpLen: 32
TCP Options (3) => NOP NOP TS: 323081797 135821704
=+=+=+=+=+=+=+=+=+=+=+=+=+=+=+=+=+=+=+=+=+=+=+=+=+=+=+=+=+=+=+=+

01/16-23:34:11.903218 192.168.1.68:45991 -> 172.16.34.18:80
TCP TTL:47 TOS:0x0 ID:44485 IpLen:20 DgmLen:203 DF
***AP*** Seq: 0x3ED87B83  Ack: 0x933AEFD3  Win: 0x16D0  TcpLen: 32
TCP Options (3) => NOP NOP TS: 323081797 135821704
=+=+=+=+=+=+=+=+=+=+=+=+=+=+=+=+=+=+=+=+=+=+=+=+=+=+=+=+=+=+=+=+

01/16-23:34:11.903262 172.16.34.18:80 -> 192.168.1.68:45991
TCP TTL:64 TOS:0x0 ID:38495 IpLen:20 DgmLen:52 DF
***A**** Seq: 0x933AEFD3  Ack: 0x3ED87C1A  Win: 0x16A0  TcpLen: 32
TCP Options (3) => NOP NOP TS: 135821708 323081797
=+=+=+=+=+=+=+=+=+=+=+=+=+=+=+=+=+=+=+=+=+=+=+=+=+=+=+=+=+=+=+=+
```

Notice how any mention of a specific alert is conspicuously absent from
these files.

If you're like us, you want to see what's happening *as it happens,* instead of
seeing what happened after the fact. Ever bake a cake with the oven light on
the whole time? It doesn't make the cake cook any faster, but it's kind of cool
to watch it rise. For those of us who need this instant gratification, Snort has
the -v switch. When logging packet data, this will send the data straight to
the console.

Since Snort is a descendant of tcpdump, it will take much of the same command line syntax as tcpdump, including expressions dictating what kind of traffic to process, and what to ignore. If you're going to try running Snort with the -v switch to watch decoded packets and you're accessing your Snort machine over an SSH connection, make sure to tell Snort to ignore your SSH traffic, otherwise your terminal will turn into an unreadable flood of data as Snort displays the headers for each SSH packet. Each packet sent back to your terminal will in turn have its headers displayed, causing an unending cycle of data streaming.

The -v switch is great for debugging purposes, but it slows down Snort considerably, and causes Snort to drop packets. Don't use the -v switch while running Snort in IDS mode, or you might miss an attack.

If you want to log more detail about each packet, you can use the -d switch to dump application layer data from each packet, and you can use the -e switch to dump the link layer data from each packet. Here, we tell Snort to ignore our own SSH packets (which operate over port 22), and print all other packets to the terminal showing the application layer as well as the link layer:

```
# snort -vde not port 22
Running in packet logging mode
Log directory = /var/log/snort/test_logging2/

Initializing Network Interface eth0

        --== Initializing Snort ==--
Initializing Output Plugins!
Decoding Ethernet on interface eth0

        --== Initialization Complete ==--

-*> Snort! <*-
Version 2.1.0 (Build 9)
By Martin Roesch (roesch@sourcefire.com, www.snort.org)


01/16-01:22:23.654699 0:10:67:0:B2:50 -> 0:A0:CC:D2:10:31 type:0x800 len:0x6A
192.168.16.50 -> 172.16.34.18 ICMP TTL:104 TOS:0x0 ID:60592 IpLen:20 DgmLen:92
Type:8  Code:0  ID:56566    Seq:16552  ECHO
AA AA AA AA AA AA AA AA AA AA AA AA AA AA AA AA  ................
AA AA AA AA AA AA AA AA AA AA AA AA AA AA AA AA  ................
AA AA AA AA AA AA AA AA AA AA AA AA AA AA AA AA  ................
AA AA AA AA AA AA AA AA AA AA AA AA AA AA AA AA  ................

=+=+=+=+=+=+=+=+=+=+=+=+=+=+=+=+=+=+=+=+=+=+=+=+=+=+=+=+=+=+=+=+
```

```
01/16-01:22:23.654842 0:A0:CC:D2:10:31 -> 0:10:67:0:B2:50 type:0x800 len:0x6A
172.16.34.18 -> 192.168.16.50 ICMP TTL:255 TOS:0x0 ID:35856 IpLen:20 DgmLen:92
Type:0  Code:0  ID:56566  Seq:16552  ECHO REPLY
AA AA AA AA AA AA AA AA AA AA AA AA AA AA AA AA    ................
AA AA AA AA AA AA AA AA AA AA AA AA AA AA AA AA    ................
AA AA AA AA AA AA AA AA AA AA AA AA AA AA AA AA    ................
AA AA AA AA AA AA AA AA AA AA AA AA AA AA AA AA    ................

=+=+=+=+=+=+=+=+=+=+=+=+=+=+=+=+=+=+=+=+=+=+=+=+=+=+=+=+=+=+=+=+=+=+=+=+=+=+
```

Yep, we're getting pinged (the keywords ICMP, ECHO, and ECHO REPLY clue us into this). If you want to see more interesting traffic than this, run the same command on your own Snort box and see what you get. If the output is too much to deal with, try playing around with different expressions to ignore different kinds of traffic. For a list of useful command-line options that pertain to Snort's logging and alerting, see the sidebar titled, "Snort's command-line switches for logging and alerting" in this chapter.

using log_tcpdump

It may come as no surprise that the log_tcpdump logging module logs data to a binary tcpdump-formatted file. Logging binary data is very fast for Snort, since it skips the binary to text conversion process associated with other forms of logging.

Once you've got log data in a tcpdump format, you can use any one of many different tools for post processing. If you've been working with networks for a while, it's possible that you already have a favorite tool for working with network packet captures. One of ours is Ethereal, a great GUI packet-sniffer that can actively capture data or display previously recorded network traffic.

The log_tcpdump output module takes only one argument when specified in your snort.conf file, and that is the destination file for logging its data:

```
output log_tcpdump: snort.dump
```

Remember, by default Snort will send all of its output to /var/log/snort unless you specify a different path, or override this setting on the command line.

When running Snort as an IDS, the log_tcpdump module is activated when packets match Snort rules and generate alerts. It will log packets that are associated with alerts only, and not log every packet that flies across the wire. Although this may sound like a limitation, it is very desirable behavior, since logging every packet on your network would quickly fill up the hard drives on your Snort system.

If you've decided that for testing or debugging purposes logging every packet on the wire is really what you need to do, you can call Snort with the -b switch to log *all* packets in binary format and specify the log file with the `-L` switch. To log all packets to a binary format, type the following at a command line:

```
/usr/local/bin/snort -b -L /var/log/snort/snort.dump
```

When you look in the `/var/log/snort/` directory, you'll see your `snort.dump` file has a dot and a bunch of numbers stuck on the end:

```
snort.dump.1074240477
```

This is a timestamp, indicating when this particular instance of Snort was run so it isn't confused with other packet-capture sessions. The number is a count of the number of seconds past "the epoch," and is a standard way of measuring time in the Unix world. (*The epoch,* incidentally, is 01 January 1970. It may be worth noting that the Unix programmer's sense of time begins at the exact moment the '60s ended.)

Snort logging to a database

So far we've talked about Snort's capability to log data in a variety of formats to flat text files, as well as its capability to log straight `tcpdump`-formatted data to a binary file.

Flat text files are a great format for reading (in fact, text is one of our favorite things to read), and they're not bad for sorting through by machine. The Unix `grep` command is by far one of the most useful tools for sorting through log files, and there are numerous programming languages devoted solely to manipulating text (such as `awk`, `sed`, and `perl`). The problem with this is that sorting through flat text files is slow, and it only gets slower the larger your files become.

Binary data in a tcpdump-formatted file is great for reading with your favorite packet sniffer, or analyzing with any of the myriad packet analysis tools available, or even replaying like a tape through Snort to test new rules or look for attacks. But analyzing these binary files takes processor power — and as with text files, the larger your binary data file becomes, the more your processor must crunch to make human-readable sense out of all the zeros and ones.

Neither of these solutions is viable when you want immediate (or close to immediate) reports on what's been happening on your network. If your Snort sensor has been running for more than a few hours, you're going to generate a tremendous amount of data, and flat text files and binary data just don't scale very well.

Snort's command-line switches for logging and alerting

Snort has many logging options that can be specified at run time on the command line. If you also specify the use of a configuration file, remember that any option listed on the command line will override that same option in the configuration file. The following options are useful when considering different logging options:

-A alert-mode This switch tells Snort to use one of various alert modes. alert-mode can be fast, full, none, or unsock (an experimental alert mode that sends alerts to a Unix socket, and is safe to ignore unless you like writing Unix socket code).

-b This option tells Snort to log packets in a tcpdump-formatted file. Using this switch, Snort will log *all packets* going across the wire, not just those that match an attack pattern or other rule. This makes Snort behave almost exactly like tcpdump — including the use of tcpdump-style expressions to specify which traffic to grab.

-B address-conversion-mask This switch converts all IP addresses of your local network, or home network in the binary logs, to the address indicated by address-conversion-mask. In this way, you can share binary Snort logs with others without revealing your home network address.

-C When logging packets as ASCII text, this switch prints the character data from the packet only without printing the corresponding hex data.

-d This switch prints Application-layer data when logging packets.

-e Displays Link-layer data in packet headers

-h home-net Use this option to specify your home network, which should be replaced in your binary logs with the network specified by the -B switch.

-l logging-directory This option will tell Snort to log to the specified directory, rather than the default /var/log/snort directory.

-L binary-log-file When logging in the binary tcpdump format, this switch specifies where Snort should dump its packets.

-N This option turns off packet logging. This is useful when you want to specify a snort.conf file that includes a packet logging option that you want to override. Snort will continue to generate alerts normally when this switch is used.

-O When logging packets as decoded plain text, this switch will change any IP addresses that get printed to "xxx.xxx.xxx.xxx", unless the "home net" is specified with the -h switch — in which case, home-net IP addresses will be changed but external addresses will be left unchanged. This is another method of hiding your home-network information when sharing your logs with others.

-P snap-length When capturing packets, this sets the packet snaplen (the amount of data in a packet that's captured) to the value represented here by *snap-length*.

-s Use this switch to send alerts to the Unix syslog facility.

-U Timestamps in all logs will be converted to UTC (Universal Coordinated Time)

-v Print packets to the console. A nearly universal Unix directive to be *verbose*. This is great for testing or debugging, but bad for production environments, since it will slow down your system, and cause Snort to drop packets.

-y Show the year in your log files.

Enter the Snort database output module. By logging your alerts and packet logs to a database, you get a very stable format that scales exceptionally well, and allows for extremely fast searching and reporting. It's not unusual to have Snort databases that are a gigabyte or so in size. By splitting each log entry into component pieces, and writing those pieces to different database tables, searching for a specific entry is fast enough that it can be done from a Web-server script to generate Web pages on the fly. Try to do *that* with a text file (you'd better have some errands to run while you wait for the output). These are some of the reasons why we chose to configure Snort for database output in Chapters 4 and 5.

With the database output module, Snort has the ability to send output to many SQL databases. As of version 2.1, Oracle, UnixODBC, MS-SQL, PostgreSQL, and the ever-popular MySQL are all supported by this plug-in.

If you plan to log your Snort data to a database, make sure you run the configure script with the appropriate flag to include support for your particular database format when you compile and install Snort. More information on compiling Snort is available in Chapter 4.

Database logging isn't available as a command-line option to Snort. Instead, it must be configured in the snort.conf file. The format to include this module is:

```
output database: <log | alert>, <database type>, <parameter list>
```

The | (pipe) between log and alert is shorthand, indicating that you need to specify either log *or* alert as the logging method.

The database module differs from other reporting modules a bit in how it handles logs versus alerts. If you have the log keyword in a Snort rule, when the rule is activated, it sends data on to the appropriate output module (usually log_tcpdump) by way of the log facility. When the alert keyword is used in a Snort rule, the `alert` facility is used, but data is also written to the `log` facility. If the `database` plug-in is configured for alerts, it will *only* receive output from rules that specify the `alert` keyword. If the `database` plug-in is configured with the `log` option, it receives output from `alert` rules *and* `log` rules. Sound confusing? Don't sweat it. The `log` option will work just fine for most situations.

So if you know that you want to use the `log` option, and you already know what database type you're going to use, you can move on to specifying the required parameters to make it all work. Some of these parameters must be specified; others will be filled in by Snort, if not by you. When written into your `snort.conf` file, each parameter is specified by a `name=value` pair, where name is the parameter name, and value is, of course, its value.

- ✔ `host`: The name or IP address of the host that's running your database server. If you don't include a hostname, Snort assumes you're sending data over a Unix domain socket. If a host name or IP address is specified, Snort will use TCP/IP to send your data. If you're running your database server on the same system as Snort, set your host to `localhost`.

- ✔ `port`: The port number your database server is listening on.

- ✔ `password`: If your database server requires authentication, this is the password to use.

- ✔ `dbname`: This is the database username used for authentication purposes when connecting to your database.

- ✔ `encoding`: Binary data isn't very portable across databases, but binary data is what we've got in our packet payload, so some form of encoding must be done to actually store the data in the database. Your options are as follows:

  - • `hex`: This is the default method. It represents binary data as a hex string, which makes for great searchability, but poor human-readability without some form of post-processing. This takes up twice as much space as binary data.

  - • `base64`: Binary data is represented as a base64 string, which is slightly larger than the binary data itself. This format isn't very searchable or readable without post-processing.

  - • `ascii`: Since not all binary data can be represented as ascii, you will loose some data if you go this route. This takes up slightly more space than the original binary format, but gives you excellent searchability when looking for a text string. And of course, ascii text is infinitely readable by us humans.

- ✔ `sensor_name`: If you want to specify a name for this particular Snort sensor, do so here. If not, Snort will come up with one for you.

- ✔ detail: How much detail of the offending packets should be logged?

- ✔ full: This is the default, which logs all the available information about the packet, including the packet payload, and its ip/tcp options.

- ✔ fast: This will only log the timestamp, message signature, source IP address, destination IP address, source port, destination port, tcp flags, and protocol.

A minimalist configuration entry for database logging would look something like this:

```
output database: log, mysql, user=snortuser password=h4wg
          dbname=snortdb host=localhost
```

Unified logging

If you've tried other logging formats, you'll soon find that once you've overcome the intimidation factor involved in installing and configuring your own databases, logging to a database is the best way to go for long-term stability and scalability of your Snort data. With the amount of software and Web-driven scripts available for pulling details from databases, database logging is the best storage mechanism to make your log details quickly available for reporting and analyzing.

But for all its advantages, the database output module is still being run on your Snort sensor, even if the results are being sent to a remote database server. In fact, it's being run by the same process that's analyzing packets. This means valuable CPU cycles are being spent converting data and talking to your database server, instead of doing what Snort does best: capturing and analyzing network traffic.

Wouldn't it be nice if Snort didn't worry about converting the binary data it gets from libpcap (or WinPCAP) to a format us puny humans can read? Or if it didn't worry about shoveling data over to your database server, or syslog server, or writing log files to directories? Without these extra tasks to bog it down, Snort could process more packets and compare them to more rules even faster than it does now.

With the new unified logging format, Snort does exactly this. It keeps all of the packet data that it gets from libpcap in its native binary form, and doesn't even bother to convert the alert data to something human-readable. Instead, it relies on an external software piece to do this work for it.

This extra bit of software is Barnyard, and combined with unified logging, it is the way of the future.

For all of the hype, configuring unified logging for Snort is actually pretty simple. Since it's really not doing anything other than dumping raw data, you just need to tell Snort to use the unified logging output and where it should write its data. Edit the `snort.conf` configuration file and add the following:

```
output alert_unified: unified_alert_filename
output log_unified:   unified_log_filename
```

As with all other Snort logging, these files will wind up in /var/log/snort by default. When you look at these files, you'll see that the filename has been appended with a bunch of numbers. This is a timestamp designed to keep different unified output files separate. As with the `alert_tcpdump` output files, the timestamp is the number of seconds past the epoch (that is, 01 January 1970).

Shazam! You've got unified logging! Now what do you do with it? Flip over to Chapter 14 and see what you can do with Barnyard.

Chapter 7

Adding Visuals and Getting Reports

So you've set up Snort and MySQL on the operating system of your choice. Everything is working fine: Both Snort and MySQL are running with no errors. Now you'd like to see the alerts, wouldn't you? For this we use the standard Web technology — a Web browser. Unfortunately, it's not as easy as pointing your browser at someone's Web site and digesting a deluge of information. You have to set up your own Web server, configure a scripting language, and install some custom scripts designed to extract and present Snort alert information from your SQL database. So plant your tuchus in a seat — because even though these various applications and scripts are pretty straightforward to set up, it takes a while to get all the components talking to each other the way they should.

The ACID Dependency Soup

For retrieving and presenting Snort alert information, we use ACID (an acronym for Analysis Console for Intrusion Detection), an open-source analysis console specifically tailored for Snort. The console (really a set of PHP scripts and a configuration file) requires the following supporting programs:

✔ A Web server that supports version 4.0 or later of the PHP scripting language

✔ Version 4.0 or later of PHP

✔ ADODB (which stands for Active Data Objects Data Base — don't ask us how to pronounce it)

✔ JpGraph and PHPlot (packages designed for graphing data retrieved by ACID)

Each of these components must be installed and properly configured for ACID to function the way it's supposed to. In the following sections, we cover each application in more detail, and then move on to installing and configuring each application.

ACID

ACID is an analysis and reporting tool for Snort that is accessible through a Web browser. ACID isn't an actual application in the strictest sense, but rather a collection of PHP scripts; working together, these scripts retrieve Snort data from your database, format what they get into easy-to-navigate Web pages, and constantly update those pages. When you have it up and working, you'll understand why ACID is probably the most widely used analysis and reporting package around. With an ACID console, you can do the following:

✔ View Snort alerts according to various criteria.

✔ View details of each alert, including source and destination IP address, full session information, and the actual vulnerability under attack.

✔ Exploit the (in most cases) helpful security information on Web sites such as those for Bugtraq and arachNIDS.

✔ Organize historical alert information in various formats and organizational techniques (such as Most Frequent by source or destination port, and Most Recent by protocol).

✔ Put all alert information in graphical format (using JpGraph/PHPlot).

✔ Search functions for all Snort data in the database.

PHP

PHP is a Web scripting language used for building dynamic Web pages. It's often used to pull information from a database application (such as MySQL) to construct Web pages. PHP is the language that the ACID scripts are written in, and must be installed and configured to operate with your Web server before ACID will function.

Web server

Naturally, if you're going to serve up Web pages, you need a Web server. As long as the Web server supports PHP 4.0 or later, you're good. In this chapter we cover two platforms: Apache on Linux, and Internet Information Services for Windows. Apache and IIS are by far the most widely used Web-server software packages on the Internet, with a combined market share of over 88 percent (according to a January 2004 Netcraft survey). For more information on other Web servers that support PHP, consult the PHP documentation at www.php.net.

ADODB

ADODB is a collection of standardized database class libraries for the PHP scripting language. Within the Snort environment, these scripts do the grunt-work of pulling out relevant Snort alert data and passing the data to ACID for display.

PHPlot and JpGraph

These plotting and graphing libraries are required in order to view graphical information derived from your Snort alerts — and both are written in the PHP scripting language:

- **PHPlot** is the plotting software and is required with Windows.
- **JpGraph** is an engine for displaying graphs from ACID data and is required for both Windows and Linux/Unix platforms.

Preparing ACID and Its Dependencies

Before you can install ACID, you must prepare all its dependencies. Unfortunately, for most of these packages, you'll only know that everything is working when you launch a Web browser and point it at ACID. Following these instructions step-by-step should have you up and running in no time.

Gathering the necessary files

Before you begin, you need to download all the necessary packages into a temporary directory on your hard drive. What follows is a list of packages used for this chapter and their relevant Web addresses. Internet Information

Services, however, is available only on your Windows operating system CD (Windows 2000 Professional, Windows 2000 Server, Windows XP Professional, or Windows Server 2003).

Internet Information Services (IIS) is the default Web and FTP server for the Windows platform, and has been since Windows NT 4.0. Windows XP Home is the exception: IIS isn't included. Table 7-1 outlines how IIS differs on the various Windows platforms:

Table 7-1	Windows IIS Platforms	
Windows 2000/XP Professional	*Windows 2000 Server*	*Windows Server 2003*
Version 5.0/5.1	Version 5.0	Version 6.0
10 Simultaneous Connections	Unlimited Connections	Unlimited Connections
1 Virtual Server (Web Site)	Unlimited Virtual Servers	Unlimited Virtual Servers

ACID

This version of the ACID console is compatible with both Linux and Windows installations. Developed by Roman Danyliw, ACID is available at his Web site

```
http://www.andrew.cmu.edu/~rdanyliw/snort/snortacid.html
```

or on SourceForge.net at

```
http://acidlab.sourceforge.net/
```

PHP version 4

Both the Linux and Windows versions are available from the PHP Web site at

```
http://www.php.net
```

Apache Web Server version 2

This is the Unix source-code distribution of the current Apache version. We cover installation and configuration of the Apache Web server for the Linux operating system in this chapter. The Apache Web server is available from

```
http://www.apache.org
```

Tar got you stuck? Zip through this . . .

If you are using the Windows 2000 (or earlier) operating system, you need a file-archive tool to decompress zipped or tar/gzipped files (any files ending with the suffixes `.zip`, `.tar.gz`, or `.tgz`). Here's a quick rundown on popular zip utilities:

✔ WinRAR is a freeware, open-source application, available at the RARLabs Web site: `http://www.rarlab.com/`.

✔ WinZip is a commercial application, available at the WinZip Web site at `http://www.winzip.com/`.

Both WinRAR and WinZip are popular file-archive tools available for the Windows platform. (Windows XP and later Windows platforms have file archiving built-in, and thus don't require a third-party application for un-zipping files. For un-tarring files, however, Windows XP still requires a third-party application.)

✔ For you Linux users, the tar and GNU Zip (`gzip` and `gunzip`) utilities come as standard parts of Linux OS distributions.

Internet Information Services

You need your Windows CD to install Internet Information Services (IIS). We cover both Windows 2000 and Windows XP configuration and installation in the "Installing and configuring a Web server" section of this chapter.

ADODB version 4

Both the Unix and the Windows versions are available from the ADODB Web site at

```
http://php.weblogs.com/ADODB
```

PHPlot version 4

This version is for the Windows platform only. (You don't need PHPlot for the Unix platform.) PHPlot is available at the following Web site:

```
http://www.phplot.com
```

JpGraph version 1

This version is for both the Windows and Unix platforms. JpGraph is available at the following Web site:

```
http://www.aditus.nu/jpgraph/
```

Installing and configuring a Web server

In this section, we cover installing, configuring, and securing the Apache Web server for Linux and Internet Information Services for the Windows platform in relation to the ACID console.

Apache and PHP on Linux

Apache is by far the most popular Web server for the Linux platform due to Apache's stability and flexibility. This section assumes that you don't already have Apache installed; we walk you through installing Apache for use as an ACID console.

Apache got its name from being "a patchy" server, built from patches submitted by a whole community of coders. That said, make sure you're using the latest version of the software; earlier versions are more likely to have security vulnerabilities in them.

Installing and configuring PHP is best done when you install Apache, so we cover PHP in this section as well.

Installing Apache

True to form, Apache has a "patchy" installation process. Here's the basic drill:

1. **Download the latest source code for Apache from**

   ```
   http://httpd.apache.org/download.cgi
   ```

   Using this page is one way to be a good Net neighbor and download Apache from a local mirror site, rather than from one central server.

2. **Download the PGP signature and/or MD5 hash from the same source.**

   Download the *tarballs* (Unix-geek jargon for archive files made with the tar utility) into /usr/local/src/tarballs and keep the un-tarred source code in /usr/local/src. Here's the code that does the job:

   ```
   $ cd /usr/local/src/tarballs
   $ wget -q http://apache.webmeta.com/httpd/httpd-
          2.0.48.tar.gz
   $ wget -q http://apache.webmeta.com/httpd/httpd-
          2.0.48.tar.gz.md5
   $ cat httpd-2.0.48.tar.gz.md5
   466c63bb71b710d20a5c353df8c1a19c  httpd-2.0.48.tar.gz
   $ md5sum httpd-2.0.48.tar.gz
   466c63bb71b710d20a5c353df8c1a19c  httpd-2.0.48.tar.gz
   ```

   From this, we can see that the MD5 sum published by Apache matches the output from our own md5sum program. Now we know for sure that the source code hasn't been tampered with. (For more information on why we did this, see the "Accept No Substitutes" sidebar in Chapter 5.)

3. **Prepare to extract the source code and start configuring and compiling Apache.**

   Apache is an extremely flexible piece of software and has numerous configuration options. For an ACID console, you won't need anything too esoteric. For a taste of what other options are available when configuring Apache, run the configure script with the —help option.

4. **Change to the directory where your source is kept:**

   ```
   # cd /usr/local/src
   ```

5. **Run the** script **command, like this:**

   ```
   # script ~/apache.install.notes
   ```

   This makes a handy transcription of all our subsequent commands (and their output) in the apache.install.notes file so we can refer to the transcript later if problems crop up in the installation.

6. **Rip open that tarball, configure Apache, and build it:**

   ```
   # tar -xvzf tarballs/httpd-2.0.48.tar.gz
   # cd httpd-2.0.48/
   # ./configure --enable-so
   # make
   # make install
   ```

7. **You're not quite done yet. Tell your system how to get to Apache's shared libraries:**

   ```
   # echo "/usr/local/apache2/lib" >>/etc/ld.so.conf
   # ldconfig
   # exit
   ```

8. **When you've finished the installation procedure, test the server.**

   By default, Apache 2.0 puts all its files in /usr/local/apache2, so you should be able to run the following command:

   ```
   # /usr/local/apache2/bin/apachectl start
   ```

   You should get one of two results:

   - If that command didn't throw out a barrage of error messages, point a Web browser at the IP address of your new Web server, and you should see Apache's lovely default Web page. Success? Excellent!

   - Oops, not yet? Check the apache.install.notes file in your home directory for errors. You can also check your /usr/local/apache2/logs/error_log file.

9. **If your Web server ran, shut it down for now.**

   Use the same command you used to start it up, only tell it to stop:

   ```
   # /usr/local/apache2/bin/apachectl stop
   ```

Internet Information Services (IIS) on Windows

IIS comes standard with Windows 2000 Professional and Windows XP Professional, which are the versions of Windows we currently recommend for use with Snort. We cover installing and configuring the services necessary to operate the ACID console in the following sections. The configuration options for PHP and ACID are covered in the sections "Installing and configuring PHP" and "Installing and Configuring ACID" in this chapter.

Installing IIS on Windows 2000 and XP Professional

To install IIS, perform the following steps:

1. **Insert the Windows CD into your CD-ROM.**

2. **Click the Start button, point to Settings, and then click Control Panel.**

3. **Click the Add/Remove Programs icon.**

   The Add/Remove Programs window appears.

4. **Click the Add/Remove Windows Components icon.**

   The Windows Component Wizard appears.

5. **Click the Internet Information Services check box and then click the Details button.**

   Details, details. You've got 'em.

6. **Check the following check boxes:**
   - World Wide Web Server
   - Common Files
   - Documentation
   - Internet Information Services Snap-In

7. **Uncheck all other check boxes and then click the OK button.**

   The Windows Components Wizard window appears.

8. **Click the Next button.**

   Windows builds a file list and installs components.

9. **At the Completed window, click the Finished button.**

   You're finished. But you knew that.

Additional setup tasks

Well, okay, we're not quite done yet. You still have to let IIS know that PHP is present and how to handle PHP scripts. In addition, you must set up the ACID Web site in IIS. We discuss all this stuff in more detail in the following section, "Installing and Configuring PHP," because PHP and ACID must be installed before these tasks can be completed.

Installing and configuring PHP

In this section, we cover installing and configuring PHP for the Windows and Linux platform, including configuring Apache on Linux and IIS on Windows to use PHP scripts.

Installing PHP for Apache on Linux

PHP is the wildly popular scripting language that enables you to publish dynamic and exciting Web pages. Like Apache, PHP is extremely flexible and functional. That functionality comes at a price when installing PHP — namely, a few software dependencies, and at least one case where a dependency has a dependency. So take a deep breath and read on . . .

PHP uses the GD library to perform image manipulations. In the old days, GD was distributed separately from PHP, and had to be compiled and installed separately. Now GD is included in the PHP distribution — but (unfortunately) many of GD's dependencies are not.

Installing GD dependencies to go with PHP on Linux

Work with us here. Before you can get PHP up and running, you have to grab and install two GD dependencies: `libpng` and `zlib`. Fortunately, these two packages are pretty straightforward to install.

Your Linux distribution might already have `libpng` or `zlib` installed. Use the `find` or `locate` commands to see whether they're already on your system (the way to use of `find` and `locate` can be found in your Linux distribution's documentation or by typing `man find` or `man locate`). Our example assumes you don't already have `libpng` or `zlib` installed.

Here goes the downloading part:

1. **Download** `libpng` **from**

   ```
   http://www.libpng.org/pub/png/libpng.html
   ```

2. **Download** `zlib` **from**

   ```
   http://www.gzip.org/zlib/
   ```

3. **For each program, check the MD5 sum for the source code.**

   That's the same step we recommend in the "Accept No Substitutes" sidebar in Chapter 5. The MD5 sums for `libpng` and `zlib` are listed at their respective Web sites.

4. **Use the** `script` **utility to generate a transcript of the installation session.**

   Doing so gives you a resource you can refer to in case of errors. Meanwhile, if the downloads are complete, install 'em if you got 'em . . .

Installing zlib

To install zlib, the basic drill starts with the path:

```
# cd path-to-your-tar-files
```

where *path-to-your-tar-files* is the directory where you store the compressed files on your system (for example, ours is /usr/local/src/tarballs). Then . . .

```
# wget -q http://www.zlib/net/zlib-1.2.1.tar.gz
# md5sum zlib-1.2.1.tar.gz
# cd ../
# script ~/zlib.install.notes
# tar -xvzf path-to-your-tar-files/zlib-1.2.1.tar.gz
# cd zlib-1.2.1/
# ./configure
# make
# make test
# make install
# cd ../
# exit
```

Installing libpng

When zlib is installed, you can install libpng Here goes:

```
cd path-to-your-tar-files
```

where *path-to-your-tar-files* is the directory where you store the compressed files on your system (for example, ours is /usr/local/src/tarballs). Then . . .

```
# wget -q http://download.sourceforge.net/libpng/libpng-
           1.2.5.tar.gz
# md5sum libpng-1.2.5.tar.gz
# cd ../
# tar -xvzf path-to-your-tar-files/libpng-1.2.5.tar.gz
# cd libpng-1.2.5/
```

This part is a little different because libpng doesn't use the typical configure script you've seen so many times before. Instead, there is a makefile already made for you in the scripts directory (what the heck, all the configure script does anyway is make a makefile). Because you're running this whole show on Linux, use the makefile.linux file, like this:

```
# script ~/libpng.install.notes
# cp scripts/makefile.linux Makefile
# make test
# make install
```

Building PHP

When you've got the GD software dependencies built, it's time to build PHP with its built-in (har, har) GD support. Assuming you've already downloaded the PHP source code from a mirror site and placed it in /usr/local/src/ tarballs, start with the following code to build PHP:

```
cd path-to-your-tar-files
```

where *path-to-your-tar-files* is the directory where you store the compressed files on your system (for example, ours is /usr/local/src/ tarballs). (Yep, there's something familiar about that command.) Then . . .

```
# md5sum php-4.3.4.tar.gz
# tar -xvzf php-4.3.4.tar.gz
# cd php-4.3.4.tar.gz
# ./configure --prefix=/usr/local/apache2/php \
> --with-config-file-path=/usr/local/apache2/php \
> --with-apxs2=/usr/local/apache2/bin/apxs \
> --enable-sockets \
> --with-mysql=/usr/local/mysql \
> --with-zlib-dir=/usr/local \
> --with-gd
```

As you can tell, there are a ton of configuration options to PHP that we want to enable at this point. So many, in fact, that they won't all fit on one line, so we split them up on the command line. Each backslash (\) tells your Linux shell that the command input is to be continued on the next line. This makes the long string of configuration options more manageable to enter.

Making PHP

When it's configured, PHP installs with simple make and make install commands. The next step is to copy the php.ini file to the apache directory on your system. Assuming you're still in the PHP source directory, here's the magic word:

```
# make
# make install
# cp php.ini-dist /usr/local/apache2/php/php.ini
```

Configuring Apache to use PHP

Three general steps configure Apache to use PHP:

1. **Edit the Apache configuration file.**

2. **Test the Apache and PHP configuration.**

3. **Set Apache to start automatically when the server starts.**

Editing the Apache configuration file

Now you need to tell Apache what to do with .php files, like this:

1. **Edit your** httpd.conf **file (in** /usr/local/apache2/conf/**) and make sure you have the following line in there:**

   ```
   LoadModule php4_module          modules/libphp4.so
   ```

   Newer versions of PHP add this line for you.

2. **Add this next line by hand:**

   ```
   AddType application/x-httpd-php .php
   ```

   The last edit lets Apache know that an index.php file can serve as a default directory index.

3. **Find the line with the** DirectoryIndex **directive, and edit it to include** index.php, **like this:**

   ```
   DirectoryIndex index.html index.html.var index.php
   ```

Testing the Apache-PHP setup

Before you go making any rash assumptions, test and make sure that PHP and Apache are working and playing well together:

1. **Make a small (and we mean *small*)** phptest.php **file in your** /usr/local/apache2/htdocs **directory, containing only one line:**

   ```
   <?php phpinfo();?>
   ```

2. **Restart your Web server, using** apachectl start.

3. **Point a browser at** http://*your.apache.server*.ip/phptest.php.

   If everything worked correctly, you should see a page detailing every aspect of PHP on your system — and this kind of information is a goldmine for system crackers. *So . . .*

4. **After you've confirmed that your system is working correctly, make absolutely sure that you move, rename, or delete this test script.**

Configuring Apache to start automatically

After you've confirmed that everything is working correctly, ensure that it works correctly after a system reboot. To do this, follow these steps:

1. **Copy the** apachectl **binary that you've used to start and stop your server to the** /etc/init.d **directory as** httpd.

2. **Set up links to the new initialization file from your default run level.**

   That would be run level 3 on Red Hat Linux, unless you're running a GUI. (If necessary, check your run level by entering the runlevel command.)

The code that accomplishes Steps 1 and 2 looks like this:

```
# cp /usr/local/apache2/bin/apachectl /etc/init.d/httpd
# cd /etc/rc3.d
# ln -s ../init.d/httpd S85httpd
# ln -s ../init.d/httpd K85httpd
```

Congratulations! You now have a working Apache Web server with working PHP.

3. **Test to make sure Apache with PHP is going to start up after a system reboot.**

   To do so, reboot your system and point it to the appropriate URL:

   ```
   http://your.apache.server.ip/phptest.php
   ```

   Go ahead, we'll wait for you. Never hurts to make sure.

Setting up PHP on the Windows platform

As with the package for Linux, the Windows PHP package consists of a collection of configuration files and executable files that the Web server uses to process PHP scripts.

Extracting the files

First order of business is to extract the PHP files and put them in an applications directory. (We keep all our Snort-related apps in a directory called `snortapps` on our C:\ drive.) Regardless of where you put your Snort-related apps, take note of the location of PHP.

To extract PHP using WinZip or WinRAR, perform the following steps:

1. **Double-click the compressed file.**

   WinZip/WinRAR opens and displays the files in the archive.

2. **Click the Extract button (for WinRAR, it's the *Extract to* button).**

   An Extraction window appears.

3. **Type a path into the dialog box provided, and then click the Extract button (for WinRAR, it's the OK button).**

   PHP extracts into a directory called `php-4.3.4-W32`.

4. **After the files are extracted, navigate to `php-4.3.4-W32` and change the name of this directory to `php`.**

The location of PHP on your hard drive is important when you configure IIS. The Web server needs to know the path to `php.exe` to properly pass PHP code to the parser. So, if you don't keep all your Snort-related applications in the same directory, be sure to record what directory you installed PHP in.

Renaming the PHP INI file

PHP needs its own initialization file. To meet that need by renaming the `php.ini-dist` file, follow these steps:

1. **Click the Start button, point to Run, type** `cmd` **in the Open dialog box, and click the OK button.**

   A DOS command window opens.

2. **Change to the directory in which you've installed PHP.**

3. **Type the following at the command prompt:**

   ```
   copy php.ini-dist php.ini
   ```

4. **Type** `exit`.

   The DOS window closes.

Editing the PHP INI file

To edit the `php.ini` file, open it in a text editor such as Notepad or WordPad. Once it's opened, edit the following lines:

1. **Change the following line:**

   ```
   max_execution_time=30
   ```

   to

   ```
   max_execution_time=60
   ```

2. **Change the following line:**

   ```
   session.save_path=/tmp
   ```

   to

   ```
   session.save_path=YOUR-TEMPORARY-DIR
   ```

   `YOUR-TEMPORARY-DIR` is the path to a temporary directory that anyone accessing an ACID console has permission to use:

   • For Windows 2000, that directory is typically `C:\Winnt\Temp`.

   • For Windows XP Professional, the temporary directory is typically `C:\Windows\Temp`.

3. **Change the following line:**

   ```
   ;cgi.force_redirect=1
   ```

   to

   ```
   cgi.force_redirect=0
   ```

The `cgi.force_redirect` line has a semicolon (;) in front of it — the standard way to tell PHP to ignore a line in a script. Be sure to remove the semicolon when you edit this line so PHP knows what to do.

4. **Change the following line:**

```
;extension=php_gd2.dll
```

to

```
extension=php_gd2.dll
```

As with the previous line, remove the semicolon from in front of the `extension=php_gd2.dll` line. No other changes are made to this line.

5. **Change the following line:**

```
extension_dir=./
```

to

```
extension_dir=PHP-Path\extensions
```

PHP-Path refers to the path to your PHP installation. For our configuration, this line reads as follows:

```
extension_dir=c:\snortapps\php\extensions
```

6. **After you've edited these lines, save the file.**

If you're in WordPad, be careful to save it as a Text Document and not as an RTF file.

7. **Exit from the text editor.**

Copying the DLL

In order for PHP to function on a Windows platform, you must copy the file `php4ts.dll` into the System32 folder in your Windows directory. The `php4ts` DLL file is located in the PHP root directory.

ACID won't run without the PHP DLL file. Before you run ACID, *you must restart Windows* so it can pick up the DLL file for processing:

- ✔ For Windows 2000 Professional, copy this file into `C:\Winnt\System32`.
- ✔ For Windows XP, copy this file into `C:\Windows\System32`.

Installing and configuring ADODB

The ADODB database-abstraction scripts require little setup on either Linux or the Windows platform. We cover installing and configuring ADODB on both platforms here, though an additional configuration task is required for the ACID console (covered in "Installing the ACID console," later in this chapter).

Getting to ADODB for Linux

The archive file for ADODB for Linux is the same as for the Windows platform: a GNU Zipped Tar file with the `.tgz` extension. All that's required is to download and extract the archive, and then make a quick change to the ADODB configuration file.

Extracting the files

Download the current ADODB archive to a temporary directory (we used `/usr/local/src/tarballs`) from the ADODB Web site at

```
http://php.weblogs.com/ADODB
```

When that's done, follow these quick steps to extract the files to the proper directory:

1. **At the command prompt, type**

   ```
   cp adodb401.tgz /htdocs-root/
   ```

   and press the Enter key. (The variable *htdocs-root* refers to the `root` directory for your Web server. The command that copied the ADODB archive to our root directory, for example, was `cp adodb404.tgz /www/htdocs/`.)

2. **Change to the Web server's `root` directory and type the following command:**

   ```
   tar -xvzf adodb404.tgz
   ```

   Then press the Enter key. The archive extracts to a directory called `adodb404`.

3. **Change the name of the directory to `adodb` by typing the following:**

   ```
   mv adodb404 adodb
   ```

   Then press the Enter key.

4. **Open the file `adodb.inc.php` with a text editor and change the following line:**

   ```
   $ADODB_Database = '';
   ```

   to

   ```
   $ADODB_Database = '/htdocs-path/adodb';
   ```

   where the variable *htdocs-path* is the path to the `root` directory for your Web server. This configuration line in our `adodb.inc.php` file looks like this:

   ```
   $ADODB_Database = '/www/htdocs/adodb';
   ```

5. **Save the file and exit.**

That's it for ADODB for the moment. We walk you through ACID's configuration concerning ADODB in the "Installing and Configuring ACID" section, later in this chapter.

Setting up ADODB for Windows

Since it's only a collection of scripts, ADODB requires little setup in Windows. Simply extract the files and make a quick change to the ADODB configuration file.

Extract the files

Extract the files from the ADODB archive to a directory on your hard drive. We chose to keep all our Snort-related applications together and extracted ADODB to its own directory under snortapps. To extract the files with WinZip or WinRAR, perform the following steps:

1. **Double-click the ADODB archive.**

2. **Click the Extract button (or *Extract to* if you're using WinRAR).**

3. **Type the path to the directory to which you want to extract ADODB.**

   For example, we extracted ADODB to C:\snortapps\adodb.

4. **Click the Extract button (or the OK button if you're using WinRAR).**

   The files extract to the directory you indicated.

5. **Close WinZip or WinRAR.**

Configuring the ADODB INI file

To configure an INI file for ADODB, follow these steps:

1. **Navigate to the ADODB directory and open the file** adodb.inc.php **in a text editor such as Notepad or WordPad.**

2. **Change the following line:**

   ```
   $ADODB_database="';
   ```

   to

   ```
   $ADODB_database='ADODB-Path';
   ```

   ADODB-Path refers to the directory where you installed ADODB. For our configuration, this line reads like this:

   ```
   $ADODB_database='c:\snortapps\adodb';
   ```

Be sure to edit this line exactly as it appears, with the single quote (') enclosing the ADODB path and a semicolon (;) at the end. If you don't, ACID won't be able to talk to the database because ADODB won't be able to find itself.

3. **After editing the line that identifies the ADODB path, save the file and exit the text editor.**

   A later section of this chapter ("Installing and Configuring ACID") shows you how to configure ACID to use ADODB as an interface to your SQL server.

Installing and configuring PHPlot and JpGraph

Installing PHPlot on Windows

All you need do to install PHPlot on Windows is extract the files and rename the directory, like this:

1. **Double-click the PHPlot archive and extract the files to a directory on your hard drive.**

   We chose to keep all our Snort-related applications in the same directory tree, thus we extracted to `c:\snortapps\`.

2. **Navigate to the PHPlot directory, click to highlight its name, and type in a new name.**

   PHPlot extracts to a directory called `phplot-4.4.6`. Rename this directory to simply `phplot`.

Installing JpGraph on Linux

To get JpGraph installed on your Linux system, all you need do is extract the files to the `htdocs` directory and then rename the JpGraph directory, like this:

1. **Change into your Apache document `root` directory:**

   ```
   # cd /usr/local/apache2/htdocs
   ```

2. **Grab the JpGraph source code from the Web site:**

   ```
   # wget
           http://members.chello.se/jpgraph/jpgdownloads/jpg
           raph-1.14.tar.gz
   ```

3. **Rip open the JpGraph tarball.**

   JpGraph extacts itself to your Apache `root` directory.

4. **Delete the JpGraph tarball.**

5. **Rename the JpGraph directory by using the move (`mv`) command:**

   ```
   # tar -zxvf jpgraph-1.14.tar.gz
   # rm jpgraph-1.14.tar.gz
   # mv jpgraph-1.14 jpgraph
   ```

That's all there is to installing JpGraph on Linux. Quite simple, eh?

Installing JpGraph on Windows

We're going to extract the JpGraph scripts, and then copy them to the PHPplot directory. Steady as she goes . . .

1. **Double-click the** `jpgraph` **archive and extract the files to a temporary directory.**

   You might as well use an existing one, but if Windows asks you to name a new one, name it `jpgraph`.

2. **From the DOS command line, navigate to the** `jpgraph` **directory and copy all** `.php` **and** `.inc` **files to the** `phplot` **directory.**

   Doing so puts all the JpGraph and PHPlot files in one place so the program can find them fast. For our configuration, the command-line call that does the move looks like this:

   ```
   copy *.php c:\snortapps\phplot
   copy *.inc c:\snortapps\phplot
   ```

3. **Delete the** `jpgraph` **directory.**

Installing and Configuring ACID

After you have all the ACID dependencies installed and configured, you must prepare MySQL for ACID's use before you can install and configure ACID. The next subsection walks through preparing MySQL.

Preparing MySQL on Linux and Windows

It's a two-stage process to prepare MySQL: Create the ACID user account in the database-management system, and then build the tables where Snort stores its data and ACID pulls its data. The commands for getting all this done are virtually identical in Linux and Windows (with the exception of the paths to certain files, which are noted in the text where appropriate).

Adding the ACID user account

To add the ACID user account, perform the following steps:

1. **Log in to MySQL as the** `root` **user and type the following at the DOS or Unix command prompt:**

   ```
   path-to-mysql/mysql -u root -p
   ```

Where *path-to-mysql* is the path to the mysql executable. If you already have the mysql executable in your path, you don't have to worry about the whole path, just type mysql -u root -p.

MySQL prompts for a password.

You set your mysql root user's password when you installed MySQL. If you used this book to do that, we walked you through it in Chapter 5. We also provided you a handy cheat sheet to write your password down on, if you didn't eat the cheat sheet (to throw off the hackers).

When the password is entered correctly, your prompt changes to mysql>.

2. **From the mysql> prompt, create the ACID user account by typing the following:**

```
grant USAGE on *.* to acid@localhost identified by
        "insert-password-here";
```

This command is case-sensitive. Type your chosen password between the quotation marks, and don't forget: Each mysql command must end in a semicolon *before* you press the Enter key.

Giving the ACID user account its proper database permissions

You created the snort and archive databases for MySQL as described in Chapter 4 or 5 (depending on whether you're installing on Linux or Windows). Now give the ACID user permissions to use these databases.

1. **Add permissions for the** snort **database.**

To do so, type the following command at the mysql> command prompt:

```
grant SELECT,INSERT,UPDATE,DELETE,CREATE,ALTER on snort.*
        to acid@localhost;
```

2. **Press the Enter key.**

3. **Grant permissions for the** archive **database.**

To do so, type the following at the mysql> prompt:

```
grant SELECT,INSERT,UPDATE,DELETE,CREATE on archive.* to
        acid@localhost;
```

4. **Press the Enter key.**

After each successful command, you receive a confirmation message from MySQL that looks like this:

```
Query OK, 0 rows affected (0.00 sec)
```

Checking the grants for the ACID user account

The next order of business is to confirm that the ACID user account now has the proper grants (database permissions). Follow these steps:

1. **Type the following command at the** `mysql>` **prompt:**

```
show grants for acid@localhost;
```

2. **Press the Enter key.**

   The permissions entered previously appear, as in the following example output:

```
+-----------------------------------------------------------------
               ---------------+
| Grants for acid@localhost
       |
+-----------------------------------------------------------------
               ---------------+
| GRANT USAGE ON *.* TO 'acid'@'localhost' IDENTIFIED BY PASSWORD
          '6ce1bf3569265b9d'     |
| GRANT SELECT, INSERT, UPDATE, DELETE, CREATE, ALTER ON `snort`.* TO
          'acid'@'localhost' |
| GRANT SELECT, INSERT, UPDATE, DELETE, CREATE ON `archive`.* TO
          'acid'@'localhost'       |
+-----------------------------------------------------------------
               ---------------+
3 rows in set (0.00 sec)
```

3. **Exit MySQL.**

Preparing the MySQL databases

Now to set up the tables in the `snort` and `archive` databases in MySQL. To set 'em up in MySQL on the Unix or the Windows platform, follow the steps in the following subsections.

Setting up the snort database tables

Before Snort can do you any good, the data it generates must have somewhere to go on your system — the Snort database tables. Here's how to set them up:

1. **At the command line, type the following command:**

```
mysql -u root -p snort < Create-MySQL-Path
```

   `Create-MySQL-Path` refers to the path to the `contrib` directory and the `create_mysql` file. This flat text file (installed by Snort) runs the routines that create the tables used by the `snort` and `archive` databases. For instance, on our Windows platform, the full command looks like this:

```
mysql -u root -p snort <
        c:\snortapps\snort\contrib\create_mysql
```

On our Linux platform, the full path looks like this:

```
mysql -u root -p snort <
          /usr/local/etc/contrib/create_mysql
```

2. **Press the Enter key.**

MySQL prompts for the MySQL `root` user's password.

3. **Type in the MySQL** `root` **user's password.**

You are returned to the DOS or UNIX command line with no messages (whether of success or errors).

Setting up the archive database tables

If you want to track attempted attacks through time to look for trends, you need a place to store vital data about the attacks — the `archive` database tables. Here's how to set those up:

1. **At the command line, type the following command and press Enter:**

```
mysql -u root -p archive < Create-MySQL-Path
```

where *Create-MySQL-Path* refers to the path to the `contrib` directory and the file `create_mysql` installed by Snort. As with the `snort` database, the `create_mysql` file runs the routines that create tables for the `archive` databases (the `snort` and `archive` databases use the same structure). For instance, on our Windows platform, the full command looks like this:

```
mysql -u root -p archive <
          c:\snortapps\snort\contrib\create_mysql
```

On our Linux platform, the full path looks like this:

```
mysql -u root -p archive <
          /usr/local/etc/contrib/create_mysql
```

2. **When MySQL prompts for the MySQL root user's password, type it in.**

You are returned to the DOS or Unix command line with no messages (whether of success or errors).

Checking your work

Better make sure those new databases work before you start relying on them. Here's the drill for checking first the `snort`, then the `archive`, database:

1. **Log in to MySQL by typing the following command:**

```
mysql -u root -p
```

2. **Press the Enter key.**

MySQL prompts you for the MySQL `root` user's password.

3. Enter the MySQL root user's password, and then type the following at the mysql> **prompt:**

```
show databases;
```

4. Press the Enter key.

The output should look similar to this:

```
+----------+
| Database |
+----------+
| archive  |
| mysql    |
| snort    |
+----------+
3 rows in set (0.00 sec)
```

If yours looks like this, all your databases are present. If it doesn't look like this, you have a problem. If you got error messages while typing in the commands, take a look and see what went wrong. If all else fails, you can start again at the beginning of this section.

5. If your databases are present, type the following:

```
use snort;
```

You should get an indication message that you are using the snort database.

6. Type the following command:

```
show tables;
```

7. Press the Enter key.

A list of 16 tables (titled, oddly enough, Tables_in_snort), appears, looking a lot like this:

```
+------------------+
| Tables_in_snort  |
+------------------+
| data             |
| detail           |
| encoding         |
| event            |
| icmphdr          |
| iphdr            |
| opt              |
| reference        |
| reference_system |
| schema           |
| sensor           |
| sig_class        |
| sig_reference    |
| signature        |
| tcphdr           |
```

```
| udphdr             |
+-------------------+
20 rows in set (0.00 sec)
```

If your tables match the ones in the preceding example, your snort database tables are set up correctly. Now to check on the archive database.

8. **Type the following command and then press Enter:**

```
use archive;
```

You should get an indication that you're in the archive database.

9. **Type the following command and then press Enter:**

```
show tables;
```

The same 16 tables we saw in the snort database should appear, in a list now titled Tables_in_archive.

If all databases, tables and users are present, you're ready, finally, to install the ACID console.

Installing the ACID console

Windows and Linux use the same ACID archive of files and (essentially) the same installation process. The differences are notated in the appropriate following sections.

Extracting the files . . .

After you get a hold of the ACID archive (see the section "Gathering the necessary files," near the beginning of this chapter), extract the files in the archive to the directory by performing the following steps.

. . . for Linux

To extract the files from the ACID archive on Linux, perform the following steps:

1. **Navigate to the directory where you downloaded the ACID archive and type the following:**

```
cp acid-0.9.6b23.tar.gz /htdocs-path
```

This copies the ACID archive to the htdocs directory. *htdocs-path* represents the path to the htdocs directory for Apache. For example, the command to copy the ACID archive to the htdocs directory for our configuration looks like this:

```
cp acid-0.9.6b23.tar.gz /www/htdocs
```

2. **Change to the htdocs directory by typing the following:**

```
cd /htdocs-path
```

Again, /htdocs-path represents the logical path to the htdocs directory. The command to change to the htdocs directory with our setup
looks like this:

```
cd /www/htdocs
```

3. **Extract the archive by typing the following:**

```
tar -xvzf acid-0.9.6b23.tar.gz
```

The file extracts to the acid-0.9.6b23 directory.

4. **Rename the directory to acid by typing the following:**

```
mv acid-0.9.6b23 acid
```

5. **Remove the archive tarball file by typing the following:**

```
rm acid-0.9.6b23.tar.gz
```

... for Windows

To extract the files from the ACID archive, perform the following steps:

1. **Double-click the ACID archive file.**

   The WinZip or WinRAR archive appears. If you're using Windows XP, a
   regular directory window appears.

2. **Extract the files to a directory.**

   We chose to group all our Snort-related apps under one directory tree,
   thus our ACID install path is

```
C:\snortapps\acid
```

3. **Right-click the ACID archive and click the Delete tab.**

Edit the ACID configuration file

Editing the configuration file is basically the same in Windows and Linux,
except for the paths to other supporting scripts (such as ADODB and
JpGraph). Differences are notated in the text where appropriate.

To edit the configuration file for ACID, perform the following steps:

1. **Open the configuration file in a text editor.**

   The configuration file, named acid_conf.php, is in the directory where
   Acid was installed.

2. **Use the text editor to modify the configuration file:**

   • For Linux, use vi or pico (run pico with the -w flag to turn off
     text-wrapping).

   • For Windows, use Notepad or WordPad.

3. Set the `DBlib_path` **variable, changing the line**

```
$DBlib_path="";
```

to

```
$DBlib_path="/ADODB-Path";
```

where *ADODB-Path* is the path to your ADODB installation. For our Linux system, the $DBlib_Path line looks like this:

```
$DBlib_path="/www/htdocs/adodb";
```

For our Windows system, the $DBlib_path line looks like this:

```
$DBlib_path="c:\snortapps\adodb";
```

4. Change the MySQL variables for ACID (they're the same for Linux and Windows) from

```
$alert_dbname    = "snort_log";
$alert_host      = "localhost";
$alert_port      = "";
$alert_user      = "root";
$alert_password  = "mypassword";
```

to

```
$alert_dbname    = "snort";
$alert_host      = "localhost";
$alert_port      = "3306";
$alert_user      = "acid";
$alert_password  = "acid_password";
```

Here "*acid_password*" is the password you assigned the user "acid" in the MySQL users table.

5. Change the following values:

```
/* Archive DB connection parameters */
$archive_dbname    = "snort_archive";
$archive_host      = "localhost";
$archive_port      = "";
$archive_user      = "root";
$archive_password  = "mypassword";
```

to

```
/* Archive DB connection parameters */
$archive_dbname    = "archive";
$archive_host      = "localhost";
$archive_port      = "3306";
$archive_user      = "acid";
$archive_password  = "acid_password";
```

Here "*acid_password*" is the password you assigned the user "acid" in the MySQL users table.

6. Set the graphics engine to suit your platform.

- **For Windows, change the following line:**

```
$ChartLib_path ="";
```

   to

```
$ChartLib_path ="PHPlot-path";
```

   where *PHPlot-path* represents the logical path to your installation of PHPlot. For our configuration, the `$ChartLib_path` line looks like this:

```
$ChartLib_path ="c:\snortapps\phplot";
```

- **For Linux, change the following line:**

```
$ChartLib_path ="";
```

   to

```
$ChartLib_path ="JpGraph-path";
```

   where *JpGraph-path* is the path to the `src` directory in your JpGraph installation. For our Linux system, the `$ChartLib_path` looks like this:

```
$ChartLib_path ="/usr/local/apach2/htdocs/jpgraph/src";
```

7. **Save the** `acid_conf.php` **file and exit the text editor.**

   If you're using WordPad to edit your `conf` files, be careful to save the file as a Text Document and not RTF.

Configuring IIS for the ACID console

After you've installed ACID and all its dependencies on the Windows platform, you must create the ACID console Web site and let the IIS Web server know to use PHP on the ACID console directory. With Apache, all this is taken care of when you install PHP and ACID. Unfortunately, the additional steps are required if you're running IIS; fortunately, the upcoming subsections break them down.

Create the ACID sonsole Web site in IIS

Before you can set up PHP, you must create the ACID console Web site in the IIS management snap-in. To create the ACID console Web site, perform these steps:

1. **Click the Start menu, point to Settings, and click Control Panel.**

   The Control Panel window appears.

2. **Double-click the Administrative Tools icon.**

   The Administrative Tools window appears.

3. **Double-click the Internet Services Manager icon.**

   The Internet Information Services window appears.

4. **In the left pane of this window, double-click the** `root` **machine.**

   Typically, it will have the same name as the hostname of your machine.

5. **Right-click the Default Web Site entry in the left pane of the Internet Information Services window.**

   A drop-down menu appears.

6. **Click the New menu option and the Virtual Directory menu option.**

   The Virtual Directory Creation Wizard window appears.

7. **Click the Next button.**

8. **Type a name for the Web site in the field labeled** `Alias`, **and then click the Next button.**

   For example, we called our virtual directory `ACID`.

9. **In the** `Directory` **field, type the path to your ACID installation and then click the Next button.**

   For example, the path to our installation of ACID is `C:\snortapps\acid`.

10. **On the Access Permissions window, ensure that the Read and Run Scripts check-boxes are checked and click the Next button.**

    The wizard finishes up, and your new ACID Web site is created.

Configuring the ACID console to use PHP in IIS

To let IIS know that how you want PHP files to be processed, perform the following steps:

1. **Click the Start menu, point to Settings, and click Control Panel.**

   The Control Panel window appears.

2. **Double-click the Administrative Tools icon.**

   The Administrative Tools window appears.

3. **Double-click the Internet Services Manager icon.**

   The Internet Information Services window appears.

4. **In the left pane of this window, double-click the** `root` **machine.**

   Typically, it will have the same name as the hostname of your machine.

5. **Double-click the Default Web entry.**

   The Web tree expands.

6. **Right-click your ACID Web site entry and select the Properties menu option.**

The Web site Properties window appears.

7. **On the Virtual Directory tab, click the Configuration button.**

   The Application Configuration window appears.

8. **Click the Add button.**

   The Add/Edit Application Extension Mapping window appears.

9. **In the Executable field, type the path to** `php.exe`.

   For our configuration, the path is: `C:\snortapps\php\php.exe`.

10. **Type** `.php` **In the** `Extension` **field.**

11. **Click the Script Engine check box.**

12. **Click the OK button.**

13. **On the Application Configuration Window, click the Apply button, and then click OK to close the window.**

14. **Click the OK button on the Properties window.**

Taking the ACID test

Finally. It's installed — but is it working? Well, you're about to find out, one handy subsection at a time.

Point a browser at it

Open a Web browser on the computer where ACID is installed. The browser window is where you complete the configuration. Onward . . .

- **For Windows:** Type the following Web address in the browser's address field:

  `http://localhost/your-ACID-console/index.html`

  Here *your-ACID-console* is the name you gave the virtual directory when you created the ACID console Web site in the previous section.

- **For Linux:** Type the following address into the browser's address field:

  `http://hostname/acid/acid_main.php`

  Here *hostname* refers to the hostname of the computer that ACID is installed on. For example, the Web address to our Linux ACID console is

  `http://frytaters/acid/acid_main.php`

Deal with the error

Sure as Murphy's Law, the first time the ACID console runs, the error shown in Figure 7-1 appears.

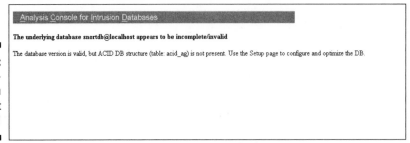

Figure 7-1:
Oh, pig-
slop! You
mean it's not
working??!!

Actually, ACID is working fine. Believe it or not, there's *one more* configuration step to go through. (Ready, *and . . .*)

1. **Click the Create ACID AG link.**

   Doing so creates additional tables in the `snort` and `archive` databases in MySQL.

2. **Click back to the index page.**

   Behold! The ACID console lives! Figure 7-2 shows the stuff it makes visible.

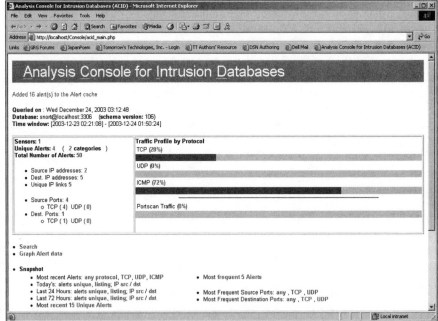

Figure 7-2:
Success is a
pig-pile of
immediate
attempted
exploits
on your
network.

Using ACID to View Snort Alerts

Pretty hefty configuration process, eh? Good thing ACID is an especially powerful alert-reporting console. It enables you to view individual alert events picked up by Snort — and you can view groups of events, organized by various criteria (source or destination addresses, type of protocol, time of day). With the addition of the graphing libraries installed in the course of this chapter, you can also view such data in a graphical format. In this section, we navigate and discuss the major features of the ACID console.

The main ACID console page

The main ACID console page gives you

- ✔ A quick view of how many alerts your Snort sensors have dumped to your database

- ✔ Some subdivided data for further investigation (such as alerts sorted by protocol/attack type)

- ✔ Graphs created by the graphing and reporting functions (installed with JpGraph and PHPlot).

- ✔ Maintenance tools related directly to the ACID application

In the following subsections, we discuss the various areas of the main ACID console page. (Figure 7-3 shows the main ACID console.)

Figure 7-3:
Quick information can be had from the main ACID console.

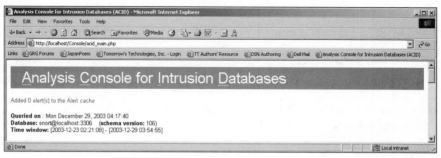

Console information

In the upper-left corner of the console window, ACID provides quick information about the console itself (as in Figure 7-3), as follows:

✔ **Queried on:** This line shows the last date and time the ACID console queried the Snort database. ACID automatically queries the database every 3 minutes or every time you click a link on the ACID console, whichever comes first.

✔ **Database:** This line shows the database, host and port that ACID is monitoring.

✔ **Time Window:** This is the time span of data that ACID has access to.

Quick Alert Information

The Quick Alert Information area of the console gives you some compiled statistics. If you have multiple sensors, all alerts are shown in these statistics. The following information is covered by this area of the main console window:

✔ **Sensors:** Displays how many sensors' data ACID has access to. Clicking the number brings you to another page with data for each individual sensor (Figure 7-4).

✔ **Alert Information:** These two criteria show you how many unique alerts have fired a Snort rule and the total number of alerts for all sensors.

✔ **IP Address Information:** Source, Destination, and Unique IP's are all quickly available by clicking the appropriate numbered link.

✔ **Port Information:** Source and Destination ports, as well as the protocols involved are listed for quick access here.

✔ **Traffic by Protocol:** The alerts by protocol are displayed in bar-graph format on the right side of the Alert Information table, showing

   • Each protocol (TCP, UDP, ICMP, and Portscan traffic)

   • A percentage of the total beside each protocol

We discuss Traffic by Protocol in more detail in the following section.

Figure 7-4:
Yeah, yeah,
we only
have one
sensor.
But, it's a
BIG one.

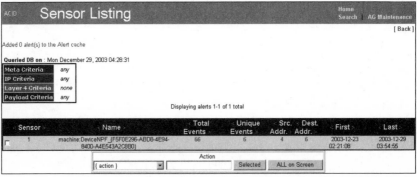

Snapshot views

The Snapshot area of the console gives you quick access to alerts in a specific grouping, such as most recent, all alerts for today, last 24 hours, last 72 hours, and others (as in Figure 7-5). The following information is available from the Snapshot view:

- ✓ **Recent Alerts:** You can view the most recent alerts by any protocol or by a specific protocol by clicking the appropriate link (any protocol, TCP, UDP, or ICMP). A separate link gives you access to the most recent 15 Unique Alerts.

- ✓ **Time Grouped Alerts:** Three separate bullet points give you access to alerts grouped by Today, the last 24 hours, or the last 72 hours. You can view by alerts, unique, a straight list, or by source or destination IP Address.

- ✓ **Port Grouped Alerts:** Two groups of links give you access to the last source or destination ports (grouped by any, TCP or UDP).

- ✓ **Frequent Alerts:** These are grouped by the 5 most frequent alerts, most frequent source or destination ports (by any, TCP, or UDP) and the most frequent 15 IP addresses (source or destination).

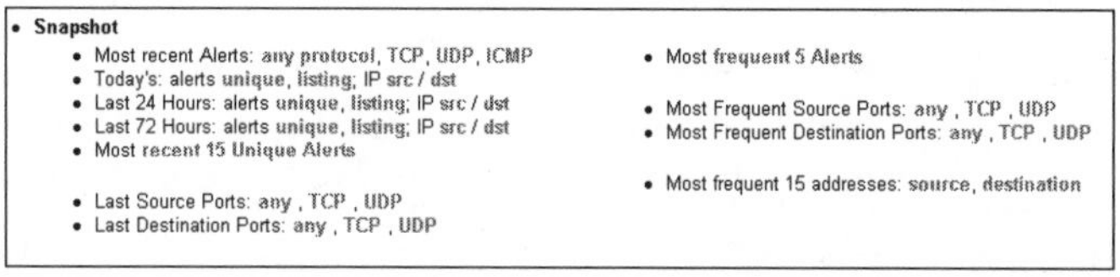

Figure 7-5:
ACID's
Snapshot
console
gives you
the from-
50,000-feet
view of
recent
alerts.

- **Snapshot**
  - Most recent Alerts: any protocol, TCP, UDP, ICMP
  - Today's: alerts unique, listing; IP src / dst
  - Last 24 Hours: alerts unique, listing; IP src / dst
  - Last 72 Hours: alerts unique, listing; IP src / dst
  - Most recent 15 Unique Alerts

  - Last Source Ports: any , TCP , UDP
  - Last Destination Ports: any , TCP , UDP

  - Most frequent 5 Alerts

  - Most Frequent Source Ports: any , TCP , UDP
  - Most Frequent Destination Ports: any , TCP , UDP

  - Most frequent 15 addresses: source, destination

Drill-down information

By clicking the links available on any of the views discussed in the preceding bulleted list, you get a wealth of information about each individual alert, including

- ✓ Unique ID # that Snort assigned the alert

- ✓ Attack signature that fired the Snort rule

- ✓ Timestamp when the alert fired in Snort

✔ Source and destination IP addresses

✔ Layer-4 (Transport Layer) protocol that the attack used (TCP, UDP, ICMP, or whatever)

For more information on the OSI networking model and how its layers match up to the TCP/IP protocol suite, see the sidebar "The lowdown on layers" in Chapter 1.

Let's take a sample alert and walk through the information you can get just by a few clicks of the mouse.

Table view of an alert

In Figure 7-6, we see a typical alert in its table view. (From the main ACID console, we clicked the "Most Recent Alerts: any protocol" link and illustrate the first one that popped up.)

Figure 7-6:
A typical alert sitting at the table.

	ID	Signature	Timestamp	Source Address	Dest. Address	Layer 4 Proto
	#0-(1.68)	[snort] ICMP Destination Unreachable (Communication Administratively Prohibited)	2003-12-29 05:19:45	24.104.93.122	172.16.1.36	ICMP

Here's what to look for in Figure 7-6:

✔ The unique identification number that Snort assigned this particular alert. All the information about this alert is stored under this ID in the database. Notice also that the ID# is a link. We talk about that in just a bit.

✔ The signature that fired this alert is displayed: ICMP Destination Unreachable (Communication Administratively Prohibited).

✔ Displayed before the alert are links to more information about this alert. In this case, only one source is listed: the snort.org Web site. Essentially, our alert is an administrative alert. Someone tried to ping our system, our firewall denied the reply to the host, and this triggered the ICMP Destination Unreachable rule. (More about Snort rules in Chapter 8.)

✔ The last four columns in the table list additional information about the alert, including

• The Timestamp that Snort applied to the alert before storing it in the database

• The IP address from which the attack originated

  • The IP address to which the attack was directed (shown as Source
    Address and Dest. Address in the table)

✔ The last column in the table lists the Layer-4 protocol that the attack
  used. In this case, it was a ping and used the ICMP protocol.

Detailed view of the alert

If you click the ID number on the alert table page, a detailed view of the alert
displays (as in Figure 7-7).

Here you have all relevant information concerning the alert, including all
information displayed in the table view, as well as specific IP information on
the datastream, and the payload of the packets received.

The IP information includes

✔ The source and destination address

✔ Additional IP information

✔ Host and domain names of both source and destination addresses

  It's a handy feature that ACID looks up the host and domain name of
  the source and destination addresses for us so we don't have to do it
  manually.

  It's important to understand that not all IP addresses will resolve to host
  and domain names. This is a "best practice" on the Internet, but not
  every organization or ISP does it. Sometimes, an IP address might be all
  the information you have to track an attacker.

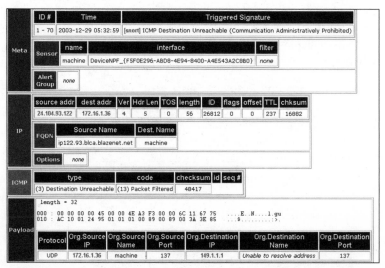

Figure 7-7:
A detailed
view of
the alert.

The Payload section of this window lists

✔ The actual bits of the network packet received in Hexadecimal (or *hex* as it's often abbreviated)

✔ A translation of the hex into a more human-readable text format

✔ The original source and destination IPs, names, and ports

Hex is often used by programmer geeks as a shorthand way to represent the zeros and ones of binary computer code. But don't worry, you don't need to read hex to understand your Snort alerts! The payload is there for informational purposes if you want to get into the nitty-gritty details of each packet, and can be useful for tweaking Snort rules. But the main things you're concerned with are

✔ Where the attack's coming from (the source)

✔ Where it's going (the destination)

✔ Which Snort alert rule was triggered

Detailed view of the signature

The link listed in the signature column in the table view of the alert takes you to an external Web page that describes the particular attack signature detected. This is really just a "for your information" Web site maintained by snort.org or other organizations that specialize in IDS signatures. The information found on these sites can help you track down both what the attack could have been targeting as well as why a Snort rule fired on that particular piece of network traffic.

Detailed view of the IP address

On any window where a destination or source IP address appears, that IP address is displayed as a Web link. If you click an IP address link, you receive what's shown in Figure 7-8:

✔ Information on the specific host

✔ Links to additional information (most of the additional information is from external Web sites, rather than your ACID console).

Figure 7-8:
Additional
information
about the
offending IP
address.

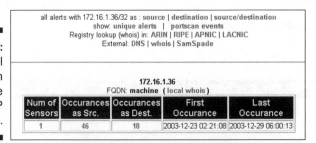

all alerts with 172.16.1.36/32 as : source | destination | source/destination
show: unique alerts | portscan events
Registry lookup (whois) in: ARIN | RIPE | APNIC | LACNIC
External: DNS | whois | SamSpade

172.16.1.36
FQDN: **machine** (local whois)

Num of Sensors	Occurances as Src.	Occurances as Dest.	First Occurance	Last Occurance
1	46	18	2003-12-23 02:21:08	2003-12-29 06:00:13

✔ Links to other occurrences of this IP address (shown at the top of the window), whether as source, destination, or both in your Snort database.

✔ Unique alerts and port scan events associated with this IP address.

✔ Some more security ammo below the information on this IP address:

- External links for more information about this host.

- ARIN, RIPE, APNIC and LACNIC links that take you to information on those respective pages about the owner of that IP address.

Usually an Internet service provider owns a range of IP addresses, of which the one you're querying is one, but the information can be as specific as an individual company or organization that the IP address range is assigned to. The ARIN, RIPE, APNIC and LACNIC registries may not have information on the specific IP address you're querying, if these IP address registries don't control that address (see the sidebar "What are these registries?" in this chapter for more about registries).

✔ Reverse-DNS (the hostname of the computer that has this IP address) using the DNS link.

✔ A link to the SamSpade Web page, where you can perform several useful functions, such as

- Following a trace route to the IP address

- Processing all the information available from the ARIN link discussed previously

We discuss hunting down and reporting attackers in more detail in Chapter 10.

Graphing and reporting

ACID's graphing and reporting functions are full-featured and easy to use, giving you graphical data on every sensor in your Snort network. The graphing functions are highly configurable, enabling you to display

✔ The number of alerts over time

✔ Source or destination IP address

✔ Source or destination ports (by protocol)

✔ Signature classification

✔ Number of alerts by sensor

To access the graphing functions of the ACID console, click the Graph Alert data link on the main console page.

What are these registries?

Four Regional Internet Registries (RIR) act as points of authority for the most basic Internet resource: the IP address. These registries control the allocation of IP address space, as well as Autonomous System Numbers and IN-ADDR.ARPA inverse mapping. What all this means to you is that these registries maintain public databases detailing where every IP address on the Internet is assigned. This is all done by querying the registry's "Whois" (as in, *"Who is the owner of this IP address?"*) database for a particular IP address or IP address range. A Whois database query can typically be done on a registry's Web site.

This information is invaluable when trying to track down an attacker that pops up in your ACID console. Conveniently, ACID provides links to the four RIR sites wherever an IP address appears on a Snort alert:

- ✔ ARIN (American Registry of Internet Numbers): America and Sub-Equatorial Africa

- ✔ RIPE (Réseaux IP Européens Network Coordination Centre): Europe, Middle East, Central Asia, Northern Africa

- ✔ APNIC (Asia Pacific Network Information Center): Asia-Pacific

- ✔ LACNIC (Latin American and Caribbean Addresses Registry): Latin America and the Caribbean

The Graph Alert data page

The main reporting page presents you with a myriad of options for reporting the alert data stored in your Snort database (see Figure 7-9). As an illustration, we discuss how to pull up a graphical report on all alerts over a span of seven days.

Figure 7-9: The main reporting page.

Select a title, chart type and period

To select a title, chart type and period, perform these steps:

1. **Type a chart title in the Chart Title text box.**

2. **Select a chart type from the Chart Type drop-down menu.**

3. **Select a chart period from the Chart Period drop-down menu.**

There are three options in the Chart Period drop-down menu. The Chart Period parameter displays all alerts in your report by

- ✔ Time of day
- ✔ Day of the week
- ✔ Both

and gives you a view of any trends in the alerts. Thus, if you look at all your alerts for the month by time of day, you probably notice that most of the alerts occur at between midnight and 4:00 a.m. For our example, we keep the default Chart Title: ACID Chart. We want a chart of all alerts over the last seven days, by day, so we select *Time (day) vs. Number of Alerts* as the Chart Type and we leave the Chart Period as *No period* because we want to see the actual dates on the graph.

Set the size, plot type and date range

To set the size, plot type and date range, perform the following steps:

1. **In the Size (width x height) text boxes, type in the size of the chart (in number of pixels).**

   The size of the chart is in number of pixels wide by number of pixels tall.

2. **Click the appropriate radio button for the Plot Type (bar, line, or pie).**

3. **Select the day, month and year for the chart to begin in the Chart Begin drop-down menus.**

4. **Select the day, month and year for the chart to end in the Chart End drop-down menus.**

For our purposes, we wanted a nice large (1024 x 768) pie chart, graphing data from December 23rd to December 29th.

Graph them there data

Once all your criteria are entered, click the Graph Alerts button. ACID chews on the data for a few seconds, constructs a JPEG image on the fly, and displays a beautiful pie chart in the lower half of the Graph Alert Data window (as in Figure 7-10).

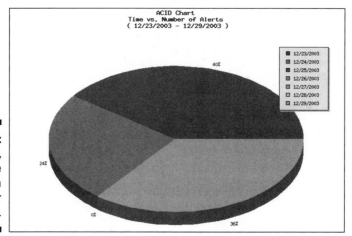

Figure 7-10:
Yeah, yeah, okay. We took a break for Christmas.

Maintenance

From the ACID console, you can view the status of the Web server, PHP, the database, and the ACID tables within the database. You can do some repairs and rebuilds of the ACID tables in the database, as well.

To access the Maintenance page, click the "Application cache and status" link at the bottom of the main ACID console page.

PHP build

The PHP Build section of the Maintenance window displays information about PHP, as well as the hardware and software PHP runs on. All this information is basic FYI and only useful if you're troubleshooting a problem with PHP.

The following information is available in the PHP Build section of the Maintenance window:

- ✔ **Client:** Information on the client (Web browser) you're currently using to view the ACID console.

- ✔ **Server:** The Web server type and version.

- ✔ **Server HW:** A bit of a misnomer, Server HW actually displays the operating system and version that's serving up the ACID console (through PHP and the Web server).

- ✔ **PHP Version:** The version of PHP running on the Web server.

- ✔ **Additional PHP information:** Including the logging level, modules and API used by ACID to generate the Web pages you're seeing.

Database

The Database section of the Maintenance window displays information about the database management system that ACID pulls data from and includes the following information:

- **DB Type:** This is the actual database-management system process ACID is pulling data from (`mysql`, `mssql`, `postgres`, `oracle`).

- **DB Abstraction Version:** ACID talks to this version of the abstraction tool to pull data from the database (in our example, we're using ADODB version 4.04).

- **Alert DB Name:** The actual database in the database management system where ACID pulls alert information (in our case, "snort").

- **Archive DB Name:** The database in the database-management system where archived alerts are stored (in our case named `archive`).

If, for some reason, these databases are not working or the data is somehow corrupted, the Database section includes a Repair Tables button that executes a repair command on the database and rebuilds the data tables. Only use this if you know that the database tables are corrupted. You'll know the database tables are corrupted if you stop receiving alerts or if duplicates or garbage text appears on the ACID console.

Alert information cache

The Alert Information Cache section of the Maintenance window gives you information on the alerts cached from the database. You can take one of two actions at this point:

- Update the Alert cache (if for some reason an alert isn't reaching the console) by clicking the Update Alert Cache button.

- Rebuild the alert cache by clicking the Rebuild Alert Cache button.

If your alerts don't seem to be reaching the console (for instance, you haven't seen one during a period of time that your normally get several), you might have a corrupted Alert Cache, and a good first-step in troubleshooting is to Rebuild the Alert Cache.

IP address cache

The IP Address Cache section of the Maintenance window includes information and functionality related to ACID's IP, DNS and Whois cache. You can update and rebuild IP and Whois cache information by clicking the appropriately titled buttons.

Here are a couple of good starting points if specific types of information aren't showing up:

✔ If you don't see hostname and domain name information in the Detailed View of the alert, you might have a corrupted IP cache, and a Rebuild the IP cache is a good first step in troubleshooting.

✔ If IP-ownership information from the registries (ARIN, RIPE, APNIC and LACNIC) in the Detailed View of the IP address isn't showing up, you might have a corrupted Whois cache. In that case, rebuilding the Whois cache is a good first step in troubleshooting.

Chapter 8

Making Your Own Rules

....

In This Chapter

▶ Exploring the gritty details of Snort's master configuration file (`snort.conf`)

▶ Dissecting Snort's pre-installed rules

▶ Exploring the many rule options

▶ Tweaking and modifying rules

▶ Creating new rules entirely from scratch

....

Although it may seem like an incredibly daunting task, sifting through the many rules that come installed with Snort can provide some incredible insight into what makes it tick. This chapter makes short order of that whole smorgasbord, and you can feast alongside the Pig itself.

This chapter dives headlong into the main configuration file (`snort.conf`) and explores the different sections and commands at your disposal. The snort.conf configuration file is a virtual buffet of rules, where you can pick and choose what it makes sense for you to feed Snort. Throw in a little spice and voilà! A feast!

The Power of the Pig

Snort has such a devoted following because the program is far more than just an alarm system for hackers. Snort's real power comes from its clever architecture. The designers didn't want a simple "signature" scanner. They created an "erector set" for network security that you can modify to match your preferences and environment. They ultimately created a "rules-based" engine, a striking and well-timed advancement in the science of network intrusion detection.

Why is a rules-based approach to intrusion detection important? Signatures don't have the flexibility of rules. Think of it this way: A "signature" is much like a printed list of stolen credit-card numbers that's kept behind the counter of an electronics store. The clerk verifies a card presented for payment isn't on the stolen-card list when a customer tries to buy something. Thus, the clerk verifies a unique aspect of the card (the presented credit-card number) against a "signature database" (the list of stolen credit-card numbers). If the presented card's number isn't on the list of stolen cards, the clerk runs the card, the transaction goes through, and someone goes home with a new plasma TV.

That's fine for the specific threat of stolen credit cards, but what about other threats that affect the store's bottom line? To continue with our analogy, "rules" are akin to a published set of guidelines given to the electronics store clerk that describes the things to look for that could threaten the store. For example, one rule may be to "Be on the lookout for patrons wearing panty-hose over their heads, brandishing weapons, and toting a bag with a '$' sign stenciled on the side of it."

Snort is a very powerful, rules-based network IDS. It's extensible via plug-ins and very customizable for any network environment. That's what gives it some of the highest marks by the security geeks who play with it day in and day out. Rules can describe things in ways that make Snort incredibly more flexible than merely matching signatures.

The Center of Snort's Universe

You've already had some modest exposure to the snort.conf configuration file if you installed and configured Snort to run in your shop. It looks long, complicated, and riddled with hieroglyphics, but it isn't nearly as bad as it seems.

Picking apart the snort.conf file

First off, the `snort.conf` file is divided into handy sections and organized very logically, even for nontechnoids. (The makers of Snort won't have poorly built configuration files with their software.) The Snort makers break down your most likely edits into four basic steps, which they conveniently refer to at the top of the file. You're interested in the Rules section, which is the last step in the `snort.conf` file.

A simple four-step process can manage the configuration parameters in the `snort.conf` file:

1. **Be like a Boy Scout: Be prepared by having a plan-of-action for what changes you want to make to snort.conf before touching the snort.conf file itself.**

   Keep a notes file of any changes (both made and proposed) and settings you're working with.

2. **Back up the** `snort.conf` **file before you edit it.**

We call ours `snort.conf.bak` and typically keep it in the same directory as the original snort.conf configuration file.

3. **Use your favorite text editor to make your changes.**

4. **Run Snort with the "-T" flag to check snort.conf.**

At the command prompt, run snort by typing the following:

```
snort -T
```

Running Snort with "-T" tests your snort.conf configuration file and rules for errors and tells you where the problems are. Testing your configuration and rules files before restarting Snort lets you correct errors *before* restarting Snort, thus keeping you from missing any alerts!

Once you've made changes to `snort.conf` (or any configuration files), restart the Snort application (which geek-types affectionately refer to as "bouncing," "sig-hupping," or even "tickling" the running snort process). If you make changes without completing this step, nothing may happen until the next time you start your computer because Snort hasn't re-read the configuration files and found the changes.

Playing by the rules

The rules section is the real meat of the `snort.conf` file. (Or should we say, "The real bacon"?) The `snort.conf` file has two important configuration entries for proper rule setup:

✔ **The location of the rules directory, configured under the** `snort.conf` **file's main variable initialization section (Step 1).**

In Step 1, the variable $RULE_PATH must be set to the location of Snort's rules — for example `/usr/local/snort/rules` on Linux or `D:\snortapps\rules` on Windows.

✔ **Near the end of the** `snort.conf` **file, in Step 4, where line after line of rule reference is placed.** Here's a snippet of a few items in our list:

```
include $RULE_PATH/local.rules
include $RULE_PATH/bad-traffic.rules
include $RULE_PATH/exploit.rules
```

Many of the configuration file's parameters and settings have analogous command-line switches. When Snort is faced with two opposing instructions (for example, when you pass the `"-fast"` logging argument to Snort, but have the alert_full output module configured in the snort.conf file), Snort ignores the configuration file and executes according to what was present on the command line. For testing and isolated sensor installation, command-line options work well, but for larger deployments, use the configuration files to make the management, editing, and distribution far easier to handle.

Rule Installation

Snort comes with more than enough rules to satiate your diet. We're always surprised to learn about new rules that inventive people have made from all over the world; many have been added to the public domain.

Our goals in building a well-tuned IDS installation is to first enable most, if not all, of the rules that come with Snort. This enabling produces a *ton* of output (most is likely irrelevant to your network environment), but it gives you a great introduction to the type and frequency of the alerts pounding on your front door. From there, tuning Snort is like Goldilocks faced with her choices: Start with the bed that's way too big and then keep refining until it's "jusssst right."

This section delves into those messy-looking rules files.

How the rules files are organized

Snort's rules directory sorts hundreds of rules into rules files according to their purpose. Although the rules are cataloged a few different ways and some of the rule categories have overlapping domains, there's certainly a method to the madness.

Rules files fit into eight major categories:

- ✔ Low-level protocols (icmp, netbios, tcp, udp)
- ✔ High-level protocols (http, ftp, dns, pop3, imap)
- ✔ Web server specific (web-attack, web-cgi, web-client)
- ✔ Exploit specific (shellcode, backdoor, exploit)
- ✔ Service impacting (dos, ddos)
- ✔ Policy specific (policy, info, misc, porn)
- ✔ Scanning and probing activities (scan, bad-traffic)
- ✔ Viruses, worms, and other malware (virus)

An in-depth rule structure

The best way to find out how the whole rule system works is to get your hands dirty with a typical example:

```
alert tcp $EXTERNAL_NET any -> $HTTP_SERVERS $HTTP_PORTS (msg:"WEB-IIS CodeRed
                v2 root.exe access"; flow:to_server,established;
```

```
uricontent:"/root.exe"; nocase; classtype:web application-attack; reference:url,
          www.cert.org/advisories/CA-2001 19.html; sid:1256;  rev:7;)
```

This rule demonstrates many of the options that you're likely to encounter with your own setup. We picked the Code Red worm alert from the `web-iis.rules` file as our starting point.

Here's a piece-by-piece explanation of that Code Red worm rule, which appeared earlier in this section:

✔ The `alert` directive (in bold in the following alert snippet) tells Snort that if the packet matches this rule, then the rule should send its output through the alert facility.

```
alert tcp $EXTERNAL_NET any -> $HTTP_SERVERS
        $HTTP_PORTS...
```

The overwhelming majority of Snort's rules use the `alert` facility, although optionally, you can use the log facility. Chapter 6 explains the difference between these two facilities.

✔ The `tcp` keyword is an argument that identifies which network protocols the rule applies to. The following alert snipped shows the tcp keyword in bold:

```
alert tcp $EXTERNAL_NET any -> $HTTP_SERVERS
        $HTTP_PORTS...
```

Because the tcp keyword is specified, Snort knows to match this rule only to network traffic using the TCP protocol (other protocols, such as UDP) will be ignored.

✔ The network source and destination arguments are highlighted in bold in the following statement:

```
alert tcp $EXTERNAL_NET any -> $HTTP_SERVERS
        $HTTP_PORTS...
```

The preceding network source and destination arguments (including port numbers) tell Snort to alert on any traffic that is either

• From the `$EXTERNAL_NET` on any port

• To any of our Web servers on the defined Web ports.

The network source and destination arguments use the variables established at the beginning of the `snort.conf` file (the arguments beginning with the $). These substitutions provide convenience and readability for managing a large collection of rules, which can easily top a few thousand entries.

✔ The last part of the rule gets even more granular with information the rule should match on, as well as what Snort should do if the rule does match . The following snippet shows what this looks like:

```
(msg:"WEB-IIS CodeRed v2 root.exe access"; flow:to_server,established;
        uricontent:"/root.exe"; nocase; classtype:web application-
        attack; reference:url, www.cert.org/advisories/CA-2001-19.html;
        sid:1256; rev:7;)
```

- A few other tests tucked away in that last section must be passed before an alert is generated. The `flow:` and `uricontent:` keywords further refine the rule. In this case, if the uricontent (URI stands for *universal resource identifier*) contains the text `"/root.exe"`. The flow says that the connection should be going to the server and should already be established. IP listed in your `var HTTP_SERVERS` section of `snort.conf`, then an alert is generated with the message `"WEB-IIS CodeRed v2 root.exe access"`.

Snort also identifies the type of attack by classifying it as a `"web applications-attack."` It further identifies the exact nature of the alert setting the `"sid"` (Snort IDentification) field to 1256. Sids are unique identifiers to Snort. They can nail down an offense to exactly one alert. The `reference:` keyword provides a log ˙ry regarding any other information that's known about the nature of the attack. References are often URLs to security-related Web sites, such as CERT, Whitehats, or SecurityFocus, which provide advisories on what the attack is and how to patch for it (if possible). In our Code Red example, we point to the CERT Web site with the following URL:

```
http://www.cert.org/advisories/CA-2001-19.html
```

Figure 8-1 shows a graphical overview of how a Snort rule is laid out. In it, you see many of the bits and pieces of a rule.

Header					Body
Rule Action	Protocol	Source Address & Port	Flow	Destination Address & Port	Additional Tests, Output Miscellaneous
alert	tcp	SEXTERNAL_NET any	→	SHTTP_SERVERS SHTTP_PORTS	(msg: "WEB-IIS CodeRed v2 root.exe access":flow:to_server, established; urlcontent. "/root.exe";nocase; classtype;web application-attack; reference:url, www.cert.org/advisories/CA-2001 19.html;sid:1256; rev:7;)

Figure 8-1: The Snort rules layout.

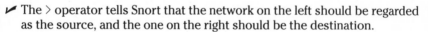

Flow or direction operators represent how traffic is traversing the network. Their use is pretty straightforward:

- ✔ The > operator tells Snort that the network on the left should be regarded as the source, and the one on the right should be the destination.

  There isn't a <- operator. All instances using it are written by flip-flopping the arguments around the > command.

- ✔ The <> operator will match any traffic between the network on the left and the network on the right, regardless of which network originated the traffic.

  The directionless operator (<>) can sometimes cause a bit of confusion with its use. It seems to makes sense that you would inspect traffic flowing both ways from one computer or network to another, but that inspection happens infrequently. Most Snort rules look something like this:

```
$EXTERNAL_NET any -> (internal host / port)
```

A rule that matches too broadly (which the preceding rule would do if it contained <>) produces a huge Snort log and unduly burdens the processing engine as it inspects everything that passes by.

Elements of the rule header

Sifting through the directory of rules shows that all the rules contain header information, though most have a jumble of different items in their bodies. The header is just a front-end filter that separates out traffic by using five key sifting factors: source IP address, destination IP address, source port, destination port, and protocol.

Rule actions

Snort comes built-in with five different rule actions. Each gives you a lot of power in building your arsenal.

Before changing the default behavior of your Snort rules, spend some time watching it operate in your environment and use its output to help you reduce noisy false positives.

Here are Snort's five rule actions:

- ✔ The log action merely logs the offending packets to the output logging that we set up when the Snort sensor was configured. The output plug-ins options are many and varied, giving you a rich set of choices. A per-rule log directive lets you customize logging down to a remarkable level.

- ✔ The alert action can print a log entry and post a notification when some event is associated with a higher priority and probably needs a personal touch.

The `alert` action is the default action for most rules that come with Snort. Snort's job, after all, is to alert us of an attack on our network!

✔ The `pass` action can ignore a matched packet and continue processing.

The `pass` action is useful when you're tuning your rules and need to disable some of the noisier ones so that you can actually see the output of what you're working with.

✔ The most powerful of the Snort actions is the `activate` keyword. `Activate` operates in concert with the `dynamic` action by triggering an alert and running what's specified by the associated dynamic rule.

The `activate`/`dynamic` pair is ideal for catching a complex series of attacks that may otherwise go unnoticed.

✔ The `dynamic` action is associated with a rule that shouldn't run until another event is encountered. You combine the `dynamic` action with the `activate` action to set up a second level of processing in certain circumstances.

The `activate`/`dynamic` pair isn't often used in common Snort setups, but it can be a handy tool for advanced intrusion detection.

Protocols

Snort, as a network IDS, must operate on the lowest level of the network to do its job. Snort grabs Ethernet frames directly from the wire. Inside of those frames are the four protocols that the free version of Snort normally scans: IP, ICMP, TCP, and UDP.

Snort's developers are attempting include other protocols, such as HTTP, 802.11, and ARP. The keywords for building your rules should include only one of the original four.

For example, let's say employees aren't allowed to use the eBay auction Web site on the job. A particular employee has been reprimanded for spending hours browsing eBay, and HR wants to monitor his behavior. The following rule logs all Web traffic that contains `ebay.com` coming from the host `192.168.1.18` with the message `eBaying`:

```
log tcp 192.168.1.18/32 any -> any 80 (msg:"eBaying"; uricontent:"ebay.com";)
```

Source/destination

The last part of a well-formed Snort rule is probably the most important piece of configuration data: The two IP address ranges that are involved with the communication. The source and destination networks are identified in a rule that takes this form:

```
(source network) (port) -> (destination network) (port)
```

CIDR (Classless Inter Domain Routing) notation is used for the network arguments. CIDR notation is that funny way of expressing an IP address using a / and another number — for example, 10.35.24.0/24, which means a Class C network of 254 hosts on network 10.35.24.0 (plus the first and last addresses that are reserved for the network address and the broadcast address, namely 10.35.24.0 and 10.35.24.255).

For the Snort rules files, you really deal with only two types of entries:

✔ Networks (which contain a /)

✔ Hosts (which omit /)

> Omitting / is a shorthand way of saying, "Just the single IP address, if you please." For example, the address 10.35.24.66 indicates just one host for matching against.

You can also enter ranges of port numbers, similar to ranges of IP addresses. Most of the examples that we cover in this chapter are single ports, such as 80 for the Web port, 443 for the encrypted Web port, and 25 for sendmail. The entire range of available ports extends from 0 to 65535.

For a range of ports, you just place a colon between the two ports. The following rule looks for any traffic containing "ebay.com" occuring on any TCP port between 1 and 1023.

```
log tcp 192.168.1.18/32 any -> any 1:1023 (msg:"eBaying";
                uricontent:"ebay.com";)
```

You can also include the maximum and minimum ports ranges by simply leaving off a number. For example :1023 means a range of ports from 0–1023, and 1024: refers to a range of 1024–65535.

Wildcards

Wildcards simplify rules. Wildcards work just like those "splat" asterisks that you can type into a DOS window or Unix shell to list only certain files. In Snort, the any keyword is the most powerful wildcard — and it's all over the place. You're allowed to use the any wildcard in both the network and port configurations: any matches everything for the category you placed it in.

In the preceding section, we used the any wildcard in a couple of places. When the host 192.168.1.18 tries to start a communication on *any* port with *any* host on ports 1–1023 with the text "ebay.com" as part of a URI, then . . . bingo! That's a match, and the message eBaying appears in the logs.

Elements of the rule body

After being mangled by the pre-processors and whittled down by the filters of the rule's header, the rule's body contains a virtual cornucopia of tests.

The most powerful test is pattern-matching what slips through for either specific keywords, phrases, or strings of binary data. Often, this inspection is the most critical, because what's being searched for is the "fingerprint" of the attack itself.

Many of the most powerful features of Snort's detection engine reside in the body of the rule. Each feature has a different style, syntax, and set of options. This flexibility can make rule management somewhat complicated, but very worthwhile.

The layout of the rule body

Snort's rule body must follow this specific structure:

- ✔ The body section of a rule is always wrapped by one set of parentheses.
- ✔ Body options (keywords, instructions, tests, and commands) are within the parentheses.
- ✔ Each body option is separated by a semicolon.
- ✔ Each body option usually conforms to this format (the value is wrapped in double quotes):

```
item: "value";
```

- ✔ The entire line is terminated with a semicolon.

While the structure contains a lot of punctuation, it helps keeps things straight for both Snort and the person managing it.

The "content" option

Content analysis flushes out specific attack signatures within the packet. The particulars of the content option is applied to each and every packet that matches the header of the rule and can be expressed in either plain text form (ASCII) or geek-speak (Hexadecimal).

Worms, viruses, and server cracks are normally transmitted onto your network as raw machine code, which, to the naked eye, looks like gobbledy-gook, but is in fact a series of instructions that harm your computers and servers.

Content matching is typically done at the application layer (Layer 7) of the OSI networking model.

Text content matching (ASCII)

As a simple scenario for demonstration purposes, let's say you're concerned about employees trading computer hacking information within your organization. You can create a rule that generates an alert whenever an e-mail is sent to your primary mail server (the mail server's IP address is 172.16.30.7) containing the word "hacking". The mail port is 25; most mail is transmitted using the TCP protocol, so the following rule illustrates how we can use the content keyword to craft a rule to meet our goal.

```
alert tcp $EXTERNAL_NET any -> 172.16.30.7 25 (msg:"Found hacking reference in
        e-mail"; content:"hacking";)
```

Content analysis (by either text or hexadecimal matching) is used in more than two-thirds of the rules that come with Snort.

Hexadecimal content matching

Hexadecimal (hex) content, although expressed differently than ASCII text, is ultimately treated the same as ASCII by the Snort processing engine. In both cases, the text is reduced to what the computer deals with best: *bits*, which is then matched against the data streaming across your network. Hex is just a shorthand way of representing the zeros and ones of binary machine code.

Hexadecimal is like a numerical alphabet that is 16 characters long, as compared with English (which has 26 letters) or decimal math (which has 10 numerals). Hexadecimal is often referred to as *base-16* because the "alphabet" it uses has only 16 "letters" (0,1,2,3,4,5,6,7,8,9,A,B,C,D,E,F). Hexadecimal strings entered into a Snort rule body contain only those characters and none others. If you create a hexadecimal string with nonhex characters, expect that Snort will turn up its nose.

Here's a real example right out of the rules directory:

```
alert tcp $EXTERNAL_NET any -> $HOME_NET 22 (msg:"EXPLOIT ssh CRC32 overflow
        filler"; flow:to_server,established; content:"|00 00 00 00 00 00
        00 00 00 00 00 00 00 00 00 00 00|"; reference:bugtraq,2347;
        reference:cve,CVE-2001-0144; classtype:shellcode-detect; sid:1325;
        rev:3;)
```

To use a hex match for content searching, wrap the hexadecimal characters to find with the pipe symbols (|). White space can separate out single bytes of hexadecimal data ("00 00"). Snort ignores the white space, which is only there to preserve the readability to the rule crafter.

The preceding rule is meant to watch for an attempted exploitation of the Secure Shell server application (sshd) by scanning traffic coming from anywhere on the external network and destined for your home network on port

22 (the sshd port). The content search is a long series of binary zeros (18 sets of two, to be exact). How can a pattern of zeros be unique? A pattern of zeros is frequently found in attack code and is often a give-away that someone is doing something you don't like.

Mixing it up

You can mix and match the style of content searching without confusing Snort. As long as the binary data you want to search for has the bookends of the pipe characters, that block of text can be intermingled with other, plain ASCII text. What follows is a good example from the back-door.rules file.

```
alert tcp $EXTERNAL_NET any -> $HOME_NET 12345:12346 (msg:"BACKDOOR netbus get-
        info"; flow:to_server,established; content:"GetInfo|0d|"; refer-
        ence:arachnids,403; classtype:misc-activity; sid:110; rev:3;)
```

Notice how the content search string is constructed: GetInfo|0d|. This string tells Snort's pattern matching subsystem to watch for the text phrase GetInfo with a carriage return at the end. Pretty nifty, eh? Inserting hex into a plain text string is useful for representing characters that can't be represented by plain text, such as a carriage return. You can drift between text and binary content all within the same search string.

The "depth" option

It would be nice if malicious content always occurred at the beginning or end of a packet. Unfortunately, malicious content can occur almost anywhere in a packet. The depth option specifies how many bytes into a packet the Snort processor should look before moving on to the next rule.

The main reason for using the depth option is to restrict the search to the most likely places where a match is found, without wasting valuable processor resources to search the entire packet. For example, if you want to find the HTTP protocol version as part of a Web site communication, look in the first few hundred bytes. Because a packet may be as large as 1,500 bytes (less the header overhead), it makes a lot of sense to give Snort a break, especially if what it must look through are millions upon millions of packets.

The following rule from the web-misc.rules file reveals that you need only 15 bytes to catch the sadmind worm. Hence, the content GET x http/1.0 is always encountered at the very beginning of the packet.

```
web-misc.rules:alert tcp $EXTERNAL_NET any -> $HTTP_SERVERS $HTTP_PORTS
        (msg:"WEB-MISC sadmind worm access"; flow:to_server,established;
        content:"GET x HTTP/1.0"; offset:0; depth:15; classtype:attempted-
        recon; reference:url,www.cert.org/advisories/CA-2001-11.html;
        sid:1375;  rev:5;)
```

The "nocase" option

The nocase option, which appears in more than a third of the rules that ship with Snort, basically says to ignore the case of the characters submitted for searching. Because the nocase directive takes no arguments, it's normally just used with a terminating semicolon. The following example from the info.rules file finds the text LOGIN FAILED or LoGIn FaIlEd on a telnet session port.

```
alert tcp $HOME_NET 23 -> $EXTERNAL_NET any (msg:"INFO TELNET Bad Login"; con-
            tent: "Login failed";  nocase; flow:from_server,established;
            classtype:bad-unknown; sid:492; rev:6;)
```

The "offset" option

Another tool that gives us a more precise scope on where in the packet to look is the offset option. Offset works by skipping over the number of bytes supplied to the right of the colon. So, offset:90 skips the first 90 bytes of the packet and then begins searching for the string given as part of the content keyword. Offset and depth work nicely together to make the search area of a packet limited to a window that is bracketed by the two. Basically, if you know where to look and what to look for, you can use these two options to help Snort get a fast grip on where to spend its time.

The Uniform Resource Identifier (URI) option

You can use the uricontent option to conduct a similar type of content searching. Its purpose is similar to the depth and offset options: to reduce the overall processing burden on Snort as it watches for more attacks to effectively do its job.

The uricontent option works much like the *content* one, except it restricts its searching to only URIs in the payload of the packet. URIs (Uniform Resource Identifiers) in Snort can specify other protocols than http, such as ftp, gopher, rsync, and https.

The uricontent option only searches for the given text in URIs that is found in the packet. If URIs aren't present, no match occurs. URI searching is good for catching malicious commands that are readily evident as they often appear in the location request to a Web server. The following rule from the web-iis.rules file shows an exploit attempt against the IIS server using both content and uricontent analysis:

```
alert tcp $EXTERNAL_NET any -> $HTTP_SERVERS $HTTP_PORTS (msg:"WEB-IIS .asa HTTP
            header buffer overflow attempt"; flow:to_server,established; con-
            tent:"HTTP|2F|"; nocase; uricontent:".asa"; nocase;
            content:"|3A|"; content:"|0A|"; content:"|00|"; reference:bug-
            traq,4476; classtype:web-application-attack; sid:1802; rev:4;)
```

A couple of interesting characteristics about this rule are worth discussing:

- ✔ When `nocase` follows a string, its effect is upon the `content` string immediately prior.
- ✔ The `nocase` option has no effect upon binary search strings. Leaving it off of those strings just helps the overall flow of the rule.

Classification

The classification options provide an overall description of a rule, along with other helpful information about the rule, that can be used by the Snort program itself and a system administrator. These options include the Snort ID, the alert message to appear in the alert log, the rule revision number, the alert priority, the alert classification, and external references for the exploit or vulnerability that triggered the alert.

Snort IDs

Quite a few options help organize and classify detected alerts. The Snort ID (sid) option is unique to the Snort system and a good way to get a handle on classifications.

The format of the Snort ID value is the same as it as other classification options. For example, a proper usage is as follows:

```
sid:<ID_VALUE>;
```

When you get the hang of building your own sets of rules, assign each custom rule a unique sid number somewhere above the 1,000,000 mark. That way, updates to the Snort rule base won't accidentally collide with your custom rule. Table 8-1 gives you a breakdown of the uses for sid ranges.

Table 8-1	Snort ID (sid) Values
Range of Values	*Usage*
1–100	Reserved for future use
100–1,000,000	For use within the `www.snort.org` distribution network
1,000,000 +	For use in customizing your own Snort rules

Priority

Snort has a built-in numerical rating for many of the rules that it ships with: The lower the priority number, the higher the risk posed by the attack that tripped the rule. By using the `priority` option, you can override Snort's default level and rate how important or impacting a particular rule is to your unique environment. For example, the following command assigns the rule associated with it the highest priority: 1.

```
priority:1;
```

Classtype

The *classtype* option can organize rules into major groups. A few dozen different classification types are spread over three priority levels, which are described in Tables 8-2, 8-3 and 8-4. For inclusion in a rule, the syntax is

```
classtype:<CLASS_TYPE_NAME>;
```

Table 8-2	Priority 1 Classifications (Critical Severity)
classtype	**Description**
attempted-admin	Attempted privilege escalation to an Administrator level
attempted-user	Attempted privilege escalation to a User level
shellcode-detect	Discovered executable code
successful-admin	Achieved successful privilege escalation to an Administrator level
successful-user	Achieved successful privilege escalation to a User level
trojan-activity	Discovered software code of a Trojan Network Attack
unsuccessful-user	Failed privilege escalation to a User level
web application attack	Identified an attack upon a Web server's application software

Table 8-3	Priority 2 Classifications (Intermediate Severity)
classtype	**Description**
attempted-dos	Attempted denial-of-service attack
attempted-recon	Attempted information collection (reconnaissance)
bad-unknown	Potentially bad traffic seen (malformed)

(continued)

Table 8-3 *(continued)*

classtype	Description
denial-of-service	Denial-of-service attack possibly underway
misc-attack	A catch-all category
non-standard-protocol	Detection or use of a nonstandard protocol
rpc-portmap-decode	Portmap decode detected
successful-dos	Denial of service detected
successful-recon-largescale	Large-scale information collection (reconnaissance)
successful-recon-limited	Limited information collection (reconnaissance)
suspicious-filename-detect	Strange or unusual filename was detected
suspicious-login	Strange username was found attempting to login
suspicious-call-detect	System call was detected
unusual-client-port-connection	A client was abnormally using a network port
web-application-activity	Access was made to a potentially vulnerable web-app

Table 8-4   **Priority 3 Classifications (Low Severity)**

classtype	Description
icmp-event	A "ping" packet was detected
misc-activity	Some behavior was detected that may be considered a policy warning
network-scan	A host or network was being scanned
non-suspicious	Regular usage activity was detected
protocol-command-decode	A protocol instruction was decoded
string-detect	A pattern of specific bytes was detected
unknown	Unknown or unclassified traffic

Revision and versions

The Snort people thought ahead and even included a way to keep a version tracking on each individual rule. The software industry uses many version management schemes because the field is so fluid and so dynamic that tight change control is almost a necessity. The format of the option is

```
rev:<#>;
```

Very few rules that come with Snort (less than 10 percent) have a revision number of only 1. Busy enterprise networks are sometimes hostile and fast-paced environments. Sometimes, rules are quickly added during the heat of a malicious event so that immediate visibility is provided to the security managers who must monitor the attack. After some analysis and a firmer understanding of the events takes shape, Snort's rules are then revised (often only subtly) to reflect what's known about the event.

Messaging and output

The mesg option creates a customized output message that can be included with any logs, alerts, and data dumps processed by the detection engine. By looking through the rules directory, you can see that the fabricators of the rules file have added messages to almost all the entries that they include. The following is an example of the format of the mesg directive in use:

```
alert tcp $EXTERNAL_NET any -> $SMTP_SERVERS 25 (msg:"SMTP sendmail 5.5.5
        exploit"; flow:to_server,established; content:"mail
        from|3a20227c|"; nocase; reference:arachnids,119;
        classtype:attempted-admin; sid:662; rev:4;)
```

See how cleverly the Snort makers had the output of this mail exploit attempt reported as "SMTP sendmail 5.5.5 exploit"? Describing the nature of an attack in plain English helps you in the long run (especially when you're searching through logs at trying to track down a breach).

External references

The second most powerful (and widely used) feature within a Snort rule is the external reference option. You can reference Web-based resources that provide you with tons of additional data on an attack or probe right in the Snort logs.

A few different formats are used. Nearly all are Web site front-ends that look up an attack based on a unique identifier. For example, using the example in the preceding section, we find the following: reference:arachnids,119;

Thanks to this command, when Snort encounters this Sendmail attack, it provides a URL where the user can find out more about the Sendmail attack. Table 8-5 gives a list of Snort's external references.

Table 8-5	Snort's External References
Keyword	*URL Base*
bugtraq	`http://www.securityfocus.com/bid/`
cve	`http://cve.mitre.org/cgi-bin/cvename.cgi?name=`
arachNIDS	`http://www.whitehats.com/info/IDS`
McAfee	`http://vil.nai.com/vil/content/v_`
Nessus	`http://cgi.nessus.org/plugins/dump.php3?id=`
url	`http://` (a general URL that's passed straight through)

Proper use of the external keyword takes this form:

```
Reference: <SYSTEM> <VALUE>
```

You can tie together any number of reference options as long as they're separated by a semicolon.

Advanced options and deep dark secrets

The advanced options give you a peek into the dark side: the stuff of the geek-chic and the wizards of computer security.

Flow control

The flow control option lets you define the direction of a network stream. All network communications have two endpoints and a direction, so Snort can be configured to alert whenever one of many other triggers is tripped. Snort's internal engine must do some fancier processing for the flow control (including some on-the-fly packet reconstruction), but it's certainly worth the overhead because it lets you know whether an attack actually worked or not.

Regular expressions

A regular expression (regex in computer-nerd circles) is the incredibly powerful voodoo of using wildcards to match substrings within other strings. Without jumping into the deep end of this black art, a regular expression combined with a Snort rule makes for powerful mojo!

Protocol options

Because of Snort's primary function to act as a low-level packet trap and filtering device, it can make lots of specific selections based on granular network protocol components. For example, sometimes hackers use specialized or fragmented packets to tease at the edge of networks for information about what they may find if they break in. These probing and recon expeditions may otherwise go unnoticed by a system administrator or a security package not configured to watch for such errant behavior. Snort's native IP rules options put a huge amount of power at your fingertips.

How does Snort deal with all those rules?

Managing the files and their contents, let alone keeping a huge decision tree running, is a fine programmatic accomplishment.

Snort keeps track of all those intricate rules (some with more than 20 different options) with some fancy data processing internally. Without getting too bogged down, the process of reading in a particular rule is governed by a *string parser,* which cuts apart the rule into its component parts, which are then stored into a series of linked lists.

Snort is a busy, complex, and low-level application. Every small or subtle error that goes undetected or that causes minor annoyances can snowball into a huge performance issue under certain circumstances. Although it doesn't happen often, a misplaced command or configuration option can cause downtime or data loss.

Rule Refinements

This section is the fun part of tweaking specific rules to match your environment. We recommend a regular strategy of nosing through your Snort output. As time passes, the composition of your network changes, and the minefield of vulnerabilities expands.

Trimming the fat

Likely the first refinement that any IDS guru recommends, almost to the point of being a broken record, is to reduce your false positives by stripping the dead wood from your rules files.

We recommend that you sit down with a map of your network and a list of your network connected assets (operating systems and exposed services are the most critical) and build a table of your computer resources that can be attacked. From there you comment out those rules that just don't matter. If you have ten Windows NT servers running MS Project Server and nothing else, there's little need for a thousand Linux/Unix rules.

Commenting out unneeded rules is a simple matter: Just edit the file containing the rule and place a "#" before the first character of the rule type (generally "alert").

Chapter 9 includes more tuning methods that reduce false positives and the reasons why removing the extra noise keeps your Snort a-snorting.

Making adjustments

Small changes to the rules files of your setup can keep your Snort installation running at peak efficiency. By refining the rules that you are already running with Snort, you generate better reports, waste less time reviewing them, and react faster.

Before editing any Snort rule file, it's highly recommended that you do the following:

- ✔ Always make a backup of that rule file.
- ✔ Make sure that you use a plain text editor that doesn't add any funky formatting or characters when you save the file. The vi program in Linux and Notepad in Windows are good examples.

Start by finding a rule that can use some tweaking. Maybe this DNS rule was misclassed:

```
alert udp $EXTERNAL_NET 53 -> $HOME_NET any (msg:"DNS SPOOF query response PTR
           with TTL\: 1 min. and no authority"; con-
           tent:"|85800001000100000000|";
           content:"|c00c000c00010000003c000f|"; classtype:bad-unknown;
           sid:253; rev:2;)
```

Out of the box, it's classified as a "bad-unknown" alert. Maybe it should be reclassified as a reconnaissance or information probe, consistent with an "attempted-recon" tag. To change the rule, just edit the dns.rules (the file that contains the rule we're modifying) and change it to something like

```
alert udp $EXTERNAL_NET 53 -> $HOME_NET any (msg:"DNS SPOOF query response PTR
           with TTL\: 1 min. and no authority"; con-
           tent:"|85800001000100000000|";
           content:"|c00c000c00010000003c000f|"; classtype:attempted-recon;
           sid:253; rev:3;)
```

We bumped up the revision number to 3 so that another person can see that something's changed.

If you plan on making lots of changes to the base rules that come with Snort, keep a local backup copy of the original version outside of the directory that Snort uses to manage its configuration. If you upgrade Snort without keeping copies of all your custom tweaking, you may accidentally overwrite the whole lot with one punch of the enter key!

Building a rule from whole cloth

In some cases, a *new* rule is needed. Situations that might require a new rule include:

- ✔ Some sort of odd behavior on the network has been noticed: Maybe an abnormal amount of data is transferred on the network after hours, or a particular server is rebooting for no apparent reason. An investigation begins to determine what these oddities mean, and based on captured network data, you can create a rule that matches the odd event.

- ✔ A new attack hits the Internet. There are no existing Snort rules that match the attack, so you decide to create a rule on your own.

For almost all configurations, the standard set of rules (if regularly updated) can be just what the doctor ordered. The need to build a whole rule from scratch isn't an everyday occurrence.

Here's a real-world situation that we can use as an example. While on-site at a customer's facility, we heard that its network was acting irrationally and that the customer needed our help in isolating the cause of it. After an hour of tracking back a huge amount of network bandwidth coming from two workstation computers, we found that they were infected with some sort of virus. We diagnosed a virus by running a packet sniffer and capturing all of those workstations' network communications.

All of that techno-sleuthing work we did can be best summarized into a packet capture, or at least a fair approximation of one. What follows is a snippet of what we were looking at:

```
15:30:05.000913 10.3.232.38.1522 > 192.168.4.81.1434: udp 376

0x0000   4500 0194 bec2 0000 6d11 d406 d963 055d   E.......m....c.]
0x0010   d8ab 0224 1069 059a 0180 6b52 0401 0101   ...$.i....kR....
0x0020   0101 0101 0101 0101 0101 0101 0101 0101   ................
0x0030   0101 0101 0101 0101 0101 0101 0101 0101   ................
0x0040   0101 0101 0101 0101 0101 0101 0101 0101   ................
0x0050   0101 0101 0101 0101 0101 0101 0101 0101   ................
0x0060   0101 0101 0101 0101 0101 0101 0101 0101   ................
```

```
0x0070   0101 0101 0101 0101 0101 0101 01dc c9b0    ................
0x0080   42eb 0e01 0101 0101 0101 70ae 4201 70ae    B.........p.B.p.
0x0090   4290 9090 9090 9090 9068 dcc9 b042 b801    B........h...B..
0x00a0   0101 0131 c9b1 1850 e2fd 3501 0101 0550    ...1...P..5....P
0x00b0   89e5 5168 2e64 6c6c 6865 6c33 3268 6b65    ..Qh.dllhel32hke
0x00c0   726e 5168 6f75 6e74 6869 636b 4368 4765    rnQhounthickChGe
0x00d0   7454 66b9 6c6c 5168 3332 2e64 6877 7332    tTf.llQh32.dhws2
0x00e0   5f66 b965 7451 6873 6f63 6b66 b974 6f51    _f.etQhsockf.toQ
0x00f0   6873 656e 64be 1810 ae42 8d45 d450 ff16    hsend....B.E.P..
0x0100   508d 45e0 508d 45f0 50ff 1650 be10 10ae    P.E.P.E.P..P....
0x0110   428b 1e8b 033d 558b ec51 7405 be1c 10ae    B....=U..Qt.....
0x0120   42ff 16ff d031 c951 5150 81f1 0301 049b    B....1.QQP......
0x0130   81f1 0101 0101 518d 45cc 508b 45c0 50ff    ......Q.E.P.E.P.
0x0140   166a 116a 026a 02ff d050 8d45 c450 8b45    .j.j.j...P.E.P.E
0x0150   c050 ff16 89c6 09db 81f3 3c61 d9ff 8b45    .P........<a...E
0x0160   b48d 0c40 8d14 88c1 e204 01c2 c1e2 0829    ...@...........)
0x0170   c28d 0490 01d8 8945 b46a 108d 45b0 5031    .......E.j..E.P1
0x0180   c951 6681 f178 0151 8d45 0350 8b45 ac50    .Qf..x.Q.E.P.E.P
0x0190   ffd6 ebca                                  ....
```

That same sequence of bytes was being repeated *ad nauseum* by the two busted computers. What we didn't know at the time was that a new worm outbreak had just started to infest the Internet. What we were seeing with that hex dump was the MS-SQL worm (also known as Slammer) in its replication stage. To bandage the situation, we unplugged the two offending computers and ran to our Snort installation, where we chopped a few bytes out of this trace to build a signature and ultimately a Snort rule to catch any more of these instances.

To illustrate, here's a string of 16 bytes that can represent this novel worm:

```
c050 ff16 89c6 09db 81f3 3c61 d9ff 8b45
```

Line number "0x0150" is an example of a segment made into a signature. Now, on to the fun part of making a Snort rule out of that gunk! The first goal is to build an appropriate header. A review of the first line of the trace dump gives all the necessary network information you need to construct a header.

```
15:30:05.000913 10.3.232.38.1522 > 192.168.4.81.1434: udp 376
```

Table 8-6 identifies the meaning of each of the preceding line's component elements.

Table 8-6	Components of Packet Trace
Description	*Value*
Time packet was sent	15.30:05.000913
Source address	10.3.232.38

Description	Value
Source port	1522
Destination address	192.168.4.81
Destination port	1434
Protocol	UDP
Packet size (bytes)	376

All that's needed from Table 8-6 are the protocol and the destination port. The source IP address, source port, and destination IP address show up differently when coming from and going to different systems. Remember, we're looking for *new* instances of this worm, not the infected systems we already know about. Coupled with the signature that was scissored from that big block of packet data, that's the complete makings of a fledgling Snort rule. All the pieces fit together like this:

```
alert udp $EXTERNAL_NET any -> $HOME_NET 1434 (msg:"New MSSQL Worm A-
           Multiplyin'"; content:"|c050 ff16 89c6 09db 81f3 3c61 d9ff 8b45|";
           sid:1000001; rev:1;)
```

The preceding example highlights the following best-practices in creating a Snort rule:

✔ We followed the path of the good Snort administrator and made the Snort ID equal to 1,000,000.

✔ The revision is marked as 1, meaning that this attempt was our first at drafting a rule to achieve the wanted results.

After testing, if our signature isn't right or other elements need tweaking, we can make the changes and increase the rev number to reflect the changes.

Chapter 9

What, Me Worry?

In This Chapter

▶ Uncovering Snort's preprocessors

▶ Tuning Snort's preprocessors to improve efficiency

▶ Trimming Snort's rules to reduce false positives

A new Snort sensor is a sensitive beast, which is good because you want Snort to be sensitive, but not *too* sensitive. After all, you need to spend your time watching for alerts and protecting your network from security breaches, not tweaking Snort day and night or going on a virtual snipe hunt for a security breach that didn't actually happen.

This chapter gives you what you need to know to increase Snort's reliability and efficiency by using preprocessors and reducing false positives.

Preprocessing Punk Packets

Snort relies on a packet-sniffing subprocess using the pcap library of functions, which it gets from either the Linux libpcap library (see Chapter 4) or the Windows WinPcap driver (see Chapter 5). Snort is a network packet sniffer, so it works by detecting well-defined patterns *(signatures)* as network traffic flows by. As Figure 9-1 shows, preprocessing is the first stop on the long train ride for a packet through Snort's systems.

The *signature analysis* that most people associate with a network IDS comes into play with Snort's detection systems, which are built by using the rules files explored in Chapter 8. Snort has a robust and flexible system of rules; that flexibility puts a lot of bullets in the belts of security administrators.

This low overhead and plug-in architecture gives Snort such a remarkable efficiency. You can turn on or off different elements as needed for every installation, which is one reason why Snort fits "just right" in most environments. If you don't need certain functions, turn them off. Preprocessing is one of the shining examples of that philosophy in action.

Figure 9-1:
Follow
Snort's nose
as data
packets
travel
through its
many
systems.

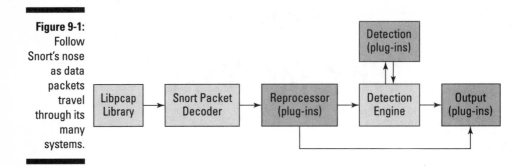

Defining preprocessing

Preprocessing fits into this whole quilt at the lowest level: the network layer. The purpose of preprocessing is to remove as much work as possible from the detection engine and associated plug-ins (which are far more processor intensive) by removing packets that just waste Snort's time.

Imagine having a million tiny balls of three different colors — red, blue, and yellow — and each ball has a number printed on it. Preprocessing is like sorting the jumbled balls into three trash cans by color and then looking through the pre-sorted balls for a specific number. If you know that only red balls can represent an attack in progress, then it makes no sense to spend time carefully checking the numbers on any of the blue and yellow balls.

Understanding the benefits of preprocessing

Preprocessing performs lots of useful tasks for a well-oiled Snort IDS. It provides a clearer picture of a stream of communications between the computers, instead of just relying on a single packet without any context. When two computers are exchanging information, the "conversation" that they're engaged in is usually called a *session*. Sessions have a well-defined beginning and end, as well as rules for who can speak and at what time.

Session analysis reduces both false positives and false negatives and gives the detection engine more visibility of the kind of behavior that is actually occurring. Packet inspection with preprocessing can reveal a lot about what tricks those wily hackers are employing to subvert the integrity of network communications, and possibly evade network security sensors.

Statefulness explained

The most useful preprocessor plug-ins are the ones that involve stream reassembly and stateful inspection. Because the normal method of communication using TCP/IP can be likened to a bucket brigade (little pails of info with "to:" and "from:" addresses being carried back and forth) they're considered a "conversation" only when viewed all together, in a stream. Stateful inspection allows Snort to understand that this stream of packets is a conversation, rather than just random, individual packets.

Because Snort's original operation was as a *packet scope,* inspecting each pail being carried, none of the context the communication was ever imparted on the detection engine. In other words, some of the information was lost. You've probably heard of *state preservation* or *stateful inspection* more from firewall vendors than from IDS vendors. But the term means the same thing whether you're talking about

firewalls or intrusion detection. You can figure out a lot of problems simply by tracking what kinds of packets are transmitted, what flags are set, and what the different elements of the envelope (the packet header) are.

By using stateful inspection, Snort can determine whether someone is *portscanning* (a process that usually is part of a hacker's initial reconnaissance while getting the lay of the land). Also, Snort can detect *stealth* or *malformed* packets, which are more likely indications of probes sent out from a would-be attacker. By comparing some of the basic building blocks of a packet across time and across different hosts, the preprocessor plug-in can get a tidy view of what would otherwise be invisible behavior. This powerful benefit is one of the many imparted by using preprocessing to round out your Snort installation.

Looking under the packet magnifying glass

When normal network communication transpires (for example, when someone is browsing for a movie showtime on Yahoo!), little bits of data go back and forth in a well-defined, choreographed dance. Some advanced packet preprocessors detect ill-formed and inconsistent packets, which are usually indicative of illicit behavior. Such network scanning tools as Nmap and Strobe allow for the manufacture of fake packets that can cause information leaks and system crashes.

Detecting anomalies

Snort implements its preprocessing functions at the *decoder level* after the packet has been broken out into its major fields and before the rule-processing engine does any pattern matching or rule analysis. This processing order gives you the most flexibility and keeps Snort operating at near-wire speed.

When you implement more and more front-end analysis, speed is sacrificed. In essence, the more examination you do, the slower the entire system, but, the better the results. One of the most important themes with tuning Snort — or any other IDS — is trying to find that fine line between too much noise and missed attacks: Eradicating false positives should be your first and foremost goal.

This goal makes Snort's method of preprocessor plug-in design a well thought-out and attractive option. If you want to expend the extra resources to scour packet streams for more data, simply turn preprocessing on. If you don't want the hassle, turn preprocessing off.

Keeping packets in a row

In this section we explore how we can setup and use the best of the pre-processors that come standard with your Snort distribution: *stream4* and *frag2*. Without *stream4* and *frag2*, your Snort system would be oblivious to scans against your network and attempts to bypass your IDS or firewall.

The stream4 preprocessor

The stream4 preprocessor was built to help Snort get a better view of TCP sessions by providing stateful inspection and session reassembly. According to its original design, Snort is basically stateless. The stream4 preprocessor, when enabled, allows Snort to monitor thousands of concurrent sessions and has the added flexibility of activating state management for user-defined ports. By restricting the preprocessor to only a few ports, you can save a lot of processing power, which would normally be wasted on trying to keep track of potentially millions of sessions in a large-scale network.

Also, you can set stream4 to alert you when sniffed packets aren't part of any session at all. This event really only occurs when a hacker is trying to masquerade as one of the computers involved in a session or is trying to insert himself into the communications stream, often called a *man-in-the-middle attack*.

Stream4 also allows the construction of rules using the `flow` keyword that can identify the direction and state of the traffic. These rules are especially helpful in determining how sessions begin and end and whether an attack is inbound or outbound from your network, as well as giving some indication as to the nature of the session. (Chapter 8 shows rules building and testing, including many rules that rely on the stream4 preprocessor for a complete analysis.)

Configuring the stream4 preprocessor

To enable stream4, open your `snort.conf` file with a text editor and make sure that the following line is uncommented:

```
preprocessor stream4: detect_scans, keepstats machine
```

The stream4 preprocessor has several different options, which you include as a comma-separated list, as shown in the preceding example. The following options govern what you can configure the preprocessor to look for (including portscans and state problems):

- ✔ `detect_scans`: The `detect_scans` option (which is normally set to Off if it's not included on the configuration file) instructs the stream4 preprocessor to alert when a portscan is attempting to avoid detection by using stealth techniques. Because the regular way TCP/IP traffic works involves a three-step handshake, which many types of stealth portscanners intentionally fail, they're snooped out by using this stream4 parameter.

- ✔ `detect_state_problems`: The `detect_state_problems` option (which defaults to Off if not explicitly set) instructs the stream4 preprocessor to analyze how the state of a flow of TCP packets is kept. This feature is intended to catch faults or failures if the state mechanism of a TCP session is somehow altered by a peer. Given how noisy this parameter can be, we don't recommend it unless you intend on doing some heavy in-depth analysis. Although good at detecting packets that are malformed, many implementations of TCP/IP have small variations that trip this sensor.

- ✔ `disable_evasion_alerts`: The `disable_evasion_alerts` option is an advanced setting that detects special cases where an attacker tries to fool an IDS detection engine into ignoring a packet, but the packet gets to the target.

  We recommend leaving this option off (which is the default). It can generate many false positives and eat lots of processing power.

- ✔ `ttl_limit`: *TTL* means *Time To Live* and is a common term used when talking about packet transmissions over a network. A TTL setting can help keep tabs on how much time a packet flow takes to reach its destination. Sometimes an attacker tries to evade detection or masquerade as being somewhere else by twiddling the TTL settings with a session. You can use the `ttl_limit` option to alert you to a big variation in the TTL setting across a stream of traffic. This parameter is hard to tune properly, but it's a safe bet to use 10 as a starting point as the maximum TTL.

✔ keepstats: The keepstats parameter accumulates a set of statistical data on the connection tracking and session state analysis, which can be logged with either the machine keyword (which actually is a text file) or the "binary" keyword, which tools such as Barnyard can read.

✔ noinspect: To curb excessive processing on a busy Snort installation, the noinspect switch can restrict the stateful inspection to only those ports listed with the stream4_reassemble preprocessor.

✔ timeout: The timeout parameter sets an idle time after which stream4 stops monitoring a particular session. Basically, if Snort doesn't see a packet as part of an active session in its table within the time specified by the timeout switch, then that session is flushed from memory. Because this option defaults to 30 seconds without even specifying it, Snort's normal behavior is to only perform stateful analysis of traffic that has been active within a 30-second window.

✔ log_flushed_streams: The stream4 preprocessor works by building a session block from the little packets that comprise the entire stream. Using this method, the preprocessor can look for anomalous behavior and perform rule testing. This session block, which is kind of like a gigantic packet, can be flushed to disk for troubleshooting and further analysis. The log_flushed_streams parameter to stream4, if used, instructs the preprocessor to drop the session block in the logs when it triggers an alert.

Our advice is to experiment with the preceding options, see what works well for you, stick with it for a time, and then go back and tune as attack trends change.

Stream4 and session reassembly

Somewhat similar to session tracking (see the preceding section), Snort's stream4 preprocessor also supports full session reassembly. By keeping a window of packets that comprise a session in memory, Snort can alert you to attacks that span multiple packets.

TCP connections can have data fragmented across a group of packets, while UDP transmissions are required to contain all the data in a single packet. Many applications that use TCP for their transfer medium are interactive in nature and often have lots of fragmentation. SSH and telnet session are notorious for splitting data in this way.

By reassembling packets, Snort's analysis and detection engines can catch the sneakiest of attacks. For example, say that you wanted notification when someone transmits a sequence of characters containing /etc/passwd (the location of the users and groups on a Unix operating system) over a telnet session. Telnet sends a separate packet for each keystroke. So, in essence, what you'd have is thousands of little packets, with one character in each, which is horrible for a rule-matching system like Snort. Reassembly globs all of those individual packets into a giant packet to which the rules engine can analyze.

Session reassembly is set up in much the same way as the stream4 pre-processor (which we discussed in the preceding section). By adding the following line to your `snort.conf` configuration file, you can enable the reassembly features.

```
preprocessor stream4_reassemble: both ports 21 23 80 110
```

The following options are available in the `stream4_reassemble` preprocessor:

- ✔ `clientonly, serveronly, both`: The first parameters given to `stream4_reassemble` identify which sides of the connection to conduct reassembly on.

  - `Clientonly` refers to traffic inbound to what you've defined as `$HOME_NET` in your `snort.conf` file.

  - `serveronly` refers to traffic outbound.

  - `Both` means reassembly of everything.

- ✔ `ports`: The `ports` parameter directs Snort's stream4 preprocessor to restrict its reassembly activity to just the ports identified with this switch.

  - By using the `default` keyword, Snort performs reassembly on ports `21 23 25 53 80 110 111 143` and `513`.

  - The keyword `all` performs reassembly on all ports, which we don't recommend (except for short periods of testing).

- ✔ `noalerts`: The `noalerts` parameter tells stream4 not to report on strange or problematic issues encountered during reassembly. For example, traffic manually inserted into a stream or modified packets is detected and logged, and `stream4_reassemble` generates an alert, *unless* this option has been indicated.

The preceding example of `stream4_reassemble` usage should be enough for most people. If you either use other protocols where you want reassembly to occur or run telnet, FTP, HTTP, or POP on nonstandard ports, change the ports listing to the appropriate application ports for your configuration.

The frag2 preprocessor

Because many varieties of devices are out there (and many can transfer data over TCP/IP), subtle implementation differences result in packets that must sometimes be reorganized and chopped into smaller packets, a process that's called *fragmentation*.

To a network-based IDS, fragmentation can result in *false negatives* (real attacks that are missed) because the attack actually spans several packets. The original offending data may have been in a single packet at the beginning of its journey, but through the normal process of routing, it may have been redistributed over several packets, which hides it well. Such fragmentation poses a special problem for Snort, but, thinking ahead, the Snort team has an answer: the frag2 preprocessor.

By enabling frag2 in your `snort.conf` file, Snort's packet decoder uses a similar reassembly process for reconstructing fragmented packets, before submitting them to the detection engine. It takes the pieces and puts Humpty Dumpty back together again.

To enable the frag2 preprocessor, use a configuration like this:

```
preprocessor frag2: timeout 60
```

Normalizing network traffic

The decoding and normalization of certain types of network traffic is an important preprocessing chore. Pattern matching systems like Snort can fail when an attacker introduces subtle variations. These variations are perfectly acceptable and even warranted in most cases, but they can be misused by attackers.

There are many ways to encode a Web page address into a URL It's possible for two encoded URLs to look completely different to the human eye, but are the same as far as a Web server is concerned. For example, the following two URLs are exactly the same, yet they look entirely different.

```
http://www.somewhere.tld/cgi-bin/form-mail.pl?execstuff
http://0/%63g%69%2d%62in/%66%6fr%6d%2d%6d%61%69%2e%70l?%65%78%65%63%73%74uf%66
```

Of course, these different notations can easily trip up a Snort rule, which matches against an exact pattern. In the preceding example, consider that a rule matches the `form-mail.pl` string of bytes, which generates a Snort alert. The second URL would sneak by the detection engine, though it's just as lethal as the first.

Snort's normalization preprocessors are an excellent way to combat these open doors. The following sections cover three of these preprocessors in more depth: HTTP, telnet, and RPC (Remote Procedure Call).

http_inspect: a preprocessor for HTTP

With Snort 2.1, the http_decode preprocessor gave way to the http_inspect preprocessor. If you use Snort 2.0, use http_decode. If you use Snort 2.1 (or later), use http_inspect.

We recommend installing and using the http_inspect preprocessor. Using http_inspect normalizes all packets containing different forms of HTTP communication into a state that Snort can easily compare and scan through its rules. A huge amount of Web traffic crosses the Net, and many attacks rely on the HTTP protocol as their transmission medium.

To configure your Snort system so that it normalizes Web traffic, you need to put a few lines in your snort.conf configuration file that look something like the following:

```
preprocessor http_inspect: global iis_unicode_map unicode.map 1252
preprocessor http_inspect_server: server default profile all ports { 80 }
preprocessor http_inspect_server: server 172.16.1.1 profile all ports { 80 }
```

The first configuration line, which contains the keyword http_inspect, is for setting up the global behavior of the preprocessor, whereas the other lines with http_inspect_server in them are for specializing the configuration for individual machines. You need to include the iis_unicode_map keyword and its argument. Without it, Snort complains and refuses to start.

The options that follow the http_inspect_server keywords include the

✔ Ports on which the preprocessor should operate (between the {}s).

✔ A series of operations that should be used when normalizing the traffic.

The options described in the next sections are some of the most useful http_inspect options. They show how HTTP preprocessing really works.

iis_unicode <yes\no>

Characters in English and Western-European languages are normally represented using the ASCII encoding system. ASCII doesn't cut the mustard for languages that require extended character sets, so a larger encoding system called *Unicode,* or UTF-8, is used. By using the iis_unicode keyword to the http_inspect_server preprocessor, all non-ASCII characters are converted back into ASCII for comparison.

The iis_unicode option is important because it alerts on attempts to hide a URL by using different encoding techniques.

double_encode <yes\no>

Double encoding is often used to preserve % in URI encoding. The percent sign is most frequently used as an escape character within a URL, giving uses the full spectrum of additional characters as part of their input. Because hackers may try to disguise their attempts using a way to obfuscate their traffic with extra %'s, this option helps trap and contain them.

iis_backslash <yes\no>

Windows and DOS systems use the back-slash character \, much like Unix systems use the / character. Web browsers, Web servers, and URLs follow the lead of the Unix world and use the forward slash as part of an encoded URL. Microsoft's IIS Web server can treat both identically, yet Snort only matches on exact sequences of bytes. The iis_backslash parameter can catch odd sequences of slashes as part of an attacker's behavior.

apache_whitespace

The apache_whitespace parameter helps when a muck of whitespace characters try to sneak around the detection engine. The apache_whitespace option automatically converts all tabs in a URL into spaces, before the detection engine compares the data in the URL against the Snort rules.

telnet_decode: a preprocessor for telnet sessions

In much the same way that http traffic can be preprocessed before being turned over to the detection engine for adjudication, telnet remote interactive command-line sessions can be sent through a preprocessor.

The two peers using the telnet protocol do their housekeeping via an inline protocol that can often trip-up the Snort detection engine. The inline negotiation channel involves such flow control parameters as discussing features the client and server support and what kind of terminal should be emulated. This noise is useless for the detection engine. By using the telnet_decode preprocessor, telnet protocol chatter can be filtered out before being analyzed for security rule matches.

The following is an example of how to configure telnet_decode in your snort.conf configuration file:

```
preprocessor telnet_decode: 23
```

The trailing 23 is the port number that the preprocessor should restrict its activity to. Telnet normally runs on port 23, but if you run your telnet daemon on a different port, then change this number to that port.

You can specify multiple ports by adding to the end of the config line, separated by spaces.

rpc_decode: a preprocessor for RPC connections

Applications that use Remote Procedure Calls (RPC connections) use a different connection method than most common network services. Servers using RPC don't listen on published well-known ports, such as TCP port 22 for telnet or TCP port 80 for HTTP. Servers using RPC bind to a random, unreserved port and publish that they're available to another application (the *local portmapper*). You may already be familiar with portmapper if you've seen what application is listening on a TCP and UDP ports 111 on a standard Unix computer.

How can you snort when you don't know where to put your nose? The answer is to decode the traffic on port 111, which is the traffic cop port. It isn't a perfect answer, but it helps get the job done.

To configure the rpc_decode preprocessor, insert the following line into your `snort.conf` configuration file:

```
preprocessor rpc_decode: 111 32711
```

The numbers that follow the colon are ports to regard for decoding. Port 32711 is a port that Sun's Solaris operating system uses for portmapper in addition to port 111.

Deciding what's normal and what's not

A big advantage of using a preprocessor plug-in is the detection of anomalous protocol behavior. With anomaly detection preprocessors, Snort can be extended to detect attacks using more advanced techniques than simple pattern or port matching.

Some of the best examples of this advanced analysis are well demonstrated with the portscan and bo preprocessors.

portscan, portscan2, conversation

Portscanning is a technique that hackers use to "get the lay of the land" of a network that they intend to target. If we compare digital attacks to real-world warfare ones, portscanning is analogous to sending a surveillance and reconnaissance team to catalog the buildings, access portals, and armed guards that protect an installation.

Typical Snort rules can't see whether an individual packet is part of a probing attack. The portscan, portscan2, and conversation preprocessors operate on both

- ✔ Individual packets
- ✔ Groups of packets

What makes a portscan a portscan? Together, several factors paint a pretty good picture of the prober's intent:

- ✔ The time over which the packets were sent.
- ✔ The number of destination ports the packets were directed toward.
- ✔ The number of destination hosts addressed by the packets.

Snort's portscan preprocessor operates by watching for a specified number of packets, sent within a certain timeframe, directed at any of the hosts on our network. For example, portscan produces an alert if it's programmed with a threshold that 100 different ports were addressed within 5 minutes all from the same IP address source.

The portscan preprocessor is configured in the Snort configuration file with a line like this:

```
preprocessor portscan: 172.16.100.0/24 10 30 /var/log/snort/portscan.log
```

For the specifics on those options, check the configuration flags, which conform to this setting:

```
preprocessor portscan: <network> <# of ports> <time period> <logfile>
```

The example shows that this instance of the portscan preprocessor is set up to produce alerts whenever someone is probing the 172.16.100.0 Class C network with at least 10 different ports within 30 seconds.

A configuration line in your `snort.conf` file can tell the system to ignore certain networks. This line is handy when you do port scans of your own network for topology mapping purposes. To configure `portscan-ignorehosts`, edit your `snort.conf` file and input a line using the following syntax:

```
preprocessor portscan-ignorehosts: network/netmask
```

To ignore networks 192.168.4.0/24 and the host 10.10.10.66, add the following line to snort.conf:

```
preprocessor portscan-ignorehosts: 192.168.4.0/24 10.10.10.66/32
```

Sneaky stealthy snoops: advanced portscan techniques

The portscan preprocessor has an interesting advanced behavior that helps you detect obvious rogues who are trying to paint a picture of what you have online. Often hackers use specialized tools to try mapping a network by slipping "broken" or "invalid" packets past Snort. Many of those packets should never be seen within the context of normal network communications, and others shouldn't exist at all. Snort can catch these stealth-scanning methods by using the portscan preprocessor's ability to detect these manufactured fake packets. Table 9-1 summarizes the most common stealth portscanning techniques.

Table 9-1	Stealth Techniques Detected by Snort
Packet Type	*Description*
FIN	Only the FIN flag in the packet header is on.
NULL	No flags are on (which should *never* happen).
SYN/FIN	Only the SYN and FIN flags are present.
XMAS	Only the FIN, URG, and PSH flags have been set.

Back Orifice (bo)

In the late 1990s, an underground hacking group named The Cult of the Dead Cow (CDC) created a remote administration application called *Back Orifice* (a play on Microsoft's Back Office program suite) to control Windows operating system computers from afar. While Back Orifice can be used for legitimate system administration, it's also a favorite backdoor program for intruders. All you must do is trick someone into installing the program, which isn't hard because it's small and easy to package with other programs.

The bo preprocessor focuses on traffic associated with the Back Orifice tool, which is an incredibly strong indication of a hacker in your midst.

The bo preprocessor can detect the first few moments of a BO connection attempt across the network and alert on it appropriately. Configuring the bo preprocessor is straightforward. Simply edit your snort.conf file and add the following:

```
preprocessor bo
```

Experimental preprocessors

A handful of other preprocessors — some developed by groups outside of the Snort development organization — are out there. These experimental and third-party can

- Handle ARP spoofing. (*ARP* stands for Address Resolution Protocol and deals with how computers' IP addresses are found on a local Ethernet network.)
- Look aggressively for unknown exploit code that hasn't been identified by a signature yet.
- Analyze the other protocols found in a standard internal network.

Fine Tuning: Reducing False Positives

You can fine-tune your Snort installation to reduce false positives. The single largest, easiest way to approach that goal is to turn off unneeded rule processing.

Removing unnecessary rules

Thousands upon thousands of rules come standard with Snort, and that number doesn't include any that you may have borrowed from elsewhere or created yourself. Probably less than half of these rules are relevant to what is running around your shop.

Cataloging your network

Probably the best place to start when you want to remove rules is with your network topology map. If you have a gigantic ocean-crossing organization, you have lots of network diagrams laying about giving you the placement of your technology assets with specific details on the hardware in use, operating system, installed applications, available services, and such access credentials as the user and group.

The best filters to strip unneeded rules from your setup are operating systems and installed network applications.

Scanning your network

Scanning your network is a quick way of finding out whether any rogue services or rogue computers are lurking on your IP network. Looking through the eyes of the enemy is often rewarding from a planning and understanding standpoint.

Your favorite tools for network or service mapping are ideal for collecting this info. For example, *NMAP* (a popular open-source network mapping tool, found at `http://www.insecure.org/`) produces a very quick understanding of how curious passers-by see your network.

Commenting out any unneeded rules

Your goal in creating this network audit is to find rules in your Snort rules directory, open them, and place a "#" before them, which disables them from being found or logged.

If you have a network of only Windows 98 workstations and those platforms don't offer any services, you can safely disable all the Linux and Unix exploits, probes, and other attacks within Snort. It's a waste of time to see them in your logs or have Snort look for them.

Coming up with an action plan

Let's say you're running a 30-person insurance claims-processing office, with lots of medical and financial records stored on four different file servers (all four running Windows 2003 Server). The company processes its own e-mail and Web services, outsources spam and virus-filtering to a third-party, and runs a few custom applications to handle the ordinary course of business. Staff members also use Windows XP Professional computers and laptops for daily activities. The office does not have any Macintosh or Unix computers (although e-mail may be moved to an open-source solution, time permitting). There's a firewall for NAT. Access Control Lists (ACLs) block everything except inbound mail to the mail server and Web traffic to the Web server.

This office's system administrator first needs to organize what's known about the network into a report. Table 9-2 summarizes the most important points from the preceding example network.

Table 9-2	Network Summary	
Host IP Address	*O/S*	*Exposed Services (Ports)*
10.0.0.1	Cisco Routers & Switches	None
10.0.0.2	Windows 2003	25, 80
10.0.0.3	Windows 2003	25, 110, 143, 993, 995
10.0.0.4	Windows 2003	80, 443, 3218
10.0.0.5	Windows 2003	80
10.0.0.6- 10.0.0.28	Windows XP Professional	Not available through the firewall

The network summary is your roadmap for removing unneeded junk from your rules and configuration files. For example, most of the rules in `web-cgi.rules` still apply. However, you can comment out almost half of the lines in `shellcode.rules` and everything in `rservices.rules`.

Usually, you decide which rules to remove based on several factors: The source and destination ports, the protocol, and the message body of the rule, which should give you an extra bit of explanation of whether the rule applies.

For example, check the following rule from the `exploit.rules file`:

```
alert tcp $EXTERNAL_NET any -> $SMTP_SERVERS 25 (msg:"EXPLOIT x86 windows
        MailMax overflow"; flow:to_server,established; content:"|eb45 eb20
        5bfc 33c9 b182 8bf3 802b|"; reference:bugtraq,2312;
        reference:cve,CVE-1999-0404; classtype:attempted-admin; sid:310;
        rev:5;)
```

✔ The header of the rule indicates that it's designed to catch an exploit directed at an SMTP (mail) service listening on the well-known port 25.

✔ The message part of the body of the rule suggests that the exploit was engineered to operate on an Intel *x*86 processor running the Windows operating system and the MailMax application server software.

Many of the stars align for this rule to match the example network, but not all of them. For example, if the mail implementation is offered using the Microsoft Exchange service instead of MailMax, the buffer overflow indicated by this rule isn't a threat. You can safely comment it out.

Using a security audit tool

A security auditing tool is an excellent way to tune your Snort installation. A vulnerability scanning tool produces a detailed view of the specific vulnerabilities that each host on your network may be susceptible to.

We recommend investigating a very robust and capable tool called Nessus (`http://www.nessus.org/`), which was written by developers guided by the same principles that drove Snort's creation:

✔ An extensible client-server architecture using plug-ins.

✔ An up-to-date set of vulnerabilities in its testing database.

✔ A robust scripting language.

The Nessus server runs on Linux and Unix systems, and a client is available for Windows systems (NessusWX).

Once Nessus has been executed against your internal network, you can use its output to locate machines that are vulnerable to attacks. If you can patch the vulnerabilities Nessus found, then by all means patch them. If you can't patch the vulnerabilities, then your Nessus output is a list of attacks you need to watch out for.

Nessus can test thousands of attacks (all developed as plug-ins). Once a Nessus report is available, we found that the most ideal method for locating and editing your Snort rules is to compare one of the unique identification tags that both systems share:

✔ The Common Vulnerabilities and Exposures (CVE) database (`http://cve.mitre.org`)

✔ The BugTraq Vulnerability Mailing List (`http://www.securityfocus.com/archive/1`)

✔ The arachNIDS signature database (`http://www.whitehats.com/ids/`)

For example, after running Nessus, you find that hackers can use CVE-1999-0494 against one of your mail servers. A little shorthand Unix grepping easily locates that rule within Snort's rule files:

```
# cd /usr/local/snort/rules
# grep "CVE-1999-0494" *.rules
pop3.rules:alert tcp $EXTERNAL_NET any -> $HOME_NET 110 (msg:"POP3 USER overflow
          attempt"; flow:to_server,established; content:"USER"; nocase; con-
          tent:!"|0a|"; within:50; reference:bugtraq,789; reference:cve,CVE-
          1999-0494; reference:nessus,10311; classtype:attempted-admin;
          sid:1866; rev:5;)
```

You found a vulnerability. Make sure that you patch it and update your Snort rules.

Chapter 10

Dealing with the Real Thing

A real attack is something we hope you never have to deal with, but you're nuts to turn a blind eye and think it won't happen. The attack may come from a skilled hacker, a script kiddie, a worm, or an insider . . . but it will come.

Fortunately, you have a Snort IDS. Snort is installed, configured for your network, tuned up, and you're watching its output using ACID. Nothing will get by you, right? Well, hopefully not, but just in case an attack does slip past your watchful eye, you need to know how to deal with it. After all, what good is *detecting* an attack if you don't know how to *respond* to it? This chapter gives you what you need to know to detect, track down, and remediate an attack against your computer systems — all the while using Snort and ACID.

Developing an Incident Response Plan

"Houston, we have a problem."

Remember in the movie *Apollo 13* when the service module's oxygen tank explodes and astronaut Jim Lovell (played by Tom Hanks) utters that oft-quoted line? The explosion sends the Apollo capsule hurtling through space and drastically reduces the crew's on-board oxygen. A *problem?* Now that's an understatement! Well, security gurus have their own understated word for any bad event that breaches the security of your network and computer systems: incident.

An *incident* can be a worm outbreak, a system cracked by hackers, a DOS attack against a network, or even an insider snooping around where he shouldn't. What all incidents have in common is that

> ✔ They affect the security of your network in a negative way.
>
> ✔ You need to be respond to them quickly.
>
> ✔ You need to be take care of them effectively (referred to as *remediation* by security wonks).

A whole subfield of information security is out there. It's called *incident response,* and it deals with how you respond and remedy incidents. Part of incident response is coming up with an incident response plan.

If you're like us, then the idea of having to actually sit down and document some kind of plan probably sounds about as pleasant as a root canal. Believe us, though: In the heat of battle against a network attack — with tempers running high, the coffee running low, and people worried about their jobs — your incident response plan is going to be the voice of reason. Hence we include the following simple steps for dealing with network security incidents:

1. **Watch for an incident.**

   Use Snort and your common sense to keep your eyes peeled for attacks .

2. **Identify the incident.**

   Use Snort and its resources to figure out what kind of attack you're dealing with.

3. **Investigate the incident.**

   Correlate your Snort logs with system logs and information gleaned from other tools.

4. **Recover from the incident.**

   After you know what happened, get your system back in working order.

5. **Learn from the incident.**

   Use what you learned about this attack to fine-tune your network security and response plan.

The rest of this chapter delves into each of the preceding five steps, and shows you how to tackle an incident from discovery to recovery.

Houston, We Have an Incident

The first step in responding to an incident is knowing that the attack happened. That's why you installed Snort, right? Snort often alerts you to an attack before the attack causes any damage, but you also have to be prepared in case Snort fails to alert you (or you fail to notice in time).

In an ideal world, Snort catches an attack and alerts you of it before the intruder gets very far. This scenario means, of course, that Snort needs to let you know when an attack is occurring. For all Snort's flexibility, the number of ways an alert can get from your Snort sensor to your eyeballs boils down to two:

- ✔ **Real-time alerts** notify you when an attack is happening. (We tell you what you need to know to generate real-time alerts in Chapter 11. Several of the tools in Chapter 16 can also generate real-time alerts.)

- ✔ **Viewable alerts** are viewed and analyzed through Snort consoles, such as ACID (which we tell you how to get up and running in Chapter 7) or by looking at the Snort alert file directly.

In addition to using real-time alerting, we recommend that you or someone in your organization be responsible for viewing and analyzing recently generated unique alerts on a daily basis. Sometimes it takes a human to recognize seemingly unrelated events, and no modern computer has the gut instinct of a person watching the Snort console every day. You can monitor these events with the ACID viewing tool (see Chapter 7).

Benign alerts

Certain alerts shouldn't cause you concern:

- ✔ **Alerts that don't apply to your network.** If you're not running Microsoft SQL or the Microsoft Data Engine (MSDE), for example, you can ignore the MS-SQL Worm propagation attempt alert, which pertains to the SQL Slammer worm. In fact, rules that don't apply to your network are good candidates to get rid of in order to reduce false positives. We tell you how you can reduce false positives on your Snort IDS in Chapter 9.

- ✔ **Ping sweeps and network scans.** Ping sweeps and network scans go on all the time, and if you tracked every single one of them, you wouldn't have time for anything else (and the source IP address may end up being spoofed anyway). You should, however, keep these alerts archived, as they're often the prelude to a more serious attack, and it may be useful in an investigation to go back and look at them. Also, look for trends in scanning, such as a large increase in the overall numbers of scans, or a group of scans focused on a particular system, as they can be the prelude to a more serious attack. ICMP PING and SCAN rules are under the attempted-recon Snort rule classification.

Malicious alerts

Alerts you should look out for on your ACID analysis console are the following:

✔ **Attempts to escalate privileges.** Privilege escalation usually shows up as an `attempted-admin` or `attempted-user` classification in Snort, meaning that someone is trying to gain administrator or user-level access to the system. A `successful-admin` classification means that a successful administrator or root login was detected.

✔ **Attempts to insert shellcode.** Shellcode is often inserted when a buffer overflow vulnerability is exploited in a program. This exploit gives the attacker the ability to run system commands as the user that the vulnerable program was running as, sometimes root or administrator. Shellcode detection shows up as the `shellcode-detect` classification in Snort.

✔ **Brute force login attacks.** By using a brute force attack, an intruder (or worm) hopes to guess the password of a given user. Brute force attacks are performed over services that require logins, such as Telnet, FTP, POP, IMAP, or HTTP authentication sessions. Brute force attacks fall under the `suspicious-login` classification in Snort.

✔ **Denial-of-service (DOS) and distributed denial-of-service (DDOS) attacks.** DOS and DDOS attacks can take down your systems or network by exhausting resources, such as bandwidth, TCP connections, memory, disk space, or CPU time. With a DDOS attack, you may not be only a victim, but also an unwitting co-attacker! DOS and DDOS attacks usually fall under the `attempted-dos` classification in Snort.

Checking an attack with ACID

Figure 10-1 shows a bit of our ACID console for a particular date. The first two *octets* (the numbers between the dots) of the IP have been blurred to protect the innocently unpatched.

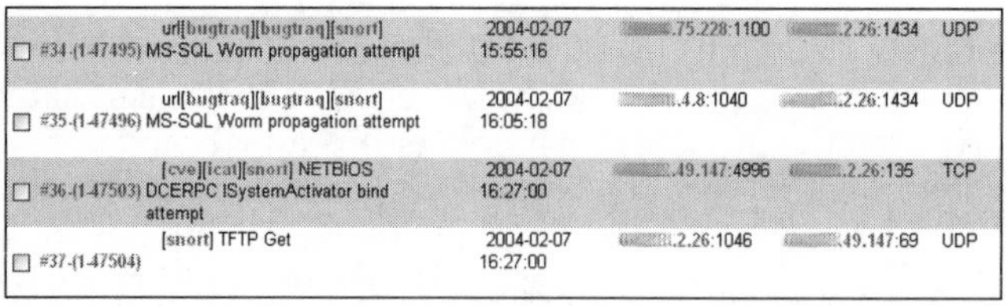

Figure 10-1:
Snapshot
of evil on
the Internet:
A partial list
of today's
attacks.

In our `alert.fast` log, the same slice of alerts looks like this (note that the numbers that were blurred in Figure 10-1 were replaced with Xs and Ys in the text):

```
02/07-15:55:16.344074  [**] [1:2003:2] MS-SQL Worm
          propagation attempt [**] [Classification: Misc
          Attack] [Priority: 2] {UDP} Y.Y.75.228:1100 ->
          X.X.2.26:1434
02/07-16:05:18.835701  [**] [1:2003:2] MS-SQL Worm
          propagation attempt [**] [Classification: Misc
          Attack] [Priority: 2] {UDP} Y.Y.4.8:1040 ->
          X.X.2.26:1434
02/07-16:27:00.305843  [**] [1:2192:1] NETBIOS DCERPC
          ISystemActivator bind attempt [**]
          [Classification: Attempted Administrator Privilege
          Gain] [Priority: 1]{TCP} Y.Y.49.147:4996 ->
          X.X.2.26:135
02/07-16:27:00.895142  [**] [1:1444:2] TFTP Get [**]
          [Classification: Potentially Bad Traffic]
          [Priority: 2] {UDP} X.X.2.26:1046 -> Y.Y.49.147:69
```

The first two alerts are MS-SQL Worm propagation attempts. Even though this worm is a Priority 2 attack and we're running Windows 2000 Server on our network, we're not running MS SQL or the MSDE, so we can safely ignore this one.

After the MS-SQL Worm propagation attempts, the log reveals an interesting one: NETBIOS DCERPC ISystemActivator bind attempt. What the heck is an ISystemActivator bind attempt? And why is the system with the IP address Y.Y.49.147 trying to bind to our server (with the IP address of X.X.2.26)? This NETBIOS DCEPRC alert is classified as an attempted-admin alert, which throws up a red flag because it's an attempt to escalate privileges.

Less than a second after the DCERPC alert, Snort logs a TFTP Get (a download attempt) from our server to the same outside system, Y.Y.49.147. TFTP is a simple, unauthenticated file transfer protocol that is mostly used for transferring configuration files and software to and from network equipment. Our server with the IP address X.X.2.26 is a Windows 2000 Server running IIS. The server shouldn't be TFTP downloading anything from anyone for any reason. It's time to delve deeper.

Using Snort to Track an Attack

So you think you're under attack, either because of a Snort alert or because your system is behaving strangely? Snort is an excellent tool for tracking and digging into an attack.

Obtaining more information on an alert

If a particular Snort alert causes you concern, your first step is to get more information on the alert. In Chapter 8, we talk about the various external resources that you can include as part of an alert rule; examples are CVE, Bugtraq, Arachnids, Icat, and URLs inserted into a rule by the rule's author. These resources provide more information on a given alert.

ACID makes obtaining more information on an alert easy. In the Signature column of an alert listing, to the left of the name of the alert and ensconced in square brackets ([]), are hyperlinks to pertinent resources. All alerts have a hyperlink to the alert's own entry in the Snort alert database. (You see this link as "[snort]" in ACID.)

As an external resource, we recommend the Common Vulnerabilities and Exposures dictionary. The CVE is nice because it gives you just the simple facts about a vulnerability, as well as links to more information. If CVE is available for the particular vulnerability you're checking on, you see a "[cve]" hyperlink.

If we take a look at a "NETBIOS DCERPC ISystemActivator bind attempt" alert (which from hereon out we call DCERPC for short, even though Snort issues several different NETBIOS DCERPC alerts): We want more information on DCERPC, so we click the "[cve]" link, The CVE description reveals that this attempt is a buffer overflow attack in the DCE interface of RPC, that it's a Windows vulnerability, and that it's commonly exploited by worms such as Blaster and Nachi.

At this point, it looks like we're the victims of an DCERPC ISystemActivator attack, either by someone using an attack tool or by a worm. But which one? And was the attacker or worm successful?

Digging into a triggered alert

If early indications are that an alert may be the real thing, you need to dig a little deeper into the packet that triggered the alert. To do so, go to the list of alerts in your ACID console. The ID column contains unique ID numbers for the alerts listed. Find the alert you want to investigate and click its ID. What appears is an in-depth look at the packet information that triggered the alert.

Meta information

In red is the Meta information on the alert, which gives you Snort-specific information, such as when the alert was triggered, the triggered alert signature, which Snort sensor triggered the alert, and any ACID-specific alert group information. The signature triggered is important because it tells you what Snort rule matched the offending packet. By knowing which Snort sensor triggered the alert, you'll know where on your network the alert was first seen.

IP packet information

In blue is the IP packet information. IP packet information is part of Layer 3 of the OSI model. (For a refresher on the layers of the OSI model, see Chapter 1.) What's most important in the IP packet information are the source and destination IP addresses, and the host and domain name for the source and destination (if this information is available via DNS). This information is useful for tracking down an attacker, or seeing which of your machines are being attacked.

TCP and UDP protocol information

In green is the TCP or UDP protocol information. (Both are Layer 4 in the OSI model.) What's most important here are the TCP or UDP source and destination ports of the attack. We're especially concerned about the destination port because that's the port that's being attacked.

Sometimes you may not recognize a TCP or UDP port (you have to remember only 65,535 of them — come on!), in which case you can use the Internet Ports Database (found at `http://www.portsdb.org`) or the Internet Assigned Numbers Authority (IANA) port numbers document (found at `http://www.iana.org/assignments/port-numbers`).

Payload information

At the bottom of the page, in purple, is the Payload of the packet that triggered the alert. (The payload is at Layer 7 in the OSI model.) This section shows you the actual contents of the packet in question, in both hexadecimal (hex) and ASCII text. This information is important because it can give you a better idea of the specifics of the attack, and how far it got.

Using the Meta, IP, Protocol, and Payload information

Figure 10-1, shown earlier in the chapter, shows DCERPC and TFTP alerts. If you click the link for the DCERPC attempt, labeled #36-(1-47503), you see a more detailed view of this attack. Figure 10-2 shows the green TCP information section. What's important here is the destination port, which is the port on the server that was attacked. In this case, it's TCP port 135. If you do a search on the Internet Ports Database site, you find that TCP port 135 is the Windows RPC port, so the alert and the port definitely match up.

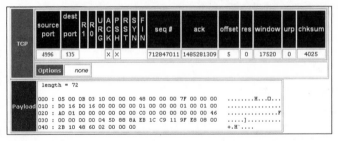

Figure 10-2:
The guts of
the DCERPC
attack.

A little further down the page in the purple Payload section (also shown in Figure 10-2) is the data that triggered the DCERPC alert. Unfortunately, the ASCII-text rendering of the hex data doesn't mean much, but it obviously meant enough to Snort to trigger the DCERPC alert.

Perhaps the extra information we need is in the TFTP Get alert? An attack often happens in a couple of different stops, resulting in several specific alerts. The TFTP Get alert occurred less than a second after the DCERPC alert, so there's a good chance they're related. To drill down into the TFTP Get alert, we click its ID link in the ID column, labeled #37-(1-47504).

As with the DCERPC alert, we're already aware of the Meta and IP information for the TFTP Get alert from the alert listing page. What really concerns us about the IP information, though, is that fact that we're the *source* IP address, so we're the ones doing the "attacking!"

We know that doing a TFTP Get isn't normal use for our Windows 2000 IIS system, so something has to be wrong. We scroll down to the green UDP information section, as shown in Figure 10-3. There we see that the destination port for the TFTP Get is UDP port 69.

If one of your systems is initiating IP traffic to an external IP address that causes Snort to throw an alert, and the type of traffic the alert shows doesn't look like something normal for the initiating system, then it's a good idea to block that traffic at your firewall. This maneuver keeps the system from initiating any further traffic destined to this port until you've had time to look into why the traffic is occurring in the first place.

Next look at the purple Payload section of the TFTP Get alert (also in Figure 10-3). There we do see something interesting: The ASCII-text translation of the hex data reveals mslaugh.exe.octet. Ah-ha! The file that our server was downloading via TFTP is a suspicious-sounding binary file called mslaugh.exe — yet another piece of evidence in our search for what's going on with this incident.

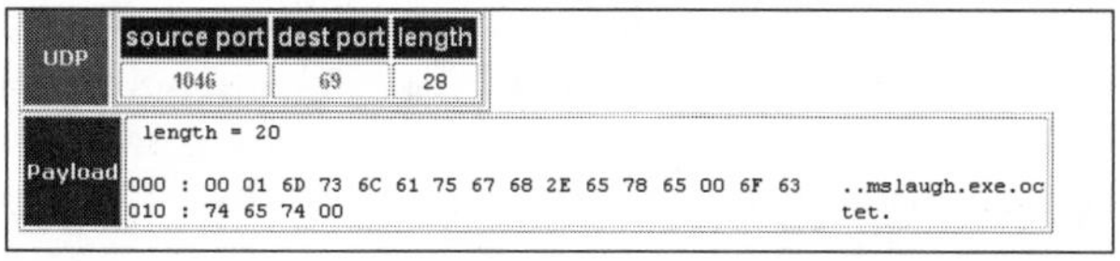

Figure 10-3:
Digging
into UDP
protocol and
Payload
sections of
the TFTP
Get alert.

```
UDP    source port dest port length
          1046        69      28

Payload  length = 20
         000 : 00 01 6D 73 6C 75 67 68 2E 65 78 65 00 6F 63    ..mslaugh.exe.oc
         010 : 74 65 74 00                                     tet.
```

At this point, we know that an external system connected to our server on
TCP port 135. Through this port, the external system attempted (possibly
successfully!) to bind to something called ISystemActivator on the
Microsoft DCE RPC service running on our server. Less than a second later,
our server then downloaded a suspicious program file from that same external system called mslaugh.exe. It sounds like we have enough to go on to try
and track down this attack.

Once you have enough basic information on an attack, you can do more
research to try and figure out if you were compromised. A good place to start
is a security Web site, such as:

✔ Security Focus at http://www.securityfocus.com/

✔ Microsoft Security http://www.microsoft.com/security/

✔ Linux Security at http://www.linuxsecurity.org/

✔ Whitehats Network Security at http://www.whitehats.com/

We also recommend searching your antivirus vendor's Web site:

✔ McAfee at http://www.mcafee.com/

✔ Sophos at http://www.sophos.com/virusinfo/

✔ Symantec (Norton) at http://securityresponse.symantec.com/

✔ Trend Micro at http://www.trendmicro.com/vinfo/

In addition, you can go to a popular search engine, such as Google (http://
www.google.com/), Google's USENET Groups (http://groups.google.
com), or Yahoo! (http://www.yahoo.com/). Sometimes what you're hunting
may be so obscure that general Internet search engines are the only places
where you can find the answer; just be prepared to wade through many,
many returned URLs.

Let's say that we're the victims of an RPC DCOM attack, and that our system transferred a file called mslaugh.exe from a foreign web site, To search on these terms, we can go to the Symantec Security Response Web site, click the Search button, and enter the following keywords: **RPC**, **TFTP**, and **mslaugh.exe**. The first result that comes back is a link to information on W32.Blaster.E.Worm. The critical piece of information is that once it compromises a system, it uses Windows 2000 and XP's built-in TFTP client to download a program called mslaugh.exe. Bingo!

Halting the Attack

Halting an attack should be your first step in investigating an incident. If an intruder still has access to your system or your system is infected by a worm, you first want to prevent the intruder or worm from causing any more damage or covering its tracks.

Pulling the network plug

If you're reasonably sure that your system has been compromised by an intruder or worm and you're concerned that it's launching attacks against other systems or networks, a quick and easy way to halt these attacks is to pull the network cable. Pulling the network plug has several advantages, including the following:

✔ Knocks a logged-in intruder off of your system.

✔ Keeps programs and processes running for further investigation.

✔ Prevents your system from being the launching point of further attacks, while still allowing programs that launch those attacks to run so that you can investigate their behavior.

Of course, simply pulling the network plug also has a few disadvantages, including the following:

✔ The intruder or worm may have left behind a program that looks for a network disconnect. When the program sees a disconnect, it may remove evidence files or try to completely destroy the file system.

✔ Any investigation you do while the system is still booted up has the chance of destroying or altering evidence, which can include something as subtle as the date and time stamp on a file.

If the system is plugged into a managed Ethernet switch, you can disable the Ethernet port the system is plugged into remotely. In many cases, disabling a switch port is as effective as physically unplugging the network cable, unless the switch itself is being attacked. The advantage to disabling a switch port is that it's possible that this can be done remotely—a definite benefit if you're managing systems across a far-flung wide area network!

Pulling the power plug

If you plan on doing a deeper forensic analysis and want to preserve evidence for a court case, then pulling the power plug — not the power switch — is your best option.

Don't shut down using the operating system's *shutdown* function or power down the system using the power switch because the worm or intruder may have left behind something that looks for these system events and causes even more destruction.

Advantages of pulling the power plug include the following:

- ✔ Knocks a logged-on intruder off of your system.
- ✔ Halts any in-progress attacks and keeps the system from being a launching point of further attacks.
- ✔ Ensures you get a snapshot of the file system while the incident is in progress, without any files or file attributes getting modified.

Disadvantages of pulling the power plug include the following:

- ✔ You don't get an idea of what programs and processes are running.
- ✔ Pulling the power plug can cause the system harm and data may be corrupted or lost.

Of course, if you pull the power plug on the system, you eventually have to plug it back in and turn it back on in order to do any type of investigation. Or you can pull the hard drives from the system and put them in a separate forensics system or in a system that creates bit-for-bit images of the hard drives without writing to them. Either way, our recommendation is that you not boot the compromised OS, but instead use forensics software that can access the system's hard drives (or bit-for-bit images made of the hard drives), but not write to them. Examples of such software include Encase (http://www.guidancesoftware.com/), SleuthKit & Autopsy (http://www.sleuthkit.org/), and SMART (http://www.asrdata.com/).

It's all good

In this chapter, we guide you through using a number of common system tools to investigate a security breach on your computer system. Unfortunately, once your system has been cracked, you can't necessarily trust those system tools, as they may have been replaced with Trojaned copies by the attacker. For that reason, we suggest that you create CDs filled with known-good copies of system utilities from a trusted system, specifically the system utilities we cover in this chapter. If you plan on pulling the power plug, another option is o use a Linux Live CD, such as Knoppix (found at http://www.knopper.net/knoppix/index-en.html), or the security-specific Knoppix-STD (found at http://www.knoppix-std.org/).

Looking through Logs

When investigating an incident, your computer's log files are your best friends. Network router and firewall logs can also provide you with excellent information for tracking down an attack.

Locating Unix and Linux logs

If you're running Unix or Linux, your system logs are likely in one of the following directories, depending on your Unix or Linux flavor:

```
/var/log
/var/adm
/usr/log
/usr/adm
```

On some Unix and Linux systems, logs are in both /var/log and /usr/log, because one is a symbolic link to the other.

You can look in your syslog.conf file (for traditional syslog) or syslog-ng.conf file (for syslog-ng) to see which logs are going where. Type the following at a command prompt to locate your syslog configuration file:

```
find /etc -name syslog*.conf
```

The preceding find command locates either the syslog.conf or syslog-ng.conf file in the /etc directory.

Once you've found your syslog configuration file, open it in a text editor or view it with a text file reader like more or less. Inside the syslog or syslog-ng configuration file is the full path to wherever your logs files are going.

Using Window's Event Viewer

Windows logs are conveniently visible through the Event Viewer. The Event Viewer is a handy tool for filtering, sorting, and searching your Windows event logs. To access the Event Viewer under Windows 2000 or Windows XP, follow these steps:

1. **Click on the Start menu on your task bar.**
2. **Choose Settings⇨Control Panel.**
3. **Click the Administrative Tools icon.**
4. **Click the Event Viewer icon.**

Windows event logs are split into the following three types:

✔ **Application:** The application log is by written is written by Microsoft or third-party Windows applications. Most programmers write their applications to write to this log. The application log usually has information on program errors, program crashes, and other significant application events (such as configuration changes).

✔ **Security:** The security log tells you about successful and unsuccessful logon attempts, account additions and deletions, and other events for which auditing is turned on.

✔ **System:** The system log is where system service start and stop notifications are written. Information about networking, remote access, and drivers is also logged here.

Knowing what to look for in your logs

If you believe a system has been compromised, what you should look for certain events in that system's logs (whether it's on Linux, Unix, or Windows):

✔ **Users added, deleted, or modified.** On Linux systems, your logs show useradd, userdel, or usermod being run when users are added, deleted, or modified. On Windows systems, the creation or deletion of user accounts shows up in the Security event log in the Event Viewer application.

✔ **Password changes on system accounts.** On Linux systems, password changes show up in your syslog logs as an execution of the `passwd` command. On Window systems, password changes show up in the Security event log of the Event Viewer application.

✔ **Users attempting to gain superuser/administrator privileges.** On Linux systems, normal users may use the `su` (substitute *user*) command to get a root shell, or they may use the `sudo` command to run a command line as root. Both `su` and `sudo` attempts are logged to syslog. On Windows systems, attempts by a user to run a program as Administrator is logged to the Security event log in the Event Viewer application.

✔ **Services starting or stopping.** A service starting or restarting can be a sign that a Trojaned version of that service is being loaded. A service stopping may mean that it's being killed off on purpose. On Linux systems, service starts and stops are logged by syslog. On Windows systems, service starts and stops appear in the Event Viewer under the System event log.

✔ **System reboots.** A reboot may be a sign of an attempt to load a Trojaned service or driver. Reboots may also occur due to cracking tools or malware that's buggy or incompatible with your system. On Linux systems, reboots are logged by syslog. On Windows systems, reboots appear in the Event Viewer under the System event log.

If you see any of the preceding events in your logs that look suspicious, write down the event, along with its date and time.

Several tools can automatically look for unusual or administrator-specified events in your logs. Three such tools for Linux systems are Swatch (the syslog-watching tool, available at `http://swatch.sourceforge.net/` — see Chapter 11), Logwatch (`http://www.logwatch.org/`), and Logcheck/ Logsentry (`http://sourceforge.net/projects/sentrytools/`). For Windows 2000, XP, and 2003 systems, you can use GFI LANguard Security Event Log Monitor (`http://www.gfi.com/lanselm/`).

Keeping your logs safe

If your computer system is compromised, you always have the threat of the intruder deleting your logs. One way to avoid this possibility is to not only log locally, but to log across the network to a centralized logging server. Logging to a centralized, remote syslog server makes sense not only for your Snort alerts, but for all your system logs. (See Chapter 6 to find out how to log to a remote syslog server.)

The importance of remote logging became apparent as we investigated a Blaster.E infection. We went to our Event Viewer in Windows 2000 Server and then to the System event log to see whether any services had been restarted.

When we clicked on a logged event to get that event's properties, we got the following warning (shown in Figure 10-4) thrown in our faces: Close all property pages before closing Event Viewer. All property pages were closed, and we weren't even trying to close the Event Viewer. Blaster.E was trying to hide what it did to our system. If we were logging to a remote syslog server, we may have caught what Blaster.E did before it disabled Event Viewer.

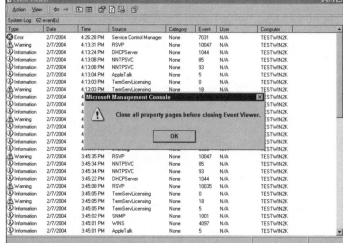

Figure 10-4:
Don't go
there!
Blaster.E
keeps
us from
checking
up on it.

Looking for Odd Running Processes

Intruders and worms sometimes leave behind running programs. Finding unusual processes can give you an idea of what the intruder or worm did to your system. Having a good idea of what's usually running on your system helps you determine whether a process is supposed to be there. We suggest keeping a hard or soft copy of a list of your normal running processes some-place safe, yet accessible, in case it's needed.

Viewing processes in Unix and Linux

The command to use under Unix and Linux to pull up a running process list is the ubiquitous ps command. While the ps command itself comes standard with every version of Unix and Linux, the syntax of the command can vary from system to system (even Linux system to Linux system) depending on whether the installed version of ps follows BSD-style syntax or Unix SysV-style syntax. Some modern versions of ps support both syntaxes.

The following `ps` commands show you a complete process list, along with the user the process is running as and the time the process started. If you're not sure which syntax your `ps` supports, it doesn't hurt to try both and see which one produces the output you need.

When using a `ps` that supports the BSD-style syntax, type the following at the command prompt:

```
ps aux
```

When using a ps that supports the SysV-style syntax, type the following at the command prompt:

```
ps -ef
```

Look for any processes that seem out of the ordinary and write down or otherwise capture the information you find, along with the date and time you obtained the information. Be sure to note the time that any suspicious process started and see whether it matches the time that you believe your system was attacked. Also note which user the process is running as.

Viewing processes in Windows

Under Windows, you can view running processes with the Task Manager. The following instructions for running the Task Manager work with Windows 2000, XP, and 2003 systems.

1. **Click on the Start menu.**

2. **Choose Run.**

3. **When the Run dialog box appears, type** taskmgr.exe **in the Open field.**

   The Task Manager appears.

4. **Click on the Processes tab.**

   The Windows process list appears.

Look for any processes that seem out of the ordinary. Write down or otherwise capture all available information on suspicious processes.

When we opened the Task Manager on the Windows 2000 server that we suspected was infected with Blaster.E, we found the suspicious process `mslaugh.exe` running (see Figure 10-5). `Mslaugh.exe` is the same program that Snort caught our server downloading from the Internet using TFTP, and the same one the Symantec site said was part of Blaster.E. It looks like we're definitely infected and are probably trying to attack other systems.

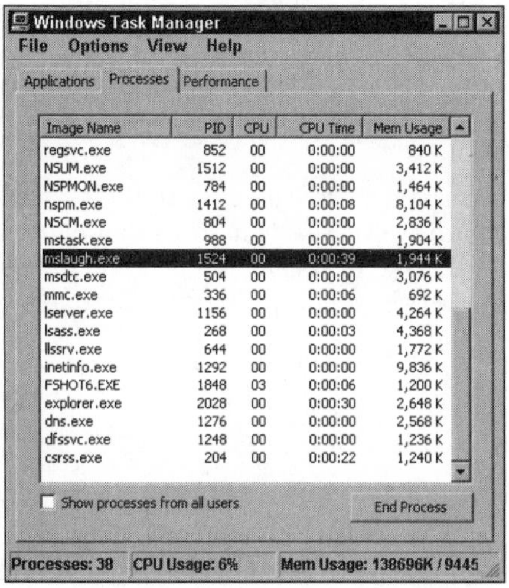

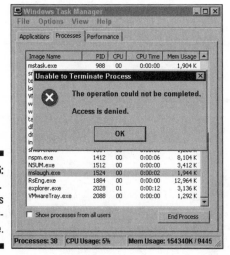

Figure 10-5:
Mslaugh.
exe isn't a
standard
part of
Windows.
Looks like
the joke's
on us. . . .

When we tried to kill the `mslaugh.exe` process using the End Task button on the Task Manager, we were denied the ability to do so and given a rude message (see Figure 10-6). The Blaster.E worm has installed itself in such a way that we can't easily remove it!

Figure 10-6:
Mslaugh.
exe is
untouch-
able.

Looking for Odd Files

Suspicious programs and files are often left around by system crackers and worms. Unfortunately, they can be named anything from random gibberish like "xxyyzz" to something legitimate-sounding like NTFS.EXE. They may also be hidden files or directories, or they can be system files that have been modified.

Rather than looking all over your hard drive for files that look suspicious by name, it makes more sense to limit your search to files that were modified around the time you suspect the system breach occurred. Use the time-stamps of your alerts in your Snort logs and ACID console to determine a good starting date.

Linux

On a Linux system, you can use the find command to look for files that were created or modified during the past *n* number of days (actually, 24-hour periods). The syntax of the command is

```
find / -ctime -n -print
```

So to find files that were created within the past 48 hours, type the following command:

```
find / -ctime -2 -print
```

You can also use the find command to look for files modified within the past *n* number of 24-hour periods by using the following syntax:

```
find / -mtime -n -print
```

So to find files modified within the past 24 hours, type the following:

```
find / -mtime -1 -print
```

Windows 2000

You can search for files created or modified within a certain amount of time on Windows 2000 systems:

1. **Go to the Start menu.**

2. **Choose Search.**

3. **Click on For Files And Folders.**

4. **When the Search Results window appears, click on Search Options.**

5. **Under Search Options, check the Date check box.**

6. **In the pull-down menu, choose either Files Modified or Files Created, depending on whether you want to look for files that were modified or created on a certain date.**

7. **Select the radio button next to the word Between and the two date boxes.**

8. **Choose the start and end date in your date boxes.**

   A good choice may be yesterday's date in the first box and today's date in the second box.

9. **Click the Search button.**

   Windows begins searching your file system for files that meet the criteria you specified.

Windows XP

On Windows XP systems, follow these steps:

1. **Go to the Start menu.**

2. **Choose Search and expand the Search sub-menu.**

3. **Click on For Files And Folders.**

4. **When the Search Results window appears, click When Was It Modified?**

5. **Select the radio button next to Specify Dates.**

6. **In the drop-down menu, choose either Modified Date or Created Date, depending on whether you want to look for files that were modified or created on a certain date.**

7. **Choose the start and end date in your date boxes.**

   A good choice may be yesterday's date in the first box and today's date in the second box.

8. **Click the Search button.**

   Windows begins searching your file system for files that meet the criteria you specified.

Once your search is complete, either using the find command on your Linux system (instructions found under the preceding "Linux" section) or Search on your Windows system, you'll have a list of files created or modified within the dates that concern you. Look for any files created or modified within that timeframe and write down or otherwise capture information on those files — including filename, creation/modification time, and file size.

When we searched our Blaster.E infected Windows 2000 server for files created on the date the DCERPC alert and TFTP Get alert were generated, we found mslaugh.exe lurking in the C:\WINNT\system32 directory. Figure 10-7 shows a directory listing of C:\WINNT\system32 with mslaugh.exe (and its creation date) at the bottom. If you refer back to Figure 10-3, you can see that mslaugh.exe was created at about the same time Snort generated the TFTP Get alert. Everything's tying together.

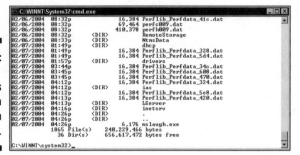

Figure 10-7: Mslaugh.exe is lurking in our system directory.

Looking for Odd Network Services

Hackers and worms often install new network services that sit on your machine and listen on a specified port. These services are usually back doors for gaining control of or attacking your system in the future. The presence of an odd network service running on an unusual port may indicate one of these tools has been installed.

The netstat utility shows you what ports are listening on your system and also provides information on what network connections are currently being made. Netstat's one of those wonderful TCP/IP networking commands that started out as a standard part of Unix systems, but has also made its way over to being a standard part of Windows systems. Even better, the syntax of the netstat command is the same for Unix, Linux, and Windows.

To run the netstat command and get a listing of all listening TCP and UDP ports, type the following at a Linux, Unix, or Windows command prompt:

```
netstat -an | more
```

The preceding command produces a list of ports your system is listening on, followed by a list of active connections. Under the column labeled Local Address is the IP address the port is listening on or the connection is taking place on (if you see a 0.0.0.0, that means *all* interfaces), with the port number itself appearing after the colon (for example, 0.0.0.0:80). Under the column labeled State is the state the port is in. For listening ports, that column says LISTEN on Linux systems and LISTENING on Windows systems. For active connections, you'll also want to pay attention to the Foreign Address column, because this system is the one that's connecting to you or being connected to.

Netstat output is another one of those things, like your process list, that you should keep a printout of what's *normally* available so that you'll be about to recognize what's unusual.

When we ran `netstat` on our system infected with the Blaster.E worm, we saw the output in Figure 10-8. We were surprised to see a number of connection attempts (which show up as SYN_SENT in the State column) from our machine to TCP port 135 on a sequential list of foreign IP addresses we don't recognize. It looks like our system is attempting to infect other systems on the Internet with Blaster.E! (Fortunately, by this time, we'd already pulled the Ethernet cable, but Blaster.E doesn't seem to know that.)

Figure 10-8:
Looks like Blaster.E's not only listening, but screaming, too!

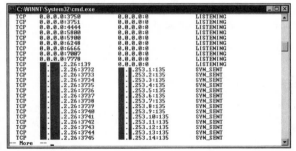

Recovering from the Incident

After you have performed your investigation, your next step is to put the pieces back together. That's primarily going to entail rebuilding the compromised system.

If your system was cracked by an intruder, we recommend that you use your Snort alerts and other information obtained in your investigation, such as file modification times and system log files, to pinpoint when the attack occurred. Using the suspected attack date as a starting point, trace backward and find the last known good backup of that system. Then completely reformat and reinstall the compromised system and recover your data using the known good backup.

Sure, you can try to locate and remove every single Trojaned system file, cracking tool, backdoor, and user account left behind by the intruder. Not only does that take forever, you can never really be sure that you got everything. The safest route is to start with a clean system.

Worms are a slightly different story. The major antivirus firms out there study each worm under a microscope. Usually within a couple of business days from a worm's release, the AV firms have a good idea of how the worm spreads, what payload it leaves behind, and how to remove it. The AV firms' Web sites usually contain specific instructions for removing individual worms. (For a list of AV company Web sites, see the section "Digging into a triggered alert," earlier in this chapter.) The antivirus programs these companies sell can also sometimes remove the worm for you. One copy of Blaster.E behaves exactly like another copy of Blaster.E (though a different variant, such as Blaster.F, may require a different set of removal instructions), so it is usually safe to follow the AV firms' instructions for removing a specific worm and expect your system to be clean.

Whether you're removing a worm from an infected system or restoring a cracked system from backup, make sure that you patch the hole the worm or intruder used to crack your system in the first place!

Learning from the Attack

An incident response plan is a feedback system that over time fine-tunes itself. You take all the information you've gathered from the time you discovered the attack and use it to prevent the attack from happening in the future. Then you can improve the timeliness and thoroughness of your response to any future attacks.

When the attack is over, your system is back up and running, and you have time to reflect, we suggest that you look at doing the following:

- **Create new Snort rules that can help you better detect the attack.** For example, we may want to create a rule specific to the Blaster.E worm that looks for the `mslaugh.exe` file being transferred over TFTP and give it a Priority of 1. (We tell you how to create new Snort rules in Chapter 8.)

- **Look at what may have led to the attack.** For example, were vulnerable systems not patched quickly enough? Do system administrators have a process in place to patch systems before putting them on the network?

✔ **Figure out whether there were any investigative tools you ended up needing that you didn't have.** If so, add those to your CD of known good utilities.

✔ **Look at any place where the investigative process broke down and try to fix it.** For example, were your system logs deleted by the intruder? If so, perhaps it's time to set up a centralized logging server.

There's always more to learn. If you want additional information on incident response, the security wizards at SANS have set up a reading room on its Web site that's chock full of free white papers on the subject. Go to `http://www.sans.org/rr/` and click on the Incident Handling category.

Part III
Moving Beyond the Basics

The 5th Wave   By Rich Tennant

"The engineers lived on Jolt and cheese sticks putting this product together, but if you wanted to just use 'cola and cheese sticks' in the Users Documentation, that's okay too. We're pretty loose around here."

In this part . . .

This part takes you into some of those more advanced features of Snort. It starts by showing you how to send yourself real-time alerts when your network is being attacked. Upgrading your Snort rules or Snort itself can seem like daunting tasks, but we show you how to do both. If you have a large network, you should take advantage of Snort's scalability and run multiple Snort sensors. Finally, this part shows you how to use Snort's unified logging feature and Barnyard to offload log processing from your Snort sensors.

Chapter 11

Reacting in Real Time

In This Chapter

▶ Integrating Snort into your overall security strategy

▶ Expanding on Snort's built-in alerting

▶ Making Snort react to traffic in real time

*S*nort's ability to analyze network streams in real time makes it a unique tool with little competition in the open-source world. With this uniqueness in mind, the developers have continued to concentrate on improving this ability, rather than slapping on functionality that may be handled better by already existing tools. For example, you may want Snort to send you an e-mail when it detects an intrusion, but you'll find this ability conspicuously absent from Snort's many talents. With a plethora of tools available to handle log analysis and e-mail alerts, Snort doesn't need to bog down your packet-capture engine in an attempt to do something that another tool already does.

The old programming adage that advises against reinventing the wheel has been taken to heart by Snort's maintainers. In fact, they not only avoid reinventing the wheel, they avoid the wheel altogether where possible. Instead, they make the best engine possible and let you choose your own wheels.

This focus on modularity results in improved scalability. Because all Snort wants to do is watch and analyze network traffic, its ability to watch *lots* of traffic is improved by off-loading other tasks to other programs. And if you're able to put those other programs on other computers, you're able to scale Snort and customize its operation to suit the demands of any large, complex, or high-volume network.

Integrating Snort into Your Security Strategy

Analyzing packets to detect network shenanigans is just one part of a comprehensive network security strategy. The ability to report these transgressions and take action against them are just as important as detecting them in the first place.

Reacting to alerts as they occur makes your Snort box more than just an Intrusion Detection System; real time reactions make Snort an impressive Intrusion Prevention System with the ability to stop attacks as they happen. Because Snort is mainly concerned with capturing and analyzing network traffic, expanding its abilities to include log analysis, e-mail alerts, and dynamic firewalling means using additional software. Thankfully, there's a glut of open-source software out there, just waiting for a clever person like yourself to put to good use.

Using Syslog-ng for log wrangling

If you like the idea of keeping your Snort alerts in a simple, flat text file for archiving or processing later, but you want some flexibility in how that text file is created, then look to syslog-ng. With its native ability to perform pattern matching on incoming log entries and shovel them to different destinations accordingly, syslog-ng makes separate log-parsing scripts unnecessary. The log destination can be a text file, a TCP or UDP port on another server, a Unix socket, or the standard input of any program you specify.

Syslog-ng also has the ability to use macros to dictate the specific file destination when logging to a text file. You can easily write logs to a filename determined by the date, the hostname of the machine that generated the log, or even the name of the program that generated the log.

Downloading and installing syslog-ng

You can find syslog-ng at `http://www.balabit.com/products/syslog_ng/` along with documentation, links to mailing lists, and other goodies. You can find the source code for syslog-ng at `http://www.balabit.com/downloads/syslog-ng/`. At the time of this writing, the latest stable version was based on the 1.6 code base, although future stable versions will be released based on the 1.9 code. If you're unsure which is the most recent version of syslog-ng when you go to download it, check out `https://lists.balabit.hu/mailman/listinfo/syslog-ng` to sign up for the mailing list or browse the archives, which will invariably have a post announcing the release of the latest stable version.

If your browser barks about the balabit.com SSL certificate, don't worry. The web site is based in Hungary, and uses a certificate authority that your browser probably doesn't recognize.

While you're downloading syslog-ng, don't forget to grab libol, a software library that syslog-ng depends on. You can get libol at `http://www.balabit.com/downloads/libol/`.

Syslog-ng requires libol to run. If you don't have the libol libraries installed, syslog-ng won't even compile, let alone run correctly.

When downloading software, check the PGP (Pretty Good Privacy) or GPG (Gnu Privacy Guard) signature of the source code. You want to make sure that what you're downloading is the code that the author wrote, and not some Trojaned tarball. For the low down on PGP and GPG, check out Chapter 4.

Download libol and check its PGP signature:

```
# cd /usr/local/src/tarballs/
# wget http://www.balabit.com/downloads/libol/0.3/libol-0.3.13.tar.gz
# wget http://www.balabit.com/downloads/libol/0.3/libol-0.3.13.tar.gz.asc
# gpgv libol-0.3.13.tar.gz.asc
```

Unless you've already checked software using Balazs (Bazsi) Scheidler's GPG signature, chances are good that you don't already have his public key. If not, the preceding step gives you the following error:

```
# gpgv libol-0.3.13.tar.gz.asc
gpgv: Signature made Fri Jan 23 05:56:17 2004 CST using RSA key ID 9AF8D0A9
gpgv: Can't check signature: public key not found
```

You can import Bazsi's public key using gpg. The preceding error message tells you which key to grab. The following text shows us importing the key:

```
# gpg --keyserver pgp.mit.edu --recv-keys 9AF8D0A9
gpg: requesting key 9AF8D0A9 from pgp.mit.edu ...
gpg: key 9AF8D0A9: public key imported
gpg: Total number processed: 1
gpg:                   imported: 1   (RSA: 1)
```

Now gpgv should be able to confirm the signature, although you may need to specify where your public keyring resides. To specify the location of your public keyring, use the `--keyring` switch to the gpgv command, as shown below:

```
# gpgv --keyring ~/.gnupg/pubring.gpg libol-0.3.13.tar.gz.asc
gpgv: Signature made Fri Jan 23 05:56:17 2004 CST using RSA key ID 9AF8D0A9
gpgv: Good signature from "Balazs Scheidler (2048) <bazsi@balabit.hu>"
```

After you know that you've got the genuine article, you can compile and install libol quickly and easily:

```
# cd /usr/local/src
# tar -xvzf tarballs/libol-0.3.13.tar.gz
# cd libol-0.3.13/
# ./configure
# make
# make install
```

After installing libol, you can proceed to download and install syslog-ng itself. Don't forget to check the GPG signature, although this time you should already have Bazsi's public key on your keyring.

```
# cd /usr/local/src/tarballs
# wget http://www.balabit.com/downloads/syslog-ng/1.6/src/syslog-ng-1.6.2.tar.gz
# wget http://www.balabit.com/downloads/syslog-ng/1.6/src/syslog-ng-
            1.6.2.tar.gz.asc
# gpgv --keyring ~/.gnupg/pubring.gpg syslog-ng-1.6.2.tar.gz.asc
gpgv: Signature made Fri Jan 23 06:11:40 2004 CST using RSA key ID 9AF8D0A9
gpgv: Good signature from "Balazs Scheidler (2048) <bazsi@balabit.hu>"

# cd ../
# tar -xvzf tarballs/syslog-ng-1.6.2.tar.gz
# cd syslog-ng-1.6.2/
# ./configure
# make
# make install
```

Shazam! You should now have syslog-ng compiled and installed on your system. If any of the preceding steps give you any guff, check out the documentation included with syslog-ng or look through the mailing list archives.

To make sure that syslog-ng starts at boot time, create an initialization script using one of the samples in the `contrib/ directory` of your syslog-ng source. You can find more detail on initialization scripts in Chapter 4.

Your syslog-ng.conf file

Syslog-ng requires a configuration file to run: /etc/syslog-ng/syslog-ng.conf by default. Some sample configuration files are included with the source code. Check the `contrib/` directory or the `doc/` directory for examples; you may be lucky enough to have a sample configuration file already tailored to your flavor of Linux. If not, an awk script called syslog2ng is in the `contrib/` directory, and it can handle generating a `syslog-ng.conf` file from your existing `syslog.conf` file.

The `syslog-ng.conf` file needs to reside in its own directory, and the install process in the preceding section doesn't create it for you. The following steps show you how to create the directory and then run the `syslog2ng awk` script to create your new `syslog-ng.conf` file:

```
# mkdir /etc/syslog-ng
# cd /usr/local/src/syslog-ng-1.6.1/contrib
# cat /etc/syslog.conf | ./syslog2ng > /etc/syslog-ng/syslog-ng.conf
```

Creating a configuration file in this manner gets you up and running with syslog-ng quickly and easily, but because this `syslog-ng.conf` file is based on your previously existing `syslog.conf` file, you can't take advantage of any extra functionality. That's no problem, though, because this chapter will walk you through hacking your configuration file to make it do all kinds of crazy stuff. . .

Customizing your configuration

Building a custom `syslog-ng.conf` file can seem like a tough task because the syslog-ng logging daemon has so much functionality. We recommend finding a sample configuration file that's been written for your flavor of Linux and then spicing it up a bit.

We include our sample `syslog-ng.conf` configuration file on the CD that accompanies this book. Our syslog-ng watches for failed login attempts, critical Snort events, and attempted Web server hacks. It pages the Sys Admin on critical events and failed logins, and it passes log entries for attempted Web server hacks to a Perl script that acts as a Jabber instant messenger (IM) client. This way, any Web developer or Admin can log in to a chat room and see who's trying to hack the server. And by using syslog-ng's ability to expand macros, we do some basic log management by writing out Snort logs based on the date. Every day, a new log file is created and written to.

We describe some of the more useful syslog-ng options in the upcoming sections. For a rundown of *all* the options, check out the `syslog-ng.conf.doc` file in the `contrib/` directory of your syslog-ng source code.

The gruesome guts of the configuration file

The `syslog-ng.conf` file has a couple of basic components: a section for global options, followed by source, filter, destination, and log statements. Each statement takes a driver, which modifies the behavior of that statement. For example, a source statement can take the UDP driver, telling it to take UDP log packets as a source. Likewise, a destination statement can take the program driver, telling syslog-ng to send log entries to a waiting program. (The following tables explain each statement and some recommended drivers.)

In the global options section, you dictate how the syslog-ng daemon behaves overall. You can apply many of the options listed in the global section to individual statements, in which case they'll override the global options. This allows you to create a sort of logging template with global options, but override it for special cases. Table 11-1 lists some of the more useful options when using syslog-ng for Snort logging.

Table 11-1	Options for Syslog-ng
Option	*Description*
`create_dirs`	No surprises here — this option automatically creates a directory for logging if one doesn't exist. You need this directory if you're using macros to write filenames.
`owner`	The owner of the newly created files.
`group`	The group ownership of newly created files.

(continued)

Table 11-1 (continued)

Option	Description
perm	Permissions on log files.
dir_owner	The owner of any automatically created log directories must be specified independently of the file owner.
dir_group	Same goes for the group owner.
dir_perm	Permissions to give automatically created log directories.

Source drivers

Once you've got a decent set of global options specified, you can start listing source statements. These lines tell syslog-ng where it should get its input from. Unless you're accepting input from remote machines, your primary source is going to be the machine itself. Table 11-2 lists some useful source drivers. Parentheses indicate required driver arguments, and brackets indicate optional arguments.

Table 11-2 **Source Drivers for Syslog-ng**

Source	Description
internal()	These messages are from the syslog-ng daemon itself.
unix-stream ("filename" [options])	These messages are from Unix sockets that are read in a connection-oriented manner. Specify /dev/log as the filename if you're running a Linux kernel earlier than 2.4.
unix-dgram ("filename" [options])	These messages are from Unix sockets that are read in a connectionless datagram mode, like kernel log messages (klogd) in the 2.4.x or later Linux kernel.

Destination drivers

Once you know where you're getting logs from, you can tell syslog-ng where to stick them using destination statements. Traditionally, syslog destinations have been flat text files, named pipes, remote machines (over UDP), or a user's console. Syslog-ng can send logs to these destinations as well as send logs to remote machines over the more manageable TCP protocol, as well as to the standard input of a program. Table 11-3 lists some useful destination drivers for syslog-ng. Parentheses indicate required driver arguments, and brackets indicate optional arguments.

Table 11-3	Destination Drivers for Syslog-ng
Driver	*Description*
`pipe( "filename" )`	The pipe driver sends log messages to a named pipe such as `/dev/xconsole`.
`file( "filename [$MACRO]" )`	The file driver writes log entries to a text file. Unique to syslog-ng is the ability to automatically expand macros when writing files. (Table 11-4 lists available macros.)
`tcp( "address" [port(port #);] )`	Forwards log entries over TCP to a remote system listening on the specified port.
`udp( "address" [port(port #);] )`	Forwards log entries over UDP to a remote system listening on the specified port.
`program( "/some/ program/name" )`	Sends messages straight to the standard input of a program. (Make sure that you know what you're doing with this one.)

When writing logs to a text file, syslog-ng can automatically expand macros to determine the filename. For example, in our `syslog-ng.conf` file, the destination statement

```
destination snort_day { file("/var/log/snort/snort.log.$MONTH.$DAY.$YEAR"); }
```

writes a different Snort log file every day. If you run with this destination statement for a couple of days, then look in `/var/log/snort`, you see

```
-rw-r-----  1 root    loggers     11k Feb  8 23:59 snort.log.02.08.2004
-rw-r-----  1 root    loggers     39k Feb  9 23:59 snort.log.02.09.2004
-rw-r-----  1 root    loggers     41k Feb 10 23:59 snort.log.02.10.2004
-rw-r-----  1 root    loggers     32k Feb 11 23:59 snort.log.02.11.2004
```

Splitting out logs based on the date may seem like a boring example, but what if you're running a centralized logging server, and you want log files split out automatically based on the hostname of the machine that sent you the logs? This destination statement has you covered:

```
destination remote_logs { file("/var/log/$HOST/$PROGRAM"); };
```

Now you've got a separate log file for each program on each remote host that sends you logs — all done with one line! Once you realize the power and flexibility you have with syslog-ng and automatic macro expansion, you'll want to install it everywhere. Table 11-4 shows some of the macros available to syslog-ng.

Table 11-4	Macros Used by Syslog-ng
Name	**Description**
$DATE	The date the message was sent.
$DAY	The day of the month the message was sent.
$FACILITY	The facility name assigned to the message.
$FULLDATE	The long form of the transaction date.
$HOUR	The hour of the day when the log was received. You can also use $MIN and $SEC, but we don't advise it unless you want a new log file created every second.
$MONTH	The month the log was received.
$MSG (or $MESSAGE)	The log entry (message) itself.
$PROGRAM	The name of the program that generated the log.
$PRIORITY or $LEVEL	The priority assigned to the message.
$TZ	Time zone, such as CST.
$TZOFFSET	The time zone as an offset from GMT.
$WEEKDAY	The day of the week the log was received, such as Wed.
$YEAR	The year the log was received. This macro is very handy for archiving logs.

If you use macro expansion to split out log files, make sure that the global options section of your syslog-ng.conf file allows syslog-ng to automatically create directories and that it sets the permissions correctly. The options create_dirs(yes), dir_owner(), dir_group(), dir_perm(), owner(), group(), and perm() can help you out here. See Table 11-1 for more details on these options.

One of the coolest destination drivers for syslog-ng is the program driver. Using this driver, you can send log entries directly to the standard input of a waiting program. We use this driver to send log entries to a Perl script, which acts as a Jabber IM client. This way, when important log entries come up, they're sent to a Jabber chat room where Sys Admins and Help Desk staff see them immediately and react appropriately.

Because this driver sends log entries to *any* program you specify, the usefulness is limited only by your creativity and programming skills. You're probably thinking, "Aha! This is what I can use to get important log entries sent to me via e-mail or pager!" and you're right.

Danger! Danger! Watch that e-mail script

A super-simple script to capture input and send it as e-mail looks no more complicated than

```
#!/bin/bash
# a simple script to take input and email it

while read input;
do
echo $input | mail -s "Snort Trouble" you@yourdomain.com
done
```

Although automatically sending log entries to the standard input of a waiting program may seem like a great way to generate real-time alerts based on log content, it can leave you open to denial-of-service attacks whenever log activity is very high. Any program you tell syslog-ng to run does so with the same permissions as sylsog-ng itself and doesn't terminate until the logging daemon does, so make that the program you choose is secure and stable. Also, make sure that you've got a good filter in place so that you don't start an e-mail flood by accident.

Log filtering

Syslog-ng is an amazing piece of software, but we haven't talked about its most wonderful feature: message filtering. With message filtering, syslog-ng looks at each incoming log entry and decides where to send it based such criteria as the priority of the message, the host that sent the message, the program that generated the message, or even whether the text of that message matches a regular expression. Using message filtering, you can filter incoming log messages and have all Snort messages with ATTACK-RESPONSES singled out for special attention. Like syslog, you can configure syslog-ng to filter logs based on the facility and priority of the message, but unique to syslog-ng is the ability to filter logs based on pattern matching. To single out ATTACK-RESPONSES log entries, use the following filter statement:

```
filter attacks { match("ATTACK-RESPONSES"); };
```

Syslog-ng's pattern matching uses standard regular expressions, which makes writing your own pattern filters easy.

The file syslog-ng.source/contrib/syslog-ng.conf.doc file has loads of useful information, including many custom filter examples.

Log statements

After you have your sources and destinations defined and you've worked a little filtering magic, you can put everything together in a log statement. This statement simply combines the source, destination, and optional filter statements and then handles the message appropriately.

The log statement from the sample `syslog-ng.conf` file on the CD takes all locally generated messages that contain the text [Priority: 1] and sends them to the administrator's pager (the filter statement and source statements are defined earlier in the sample syslog-ng.conf file):

```
log { source(local); filter(snort_crit); destination(page_admin); };
```

You can combine multiple log statements to send the same message to two different places.

Using Swatch to Watch Your Log Files

Swatch, the Simple WATCHer, is an excellent log-monitoring tool that has been around for years. Unlike syslog-ng, Swatch has the ability to throttle back its alerts, so if you get 20 of the same alert in a minute, you won't get 20 e-mails as well. Swatch can also react according to the time of day; if you don't want low priority alerts going to your pager in the middle of the night, Swatch can oblige.

Downloading and installing Swatch

Swatch now lives at `http://swatch.sourceforge.net` where you can find links to the source code itself, mailing lists, and forums to seek the help of Swatch gurus. To download Swatch, follow the download links and choose a download mirror that's close to you. Once you have the source code downloaded, extract it and get to work. We use `/usr/local/src/tarballs` to keep downloaded source code in `.tar.gz` format and `/usr/local/src/` to keep the extracted code. Untarring Swatch isn't any different than untarring any other piece of software:

```
# cd /usr/local/src
# tar -xvzf tarballs/swatch-3.0.8.tar.gz
```

Swatch is written in Perl and installs like a Perl module. Instead of the now familiar `./configure`, `make`, and `make install`, Swatch installs with these commands:

```
perl Makefile.PL
make
make test
make install
make realclean
```

Swatch depends on four additional Perl modules:

```
Date::Calc
Date::Parse
File::Tail
Time::HiRes
```

Your Linux distribution may already include these modules, but if Swatch gripes about any of them not being present, download and install them separately. The easiest way to download and install Perl modules is to use the Comprehensive Perl Archive Network (CPAN). At a command prompt, type the following:

```
perl -MCPAN -e shell
```

When you see the cpan> prompt, type the following command:

```
o conf prerequisites_policy follow
install Date::Calc
```

What follows after entering this command is *voluminous* output, which is not printed for the sake of brevity. Most admins don't even read the output that closely, because Perl takes care of just about everything for you when you install modules this way.

Repeat the install command for each of the other modules you need.

If you're worried about automatically downloading, compiling, and installing software that someone else has written, it means you're doing a good job at network security. To make sure that you're not getting something you didn't ask for, install the MD5 package from CPAN. Once you've run perl -MCPAN -e shell from your command line, type **install MD5** to get the job done. Any subsequent downloads are checked against their MD5 sum to verify authenticity.

After you have all the module dependencies downloaded and installed, get back to compiling and installing Swatch:

```
perl Makefile.PL
make
make test
make install
make realclean
```

Configuring Swatch

Swatch won't run without its configuration file. When a user runs Swatch, it looks in that user's home directory for a .swatchrc configuration file. You can override this action on the command line with the -c switch.

The `.swatchrc` file is relatively straightforward. Its format consists of a string to watch out for, followed by an action to take should it see that string.

If you prefer to hack existing files rather than create them from scratch, you're in good company. Check out the `examples/` directory from within your Swatch source code for some great example `swatchrc` files.

To tell Swatch what to watch for, use the `watchfor` command. The `watchfor` statement is not only a good idea, it's required for Swatch to run. We use syslog-ng to watch out for ATTACK-RESPONSES in Snort logs; you can tell Swatch to do the same with this line:

```
watchfor /ATTACK-RESPONSES/
```

Seems easy enough, right? You don't have to put the exact text of what to watch out for in this command, although it's the easiest way to go. You can put any regular expression in this place, and Swatch will watch for any string that matches it. An excellent site for all things Perl, including handy tutorials on writing regular expressions, is http://www.perlmonks.org.

You can also tell Swatch to ignore certain text strings or regular expressions. If you've got a Windows system that has the messenger service turned off, you may want to ignore NETBIOS DCERPC Messenger Service buffer overflow messages (they wouldn't apply to your system), but you may want to watch for NETBIOS DCERPC ISystemActivator bind attempt messages. You could apply this selective watching bycombining an ignore statement and a `watchfor` statement:

```
ignore /Messenger Service/
watchfor  /NETBIOS DCERPC/
```

After you tell Swatch what to watch out for, you need to tell it what to do when it sees something it's been watching for. Table 11-5 lists some of the more useful actions that Swatch can take when it catches something in the logs.

Table 11-5	Swatch Actions
Action	*Description*
echo [modes]	Sends the text of the matched line to standard output. Use to send data to the console from which Swatch was launched or to populate the text of an e-mail message. For your Technicolor life, you can specify a color for the modes option to have your text echoed in that color in your console.
bell [n]	Sounds the system bell when a log message is matched. Put a number *n* after this action to make your system beep *n* times.

Action	Description
`exec command`	Use this action to execute a command when text is matched. Analogous to the program destination driver in syslog-ng, except that Swatch will execute the program and then terminate it when done. To use elements of the log entry itself as arguments to the executed command, use $n to use the *n*th field of the log entry. To use the entire entry, use $* or $0.
`mail [addresses= someguy@somedomain. com:someotherguy@ someotherdomain.net], [subject=`*your catchy email subject here*`]`	Sends alerts via e-mail. If you want e-mail to go to a whole bunch of people, consider setting up a list in your /etc/aliases file. Swatch uses Sendmail, so make sure that you've got either a working Sendmail install or a suitable SMTP mailer package that actually replaces the sendmail command.
`pipe command [,keep_open]`	Makes Swatch act like the syslog-ng program driver: It will pipe matched text to the standard input of a command. If you use the `keep_open` option, the pipe stays open until a different pipe action is run or Swatch exits.
`write [user:other_ user:...]`	Uses the Unix write command to send matched log entries to a user's console. Useful as long as the user is logged in.
`throttle hours: minutes:seconds`	Keeps Swatch from going crazy when your logs are going crazy. The throttle action limits the number of times a specific action is run for a specific matched pattern. List the time interval to keep Swatch from reacting to a matched message for the length of that interval.
`when=day_of_week: hour_of_day`	Limits the execution of all the preceding options to certain times. If you're watching for Priority: 1 alerts and using the mail action to send you e-mail accordingly, maybe you want to have a separate rule that sends e-mail to your pager after office hours instead of an unmanned inbox.

The following sample .swatchrc file points out some of the more useful actions and options when running Swatch on your Snort logs. Note how the colon after `Priority` has a backslash in front of it; without this slash, your colon would be considered part of your regular expression incantation and not part of the pattern you're trying to match.

```
watchfor /Priority\: 1/
    echo
    mail addresses=admin\@yourdomain.com,subject=Snort_Alert,when=2-6:8-17
    # Sends regular email to your admin during work hours

watchfor /Priority\: 1/
    echo
    mail addresses=admin_pager\@yourdomain.com,subject=Snort_Alert,when=1-7:1-24
    throttle 0:10:0
    # Sends pager email to your admin at all hours. The throttle option will only
            react to one alert every 10 minutes.

watchfor /Priority\: 2/
    echo
    bell 5
    # Your coworkers will *love* this one. Causes your terminal receive the log
            entry and beep 5 times when a Priority: 2 Snort alert is detected.


watchfor /su\:/
    echo=red
    # Red Alert! This will send an alert to your terminal when someone runs su
```

This sample is just a taste of what you can do with Swatch watching your log files. For more information, check out the Swatch man page by typing "man swatch". Like most powerful Unix tools, Swatch gives you some basic functionality and lets you decide how to use it. So be creative and experiment!

Starting Swatch

Swatch has a number of command-line options that affect how it starts and how it runs. A few of them are highly recommended, almost to the point of being mandatory — though Swatch still runs without any arguments. If Swatch is called without any arguments, it runs as if called as

```
"swatch --config-file=~/.swatchrc --tail-file=/var/log/messages"
```

or, if no /var/log/messages file exists, as

```
"swatch --config-file=~/.swatchrc --tail-file=/var/log/syslog"
```

Table 11-6 details some of the more useful command line options for Swatch.

Table 11-6	Swatch Command-Line Options
Option	*Description*
-c	Specifies a configuration file other than ~/.swatchrc.
-t	Tells Swatch which file to tail.
—input-record-separator	By default, treats the new line character, \n, as the input record separator. Use this switch to specify a different delimiter — for example, if log entries are written in multiple line chunks, with a blank line between them, use —input-record-separator="\n \n".
—daemon	Perhaps the most useful switch of all, starts Swatch in daemon mode, where it runs continuously in the background.
-p command	Use this switch followed by the command if you want Swatch to watch output from a command rather than input to a log file.
-f filename	Use this switch if you want Swatch to read over a file that's already been written rather than read a log file as it's being written.

To start Swatch and let it read your Snort logs as they're written, you can use a Swatch configuration file in /usr/local/snort/etc/swatchrc (rather than a .swathrc file in your home directory where other Admins couldn't read it) and call Swatch as

```
/usr/local/bin/swatch -c /usr/local/snort/etc/swatchrc -t
              /var/log/snort/snort.alert --daemon
```

Firewalling Suspicious Traffic in Real Time

With Swatch and Syslog-ng you've got a way to monitor logs as they're written and execute commands based on what those log entries contain. You're probably thinking, "Why, I could use this to dynamically change my firewall rules to block all those baddies from hitting my network!" Technically, you'd be right. In fact, we've done exactly this step in the past and gotten it to work. However, it borders on the bailing wire and duct tape model of network engineering, and isn't recommended.

Here's another place where the open-source model comes to the rescue. Because the developers of Snort concentrate their efforts on making Snort the best traffic analysis system possible, they don't worry about other tasks that folks might like Snort to handle. Instead, they make the source code freely available for anyone to tinker with and leave the optional extras up to other folks on the Net. One result is the SnortSam tool for blocking attacks.

Blocking malicious network traffic with SnortSam

SnortSam consists of two different pieces of software. One piece is a set of modified source files, which extend Snort by adding a new output module: `alert_fwsam`. (See Chapter 6 for more information on output modules.) The other piece is an agent that talks directly to your firewall.

This agent can reside on the firewall itself if you're running IPTables on a Linux firewall, or pf on a BSD, or Checkpoint's Firewall-1 on a Windows host. If you're using a hardware firewall, like a Cisco PIX, you must run the Snort Sam agent on a separate machine dedicated to conversing with your PIX. Using a client-agent model lets you scale SnortSam to match the size and complexity of your network, allowing you to use it with multiple Snort sensors and multiple firewalls.

So, Snort watches traffic, and when a defined rule gets triggered, Snort sends output to the `fwsam` module. The `fwsam` module then sends an encrypted message to your SnortSam agent. The SnortSam agent checks the message to make sure that it came from an authorized source and then decrypts the message. Once the message is decrypted, the SnortSam agent checks the request to see what IP address you're asking SnortSam to block, and SnortSam checks that IP address against a whitelist of systems that should never be blocked. If the IP address isn't on the whitelist, then SnortSam tells your firewall to block that address for a definable time period.

Downloading and installing SnortSam

SnortSam lives at `http://www.snortsam.net`. Ample links exist to documentation, mailing lists, example configuration files, and, of course, the source code itself. In addition to the source code, precompiled binaries are available for many popular platforms.

SnortSam has two components: the patches to incorporate SnortSam into Snort, and the agent that talks to your firewall. For our discussion, we detail using the SnortSam agent on a Linux firewall running IPTables.

Installing the SnortSam agent is a breeze. Grab the source code, untar it, make the included installation script executable, and run it. Remember the agent is the piece that talks to your firewall, so SSH on over to your Linux firewall and get to work!

```
# cd /usr/local/src/tarballs
# wget http://www.snortsam.net/files/snortsam-v2_multi-threaded/snortsam-src-
          2.23.tar.gz
# cd ../
# tar -xvzf tarballs/snortsam-src-2.23.tar.gz
# cd snortsam/
# chmod +x makesnortsam.sh
# ./makesnortsam.sh
```

Simplicity itself, eh? You should now have a `snortsam` file in your SnortSam source directory. Do yourself a favor and copy it somewhere in your path, like `/usr/local/bin/`.

Installing the SnortSam patches to Snort can be a little more difficult. The SnortSam patches are a collection of modified Snort source code files. By wedging these modified files into your Snort source code directory (always keep your source code directory around for times like these), you can extend Snort's native abilities to include the ability to talk to your SnortSam agent. Using modified Snort source code means that once the patched source files are moved over, you need to reconfigure and recompile Snort.

Recompiling Snort with the latest SnortSam patches applied requires GNU automake Version 1.6. Not Version 1.4 or Version 1.8, but 1.6. Automake 1.6, in turn, may require an updated `autoconf` package. The specific versions of `automake` and `autoconf` may already be available on your system, but they weren't on ours, which is why we mention it. To find out what version of each you have, you can run `autoconf --version` or `automake --version`. (Who says Linux commands are arcane?) If you find that your system lacks these version, you can grab them from `http://www.gnu.org/software/autoconf/` and `http://www.gnu.org/software/automake/` respectively. Because the download and compile process for each of these is not overly complicated, we include those steps in the following SnortSam install.

Downloading and extracting the SnortSam patches is the same as any other software package, but instead of the familiar `configure`, `make`, and `make install` process, the patches use a shell script similar to the SnortSam agent to patch Snort. After you extract the SnortSam source code, make this shell script executable before running it.

Here are the steps to download and install SnortSam patches, as well as GNU automake. We even include the steps to recompile Snort:

```
# cd /usr/local/src/tarballs
# wget http://ftp.gnu.org/gnu/automake/automake-1.6.3.tar.gz
# cd ../
# tar -xvzf tarballs/automake-1.6.3.tar.gz
# cd automake-1.6.3/
# ./configure && make && make install
# cd ../tarballs/
# wget http://www.snortsam.net/files/snort-plugin/snortsam-patch.tar.gz
# cd ../
# mkdir snortsam-patch
# cd snortsam-patch/
# tar -xvzf ../tarballs/snortsam-patch.tar.gz
# chmod +x patchsnort.sh
# ./patchsnort.sh /usr/local/src/snort-2.1.0/
# cd /usr/local/src/snort-2.1.0/
# ./configure --with-mysql=/usr/local/mysql
# make
# make install
```

Configuring Snort for SnortSam

After patching and recompiling Snort, you're ready to configure Snort to use SnortSam. The first step is to tell Snort that you have a new output module for it to use. Add the line

```
output alert_fwsam:   <snortsam_agent_system>
```

to your `snort.conf` file, where `snortsam_agent_system` is the name or IP address of the system where the SnortSam agent is running. In our case, because we're using a Linux firewall, we use the IP address of the firewall. If you want to have the SnortSam agent listen on something other than the default port (898) or use a password for verification, include those on this line as

```
output alert_fwsam:<snortsam_agent_system>:<port>/<password>
```

For example:

```
output alert_fwsam:10.100.0.1:8347/bacOn
```

Now that Snort knows how to use this extra output module, configure which specific rules you want to trigger SnortSam. Remember that this software is some pretty serious stuff, and it can be all too easy to over react and inadvertently block legitimate traffic. It should be seen as a blessing then, rather than a burden, that you must edit individual rules to take advantage of this plug-in. Can you imagine the chaos that would ensue if you automatically blocked every IP address that tripped your Snort sensor?

To configure Snort rules to use SnortSam, first find a rule that you want to block traffic on. The WEB-MISC rule that indicates someone trying to poke at root's home directory looks good, not only because it's an indication of serious shenanigans and unlikely to happen by accident, but because it's one that we can easily test using Nikto, a popular Web security scanner. Here's the rule without any modifications:

```
alert tcp $EXTERNAL_NET any -> $HTTP_SERVERS $HTTP_PORTS (msg:"WEB-MISC /~root
            access"; flow:to_server,established; uricontent:"/~root"; nocase;
            classtype:attempted-recon; sid:1145;  rev:6;)
```

And here it is again modified to use SnortSam:

```
alert tcp $EXTERNAL_NET any -> $HTTP_SERVERS $HTTP_PORTS (msg:"WEB-MISC /~root
            access"; flow:to_server,established; uricontent:"/~root"; nocase;
            classtype:attempted-recon; sid:1145;  rev:6; fwsam: src,
            10 minutes;)
```

We've added the fwsam: src, 10 minutes to tell Snort to use SnortSam and to block the source of the attack for 10 minutes.

Don't forget to restart Snort after you've changed its rules.

Configuring the SnortSam agent for your firewall

After you configure Snort for SnortSam, configure the SnortSam agent to talk to your firewall. The SnortSam agent looks for /etc/snortsam.conf by default.

At a bare minimum, you need to tell the SnortSam agent what machines are allowed to connect to it, and what firewall it's going to talk to. Our barebones /etc/snortsam.conf file looks like this:

```
accept 64.123.2.28/32
iptables eth1 syslog.info
logfile snortsam.log
```

Okay, so it's not *totally* bare bones. We do include a logging statement to log all of SnortSam's activity to /var/log/snortsam.log.

While automatically blocking malicious network traffic may sound like the best thing since tiny flashing lights, Snort's false positives suddenly go from an annoyance to debilitating when you implement automatic blocking. To prevent your reactive IDS from blocking trusted hosts due to false positives or spoofed traffic, make sure that you use a whitelist containing IP addresses that should never be blocked.

The snortsam.conf file is the place to list remote systems that you never want to block. You can list these systems using the dontblock statement. It's wise to include your upstream routers, root DNS servers, and so on. If you want to manage thislist in separate file, you can use an include statement to point to your whitelist. Of course, you can do both:

```
includewhitelist_file
dontblock 192.168.1.1
dontblock a.root-servers.net
dontblock b.root-servers.net
```

For an exhaustive list of all the options to trick out your snortsam.conf file, take a peek at the README.conf file in your SnortSam source directory. Don't forget to include a list of IP addresses to never block in this file.

Once you have a custom tailored snortsam.conf file whipped up, start up SnortSam. The only command line option that it wants is the location of your configuration file:

```
# /usr/local/bin/snortsam /etc/snortsam.conf &
```

Make sure that you configure your firewall to accept SnortSam traffic from your Snort sensors. Otherwise, your sensors chatter away with no resulting action on the firewall.

Chapter 12

Keeping Snort Up to Date

· ·

In This Chapter

▶ Getting new Snort rules

▶ Updating Snort rules

▶ Upgrading Snort sensors

▶ Making sure everything works afterwards

· ·

When you have a running Snort sensor, you must regularly manage updates. The rules files are the most frequently updated part of Snort; updates, modification, and deletions occur daily. Snort itself is frequently updated. From December 2003 to February 2004, Snort went through half a dozen minor modifications and two major upgrades (Snort 2.0 and Snort 2.1.0). Keeping all these modifications current can be a hectic process, especially if you manage multiple sensors. This chapter gives you some tools and tips for keeping everything up to date.

Updating Rules with Oinkmaster

Oinkmaster is a Perl script that downloads, modifies, and puts into production Snort rules files from `snort.org`. The configuration file enables or suspends downloads, modifications, and production rule sets.

While Oinkmaster can help you update your rules files, don't rely too heavily on it to do higher-level tasks such as keeping your modified rules straight, updating your `snort.conf` file, or otherwise running as an unattended process — especially in a production environment. Oinkmaster is not robust enough to be an unattended Snort manager, and it can corrupt your rules or configuration files if something goes haywire.

Obtaining and installing Oinkmaster

Oinkmaster is free software covered under the GNU General Public License. You can obtain the Oinkmaster from either of the following sites:

- ✔ The Snort Web site: `http://www.snort.org`
- ✔ The Oinkmaster Web site: `http://oinkmaster.sourceforge.net/`

The current version of Oinkmaster is 0.9; its rules update procedures support up to Snort 2.1.

Platforms and dependencies

Oinkmaster runs on most Unix-based systems and on the Windows platform. To run Oinkmaster, you must have a Perl interpreter and the `tar`, `gzip`, and `wget` programs.

Most Unix systems have these programs standard. To run Oinkmaster on the Windows platform, however, you have two possible approaches:

- ✔ **Track down the tools you need —** `wget`, **a Perl interpreter, and a file-compression/decompression tool.**
  - If you don't have Perl, you can find it at `http://www.perl.com/`.
  - You can get `wget` for Windows at `http://www.interlog.com/~tcharron/wgetwin.html`.
  - The file-archiving tool `tar` is available for the Windows platform at `http://gnuwin32.sourceforge.net/packages/tar.htm`.
  - You can get hold of `gzip` at `http://www.gzip.org/`.
- ✔ **Install Cygwin (a Unix-like environment for Windows systems).**
  - You can find Cygwin at `http://www.cygwin.com/`.
  - Perl also comes as a Cygwin package at `http://www.perl.org`.

Installing Oinkmaster

Oinkmaster is extremely easy to install. It's really a single Perl script and a configuration file. To install Oinkmaster, follow these steps:

1. **Download the Oinkmaster archive.**

2. **Go to your source directory and type the following:**

```
# tar -xvzf oinkmaster-0.9.tar.gz
# cd oinkmaster-0.9.tar.gz
# cp oinkmaster.pl /usr/local/bin
# cp oinkmaster.conf /usr/local/etc
```

If you put `oinkmaster.conf` in a different directory, you must use the -C *path-to-confile* option when running Oinkmaster.

3. Ensure that Oinkmaster can read and write to the Snort rules directory.

The easiest way is to change the ownership of the Oinkmaster files to either

- The `snort` user (the user account that owns the Snort files).

- The `snortgroup` (the group that the `snort` user belongs to).

On our installation, the directory is `snortuser`:

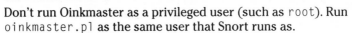

```
# chown snortuser:snortgroup /usr/local/bin/oinkmaster.pl
# chown snortuser:snortgroup /usr/local/etc/oinkmaster.conf
```

Don't run Oinkmaster as a privileged user (such as `root`). Run `oinkmaster.pl` as the same user that Snort runs as.

And that's the entire installation "process."

Mastering Oinkmaster

Oinkmaster's configuration is quick and easy. Its configuration file is similar to the `snort.conf` and `barnyard.conf` configuration files: A flat text file that tells Oinkmaster precisely what you want.

Configuring Oinkmaster

For Oinkmaster to run, it only needs to know two configuration options:

- ✔ The path to `wget`, `tar`, and `gzip`
- ✔ The types of files to update (the `update files` statement in `oinkmaster.conf`)

To perform its functions, Oinkmaster needs a few more configuration options enabled and tweaked, including these:

- ✔ Where to get rules updates.
- ✔ What to do with the rules updates once Oinkmaster has the updates.
- ✔ Whether to modify the rules in production or issue a report concerning the changes.

Open `oinkmaster.conf` in your favorite text editor and look through the configuration switches.

General options

General options in the `oinkmaster.conf` file give `oinkmaster.pl` important information about where to download Snort's rules updates and where to find the tools Oinkmaster needs to download and extract the rules files.

Oinkmaster can use the following protocols and methods to download Snort rules files:

`http`	Uses the standard Web protocol to download the rules archive.
`https`	Uses the standard secure Web protocol to download the rules archive.
`ftp`	Uses the standard File Transfer Protocol to download the rules archive.
`scp`	Uses Secure Copy to download the rules archive. You must have `scp` installed on your system for this to work.
`local copy (file://)`	The `file://` method copies the rules archive from a local directory. This protocol is most often used when you want to manually download the rules archive, read through the rules changes, and make your own modifications before deploying rules to your sensor.

The general format for the rules-archive download is

```
url = downloadmethod://address-or-path-to-rules-files.tar.gz
```

For example, our rules archive download statement looks like the following:

```
url = http://www.snort.org/dl/rules/snortrules-stable.tar.gz
```

The rules download command must end in the file type `tar.gz`. Oinkmaster initiates an `untar` and `un-gzip` procedure by default once the file is downloaded.

Path statement

The `path =` statement in the General Options portion of `oinkmaster.conf` must be properly defined for Oinkmaster to function. The path should include the location of `tar` and `gzip` on your system and `wget` if you are using `http`, `https`, or `ftp` to transfer your rules archives. For most Unix systems, the paths to these programs are `/usr/bin`, `/bin`, or `/usr/local/bin`. The default value in the `oinkmaster.conf` file includes all three paths:

```
path = /bin:/usr/bin:/usr/local/bin
```

More path statements are included for the Windows and Cygwin platforms, though you probably must change these settings, depending on where `tar`, `gzip`, and `wget` are installed. The following lines are default values for each setting; both are commented out by default:

- ✔ The native Windows format uses a semicolon (`;`) in the `path` statement to delineate additional path locations:

  ```
  # path = c:\oinkmaster;c:\oinkmaster\bin
  ```

- ✔ Here's how it looks on the Cygwin `bash` shell running under Windows:

  ```
  # path =
          /cygdrive/c/oinkmaster:/cygdrive/c/oinkmaster/bin
  ```

Temporary directory

Set a temporary directory for Oinkmaster to download the Snort rules archive to untar and unzip the files and process them. The default is the `/home/oinkmaster/tmp` directory in Linux and `C:\tmp` for Windows, but you can specify any directory you want with the following commands:

- ✔ For Unix:

  ```
  # tmpdir = /home/oinkmaster/tmp/
  ```

- ✔ For Windows:

  ```
  # tmpdir = c:\tmp
  ```

- ✔ For Cygwin:

  ```
  # tmpdir = /cygdrive/c/tmp
  ```

To enable this setting, uncomment (remove the `#` sign) the statement relevant to your platform and set the correct path to the temporary directory you want to use.

The directory you list in the Temporary Directory section of `oinkmaster.conf` must exist when Oinkmaster runs.

Update configuration options

The Update section of the configuration file tells Oinkmaster what filename to look for when it checks for file updates in the expanded archive. The default contains everything you probably need, so changes in this section are unnecessary. The `update_files` setting (either the default or your specific changes) is needed for Oinkmaster to run, so don't comment the line out by accident. This is the default setting:

```
update_files = \.rules$|\.config$|\.conf$|\.txt$|\.map$
```

The preceding configuration option tells Oinkmaster to look for all files with the `.rules`, `.config`, `.conf`, `.txt`, and `.map` regular expressions in the filename for possible updates.

Skipfile configuration option

In some instances, you may want Oinkmaster to skip analyzing and updating files it receives — especially if you created any custom rules in your `local.rules` or `snort.conf` files. If Oinkmaster updates the `local.rules` file with a "new" version, you lose all your modifications. (In most cases, you end up with a blank `local.rules` file.) If Oinkmaster updates your `snort.conf` file, you end up with a generic `snort.conf` — again, losing all your modifications.

Have Oinkmaster compare the generic `snort.conf` with the updated `snort.conf` file to alert you to changes that you may need to make in your production copy of `snort.conf`, like when more features or settings are introduced. We talk more about that task in the section "Running Oinkmaster," later in this chapter.

To configure Oinkmaster to skip a particular file, the format is simple:

```
skipfile filename
```

If you want Oinkmaster to skip analyzing the `local.rules` file, the configuration looks like this:

```
skipfile local.rules
```

Modifysid options

Oinkmaster can modify the downloaded rules on the fly according to your configuration options. As stated in the `oinkmaster.conf` file, though, this operation is only for the "skilled/stupid/brave."

No checks and balances prevent you from screwing up the rule beyond repair. While it's fun to fly by the seat of your pants, having Oinkmaster download and modify rules files on the fly can both cause Snort to gag *and* allow an important attack to slip through Snort's nose without firing an alert. To disable certain rules instead, see the "`disablesid` options" section later in this chapter.

The format of the `modifysid` option is

```
modifysid SID "replacethis" | "withthat"
```

Item by item, here's what's going on in the modifysid option:

- ✔ The *SID* variable is the actual SID (*Snort rule ID* number) of the rule you want to modify.

- ✔ The "*replacethis*" variable stands for the *search string,* the regular expression text string you want to find in the rule.

- ✔ The "*withthat*" variable stands for the *replace value,* the new text string with which you want to replace the regular expression.

  Both the search string and the replace value are in quotation marks. Both values are also case-sensitive.

The oinkmaster.conf file also contains several examples of using the modifysid option.

enablesid options

The enablesid option can enable rules that are typically disabled by default. The format is simple:

```
enablesid SID1, SID2, SID3
```

Here *SID1, SID2,* and so on stand for the actual SID number(s) of the rule(s) you want to enable.

Functionally, the enablesid option removes the # from in front of the rule so the rule is processed by Snort. You can enable multiple SIDs in two ways:

- ✔ Separate enablesid calls
- ✔ One enablesid call with comma-separated SID numbers

disablesid options

The disablesid option is the opposite of the enablesid option. Functionally, it inserts a # sign in front of the given rule (by SID) to disable it from rules processing. The format is the same as for enablesid:

```
disablesid SID1, SID2, SID3
```

This option is far more common than any of the others, especially if you run a targeted Snort sensor — for example, one that's only monitoring Web services for a host or subnet. (See Chapter 13 for all the information you need to set up a Snort sensor for specific network services on a host or subnet.)

Mastering Oinkmaster

Oinkmaster is at its best when it alerts you to changes to updated rules archives.

Don't use Oinkmaster to automatically change your production rules. Even the developer warns — throughout the installation and configuration files — that the faint of heart shouldn't use Oinkmaster as an automated rules updater.

Configuring Oinkmaster

To start configuring Oinkmaster, set the General options that apply. For us, we use the latest stable version of Snort and thus use the latest stable version of the rules.

✔ Download the rules to a temporary directory in the /etc/oinkmaster subdirectory. Oinkmaster is installed in /usr/local/bin. We want to see all the changes to all the rules. The meat-and-potatoes of our oinkmaster.conf file looks like this:

```
url = http://www.snort.org/dl/rules/snortrules-stable.tar.gz
path = /bin:/usr/bin:/usr/local/bin
tmpdir = /usr/local/etc/oinkmaster/tmp
update_files = \.rules$|\.config$|\.conf$|\.txt$|\.map$
```

✔ Because we don't want Oinkmaster enabling, disabling, or modifying rules on the fly, we need to tell it not to process our local rules, snort.conf, or the deleted.rules files included in the rules archive. We usually review the deleted.rules separately and don't want Oinkmaster mucking around with it. As a result, the next section of our oinkmaster.conf file looks like this:

```
skipfile local.rules
skipfile snort.conf
skipfile deleted.rules
```

Backing up your production environment

You should do a thorough backup before making any changes to your Snort environment in case something goes screwy with Oinkmaster, and your Snort installation becomes corrupted. Back up these essentials:

✔ Your rules

✔ Your snort.conf file

✔ Any other configuration files relevant to Snort (such as the barnyard.conf file if you use Barnyard, as described in Chapter 14)

After everything's secured, you can run Oinkmaster.

Running Oinkmaster

From the command line, we run Oinkmaster with these options:

```
# oinkmaster.pl -o /usr/local/snort/rules/tmp
```

This command tells Oinkmaster to

✔ Read its `oinkmaster.conf` file.

✔ Download the file as configured in the configuration file.

✔ Compare the new rules to the rules in `/usr/local/snort/rules/tmp`.

Upon execution, Oinkmaster gives you two-part output:

✔ It reports the following information:

```
Loading /usr/local/etc/oinkmaster.conf.
Downloading rules archive from http://www.snort.org/dl/rules/snortrules-
       snapshot-2_1.tar.gz... done.
Archive successfully downloaded, unpacking... done.
Processing downloaded rules... disabled 0, enabled 0, modified 0,
       total=1987.
Setting up rules structures... done.
Comparing new files to the old ones... done.
```

✔ It shows you the changed rules (similar to the following):

```
2338 || FTP LIST buffer overflow attempt || bugtraq,8486
    2339 || TFTP NULL command attempt || bugtraq,7575
    2340 || FTP SITE CHMOD overflow attempt || bugtraq,9483
```

Armed with this knowledge, perform the following steps:

1. **Decide which rules to update and which to ignore.**

2. **Set up the** `oinkmaster.conf` **file to ignore the specific rules that you don't want.**

   Use the `disablesid` option in the `oinkmaster.conf` file.

3. **Run Oinkmaster to update your production rules, like this:**

   ```
   # oinkmaster.pl -o /usr/local/snort/rules
   ```

   Oinkmaster updates all the rules in your production rules directory.

4. **Restart Snort and test to make sure that everything's working properly.**

   As a Snort "best practice," run Snort with the `-T` flag after a major modification (such as an Oinkmaster rules update). The `-T` flag runs Snort in test mode, which tests the Snort configuration and outputs either success or failure.

If Snort's running fine, you're in business.

Upgrading Snort

Upgrading Snort can be a time-intensive process, especially if several sensors are spread over your entire enterprise.

No tools or proven methods can simplify this process, but the following guidelines can help make your Snort upgrade as smooth as possible.

Preparing for the upgrade

To prepare for a Snort upgrade, you must understand what's changed in the new version of Snort, back up all your relevant configuration information, and possibly set up a test sensor to ensure that the changes won't break your production environment.

Understanding what's changed

The release notes, available with each Snort distribution, describe changes to the program, as well as changes needed in the configuration file and rules.

Before you start upgrading, read the release notes and the Snort message boards to find out as much as you can about the changes and how they can affect your environment.

Backing up everything

A few minutes backing up now makes sure that you can recover quickly from potential upgrade problems.

Backing up important files is never more important than when you're running Snort. You may have spent tens of hours devoted to rules tweaks, configurations, and database setup. Save that work; back it up.

You should back up the following Snort files regularly, but especially before you deploy an upgrade:

- ✔ `snort.conf` configuration file
- ✔ Rules files

In addition, even though it's not always a part of every Snort deployment, regularly backing up your Snort database is a good idea.

If you use `syslog` or another output method, make sure that your logging configuration information is properly archived before you do a Snort upgrade.

You are not alone

To see how Snort's changes affect Snort "in the field," sign up for Snort's mailing lists. Most members of the mailing lists, message boards, and other online forums are true Snort eggheads who can tell you what's changed and what it means to Snort's operation.

We provide a list of Snort information resources for you in Chapter 16.

Finally, if you use ACID, Barnyard, or one of the other fine tools available to help Snort do its job better, you'll want to back up the relevant files from these applications as well, including any configuration or log files related to the applications. (ACID is covered in Chapter 7 of this book. Barnyard is covered in Chapter 14.)

Completing the upgrade

Upgrading Snort is as easy as three simple steps:

1. **Download the files.**
2. **Make your changes.**
3. **Update your sensor with the new executables, configuration files, and rules.**

Use the information on installing Snort in Chapter 4 (for Linux) or Chapter 5 (for Windows) if you're not sure how to update your sensors.

The new version of Snort is always available from the snort.org Web site. If you monitor the mailing list or the Web site, you should have ample warning that a new version is pending.

Testing

When deploying any complex system into your enterprise environment, a laboratory test is always a good idea if you have the hardware to spare. You should first make sure that the new version of Snort runs at all in your environment. Then, test any quirks of your configuration in the lab environment.

Make sure that the following statements are true about your Snort environment:

- ✔ The output is in line with what you want to see.
- ✔ Snort can talk to your database properly.
- ✔ Your rules are firing in just the way you're used to.

An ounce of testing is worth a pound of troubleshooting. Always set up a test sensor when a new version of Snort comes out to make sure that it works in your environment before deploying it for real in the production environment.

1. **Run your new Snort sensor in foreground mode.**

   Doing so tells you whether Snort gags on the configuration file, stumbles over any rules files, or gives you any grief when an alert is issued.

2. **Test any new pre-processors.**

   The developers at snort.org are constantly replying to their (often very vocal) users by providing new Snort functionality. See if any new pre-processors solve existing problems for you.

3. **Determine whether the new version of Snort requires more horsepower.**

   It's always best to be surprised about performance changes in a lab environment, rather than having to learn it in the school of hard knocks after your production Snort sensor slows down to a crawl.

4. **Test your new Snort sensor.**

   For example, you can run an automated vulnerability assessment or use a tool such as Nmap (available at http://www.insecure.org/) to make Snort fire on a rule and issue an alert.

5. **Trace the alert from the console (where you run Snort in foreground mode), to the log file (if applicable), or to the database by either logging in directly to the database or by using your ACID console.**

   Did the alert get to where it was supposed to go? Great! No? Track down the problem and try again.

Once all the bugs are worked out, run Snort as a daemon or service. You're in business with a brand new Snort release.

Chapter 13

Filling Your Farm with Pigs

· ·

· ·

*Y*ou probably already know you need Snort. You may have installed it, kicked it, tested it, kicked it, tried it on various platforms, and kicked it again. Don't put those heavy boots away yet! In this chapter, we show you how to make all your pigs oink in the same direction. With Snort's ability to log to various sources, monitor a variety of network architectures, and make an overall contribution to your network security, you can live your true dream as a pig farmer.

Pigs on the Perimeter

Why would you want more than one Snort installation on your network? Multiple installations of Snort leverage Snort's benefits and reduce its liabilities. Snort does some things very well: analyzing network traffic and alerting on its rules. It doesn't do anything else well.

If you ask Snort to do much stuff it doesn't do well, it can't do the things well that it does so well.

With the flexibility of monitored services and traffic, platform support and output plug-ins, Snort can (and should) be installed wherever attackers come knocking, sniffing, stomping, or breaking down the door. Chapters 4 and 5 show you how to install Snort as a single-machine network IDS logging to a database (or other logging feature) on that same machine. That setup is terrific for testing purposes, but a single-machine deployment is both resource intensive and a security risk. If intruders beat the single machine, intruders get to play with all your toys.

The following sections show you how to

- ✔ Set up multiple Snort sensors across your network on various hosts to perform a variety of intrusion detection tasks.
- ✔ Point all those Snort sensors to a central logging repository.

Preparing for deployment

Before you can deploy multiple, targeted Snort sensors, you need to plan.

Before you even gather the hardware and software:

- ✔ Decide where best to place your sensors in your network environment. Chapter 2 shows you how to deploy Snort sensors in a variety of situations.
- ✔ Start with a clean house. Chapters 8 and 9 help you make sure that your new Snort sensors run as efficiently as possible.

It's unlikely that you're installing a stand-alone host network sensor on your network. Though this setup is possible, such a configuration doesn't leverage Snort's distributed, scaleable nature. You probably want other Snort sensors monitoring various aspects of your network; these sensors may be logging to a centralized server. You need the following information to configure each of the network sensors to operate and log properly in your Snort environment:

- ✔ **Database information:** If you use a database to collect alerts from several Snort sensors, you need the hostname and IP address of the database server, and the database name, username, and password for the Snort database. If your database runs on a nonstandard port — for example, if MySQL is listening on a port other than 3306 — you need that information for your Snort sensor configuration.
- ✔ **Snort sensor conventions:** If you have several Snort sensors, create a logical naming and numbering convention to help recognize where alerts are coming from when you review your logs or database.
- ✔ **Plug-in and logging conventions:** If you use a logging plug-in (such as Barnyard or syslog-ng), you need all the configuration and architecture information for these services.

Once you have all this information, you can set up your new Snort sensors.

Setting up a Snort sensor for an internal network

When configuring a Snort sensor for an internal network, you want to enable only those features, rules, and configuration options that apply to that network. Everything else just eats processor time and memory and may report false positives. If a Snort sensor monitors your user LAN behind a firewall with all hosts running Windows XP, you want to monitor the subnet only for those network services that are present on Windows XP. You may also want to enable certain rules for detecting anomalous activity, such as portscans originating from an internal source, or client-based services, such as AOL Instant Messenger. In most cases, network traffic coming from a source outside your network to a host on your user LAN should be very rare and either stopped by your firewall or detected by a Snort sensor between the originating host and the destination.

Positioning the subnet sensor

Snort works best when it can sniff all the traffic going across the wire.

- ✔ In a switched environment, your Snort subnet sensor needs to listen on the Spanning or Monitor port of your network switch.

- ✔ If your subnet operates on a hub, the Snort sensor should have access to all the traffic it needs for its job.

Once you have all the information you need and install your hardware and Snort, open `snort.conf` and tweak that configuration.

Setting network variables

For the subnet sensor, you only need to set the HOME_NET variable to the size of your subnet.

In our case, we have space for an entire class C on the user network, so our HOME_NET variable looks like this:

```
var HOME_NET 172.16.1.0/24
```

In a switched environment, with Snort physically capable of monitoring only the subnet it's attached to, you can use the HOME_NET variable any to monitor all addresses on the subnet. The EXTERNAL_NET should be set to any.

Configuring SERVERS variables

The configuration of the SERVERS variables depends on

- ✔ What subnet you're monitoring
- ✔ What's running on that subnet

For our scenario, we have no servers running on the subnet, so we commented out all the SERVERS variables. One SERVERS variable to check is the AOL Instant Messenger service, especially if you're setting up a Snort sensor to monitor a user subnet. The AIM client allows for interclient chatting, file transfers, and ads from an AOL push server. If you don't specifically block AOL traffic on your subnet, make sure that you enable the following SERVERS variable in the snort.conf file:

```
var AIM_SERVERS
        [64.12.24.0/24,64.12.25.0/24,64.12.26.14/24,64.12.
        28.0/24,64.12.29.0/24,64.12.161.0/24,64.12.163.0/2
        4,205.188.5.0/24,205.188.9.0/24]
```

Choosing your preprocessors

In a subnet, deciding which preprocessor to use is as variable as the SERVERS configuration. Chapter 9 explains what each preprocessor does.

Each preprocessor uses memory and processor time. Enable the ones you know you need and comment out the rest. For our user LAN scenario, we chose the following preprocessors to detect the protocol anomaly:

```
preprocessor stream4: detect_scans, disable_evasion_alerts
preprocessor bo
preprocessor arpspoof_detect_host: 192.168.40.1
        f0:0f:00:f0:0f:00
```

Firewalls should protect the local LAN from TCP tricks. We recommend x to protect against the silly things that users do.

- ✔ The bo preprocessor is designed to detect BackOrifice (a nasty Windows-based Trojan horse program) network traffic.
- ✔ ARP spoofing is all the rage with the kids on the local LAN. By pretending to be a host that he or she's not, an internal attacker can monitor traffic meant for another host while escaping detection. With the arpspoof_detect_host, the spoof kids must actually do their work, instead of spying on their coworkers.

Configuring for your output method

Configure it to log to the proper host for your output method, such as Barnyard or syslog-ng.

Because we're logging directly to a MySQL database, our only output option looks like this:

```
output database: alert, mysql, user=snorty password=shutup
          dbname=snort host=172.16.1.34 port=3306
          sensor_name=LANsensor1
```

Enabling rules, rules, rules

The rules files that you enable cost you processor cycles and memory, so you don't want Snort parsing traffic against all the rules in your `rules` directory. The rules for your subnet are better left for you to decide depending on

✔ What runs on the subnet

✔ What you think is important to monitor

For our x subnet, we have very few rules enabled:

```
include $RULE_PATH/bad-traffic.rules
include $RULE_PATH/exploit.rules
include $RULE_PATH/icmp.rules
include $RULE_PATH/netbios.rules
include $RULE_PATH/other-ids.rules
include $RULE_PATH/backdoor.rules
include $RULE_PATH/chat.rules
include $RULE_PATH/p2p.rules
include $RULE_PATH/local.rules
```

The `bad-traffic`, `exploit`, and `icmp` rules apply to the `stream4` preprocessor.

✔ Because the `bo` preprocessor is enabled, the `backdoor.rules` is enabled, and `chat.rules` is enabled for AOL.

✔ Because this subnet has Windows-based systems, `netbios.rules` is enabled.

✔ To detect when users do bad things, such as using a peer-to-peer network client (such as Kazaa or BearShare), `p2p.rules` is enabled.

Snort sensor in the DMZ

Snort in the DMZ is more a traditional, all-purpose network sensor installation (see Chapters 4 and 5). This sensor monitors almost anything and everything, although you still should enable only those features that you know you need. For example, if you don't have Windows IIS Web servers, you don't need rules to parse for IIS-centric attacks. Attackers (and their custom-made scripts) still scan your hosts for these vulnerabilities, but the vulnerabilities aren't there. Why clutter your logs with semi-false positives?

Centralized management and logging

Deploying a Snort sensor on your DMZ assumes that you have other sensors in your environment, like those described earlier in this chapter. With so many sensors, use as many centralized management and logging tools and methods as you can. It both reduces the workload when you update software packages and rules files and gives you a clearer picture of your entire network's security profile. With ACID or another centralized console, you can see an attempted exploit, such as a portscan alert on your DMZ sensor and then again on all the other sensors that the attempted exploit touches.

With a single, properly configured, protected and backed-up database server, all your alerting is stored in one place, is easily accessible by you, and is safe from attackers. With the addition of such response and management tools like IDS Center for Windows and others, you can update rules, manage alert responses, and basically control everything from a single management interface. We summarize IDScenter and other cool Snort tools in Chapter 15.

Secure communications

- ✔ Traffic both to and from the Snort box should be secured.

- ✔ Management of the Snort computer itself should be conducted with SSH or another encrypted communication protocol.

- ✔ Output logging should be conducted over encrypted protocols, such as stunnel.

We provide tons of information on stunnel and other secure communications in the "Getting Snort through a Firewall" section, later in this chapter.

Snort configuration

A DMZ sensor should be tailored as closely as possible to the vulnerabilities that may be exploited on your DMZ. If you don't have a Web server in your DMZ, you don't need rules for Web servers. You not only have those unused ports blocked at the firewall (or firewalls) between the DMZ and the rest of the world (both internal and external), you also probably have unused ports and services disabled on the servers themselves. Most common in an enterprise DMZ is a plethora of network services (for both internal and external users) managed in a barely controlled chaos of hardware, software, and bandwidth. Snort, in turn, should be configured to process as much traffic as its hardware can handle and alert on anything suspicious that passes through your firewall.

The best method for accomplishing this is to

- ✔ Install Snort with every SERVER variable, rule, and preprocessor enabled.

- ✔ Tweak the configuration with either standard components or custom rules to catch the right mix of threat traffic on your enterprise network.

Catching All the Oinks

Snort (and its associated output plug-ins) allow you to format output to almost any usable source, such as databases, syslog, and flat comma-delimited text files. In this section, we show you how to configure Snort to output to multiple output sources, as well as manage this output centrally with multiple ACID consoles.

Multiple output configuration

Snort outputs to a variety of sources via several methods at the same time. In addition to logging alerts to a database (locally, remotely, or both), you can dump alerts to any combination of

- ✔ syslog
- ✔ tcpdump
- ✔ Snort's binary output format for processing by Barnyard or another output plug-in

This section presents a couple of scenarios where multiple output makes sense and how best to use Snort's output flexibility.

Logging to more than one database

Snort can log alerts to more than one database. In many cases, this is a good idea if you're running a database locally on the Snort sensor machine and have a centralized database for logging all Snort sensors. This keeps a backup of Snort's alert output in database format on the local machine, in case the central database is unavailable or somehow compromised.

This procedure is resource intensive because Snort must duplicate its data translation and normalization efforts while trying to keep up with the network traffic it's supposed to sniff and analyze. If you're on a high bandwidth network and your Snort sensor is performing analysis for a large part of that network, consider using the unified output and have Barnyard process the binary file and output to the database. (See the section "Multiple Unified Alert Files," later in this chapter.)

Configuring for multiple database logging

Follow these steps to configure Snort to log to multiple databases:

1. **Open the** `snort.conf` **file and find the introduction line for database output:**

```
# database: log to a variety of databases
```

2. **Configure the proper** `output database` **lines for both databases to include the** alert type, database type, and relevant login, host, and port information.

   In our case, our `output database` lines look like this:

```
output database: log, mysql, user=snortman, password=shutup, dbname=snortdb
        host=localhost
output database: log, mysql, user=snort, password=uh$$huh, dbname=snortdb,
        host=172.16.1.34, port=3306, sensor_name=websensor.
```

Both databases are updated with the same alert information as Snort outputs it.

Logging to a database and syslog

Different network environments have different logging needs, and Snort can accommodate any number of logging combinations.

A common output combination is to log Snort to both a database and a centralized syslog server:

- ✔ Logging to both sources allows for a backup of alerts in case one of the centralized data servers is down.

- ✔ Many enterprise network management and security management packages rely on the generic nature of syslog to process alert, error, and informational messages from all kinds of network, host, and server gear. Many organizations send all their IT devices' logs to a central syslog server.

- ✔ You may want to log to a database because ACID reads its data from there.

With Snort, the configuration is easy (if still resource intensive) because it's double logging again.

1. **Open the** `snort.conf` **file.**

2. **Go to the alert syslog configuration section and then make sure that the following is uncommented (remove the pound sign):**

```
output alert_syslog: LOG_LOCAL3
```

3. **For the database configuration, simply use the information from the preceding section.**

4. **Restart Snort after making these changes.**

For more information on logging configuration in Snort, see Chapter 6.

Securing Snort's Output

Snort's binary output data (while not human readable) is vulnerable to being read and used by attackers. When you ship this sensitive security information around your LAN or WAN or across the Internet, that data must be extremely secure. This section presents the lowdown on securing Snort's output data from Snort to the final destination, whether the destination is a database, syslog, or another logging function.

Giving an attacker any information about your security profile is akin to the U.S. government sending the plans for Fort Knox to a group of thieves. It may not be useful by itself, but it's really not recommended. When an attacker receives information about your network, you can guarantee that these skittering roaches share that information with all their fathead hacker buddies. It's the nature of the beast.

What's the danger of not securing Snort's output traffic? Check the juicy bits of information that Snort outputs in a given alert and what it communicates to a database just for access:

- ✔ **Database IP/hostname, port, username, and password:** Every time Snort starts, it logs in to the database with information that can be devastating in the hands of an attacker.

- ✔ **IP addresses of systems against which attacks are perpetrated:** It's an inefficient way of reconnoitering a network, but each piece of information adds to the risk that your network resources will be someone's warez server.

- ✔ **Services that you're monitoring:** Information about the services you're monitoring indicates that you're running services. An attacker can use this information to target attacks.

- ✔ **Exploits that you monitor:** The rules you enable may be as useful to an attacker as the services you're monitoring. The attacker can customize the attacks to specifically avoid triggering Snort rules.

- ✔ **Actual packet data:** If a Web application requires login and password and also trips a Snort rule, it captures the session and barfs an alert to the unsecured wire. Nice. Free passwords.

What's the solution? Stunnel. This program can secure network traffic between communication ports using Secure Sockets Layer (SSL). Stunnel is most useful when your spewing Snort alerts either inside your local network or through a firewall from a remote Snort sensor to a centralized database or a logging server.

Getting and installing stunnel

Stunnel lives at `http://www.stunnel.org`. Stunnel's prerequisites are few. You need SSL installed on your system. (Our examples use OpenSSL on both Windows and Linux.) At the time of this writing, the latest stable version of stunnel was based on the 4.05 code base.

Download the `stunnel-version-tar.gz.asc` file to check the PGP (Pretty Good Privacy) or GPG (Gnu Privacy Guard) signature on the source code — that is, unless you'd like to help out needy script-kiddies out there by providing your server as another free porn archive.

Follow these steps for stunnel source download success:

1. **Switch your the source directory:**

   ```
   # cd /your-source-directory
   ```

   Ours is `/usr/local/src`

2. **Grab stunnel using the following commands from your Linux prompt:**

   ```
   # wget http://www.stunnel.org/download/stunnel/src/stunnel-4.05.tar.gz
   # wget http://www.stunnel.org/download/stunnel/src/stunnel-4.05.tar.gz.asc
   ```

3. **Get Michal Trojnara's PGP key (he's the developer who signs the source):**

   ```
   # gpg --keyserver pgp.mit.edu --recv-keys 74C732D1
   gpgkeys: WARNING: this is an *experimental* HKP interface!
   gpg: key 74C732D1: public key "Michal Trojnara
               <Michal.Trojnara@centertel.pl>" imported
   gpg: Total number processed: 1
   gpg:               imported: 1
   ```

   gpgv can confirm the signature, although you may need to specify where your public keyring resides:

   ```
   # gpgv --keyring ~/.gnupg/pubring.gpg stunnel-4.05.tar.gz.asc
   gpgv: Signature made Sat Feb 14 08:31:39 2004 CST using DSA key ID 74C732D1
   gpgv: Good signature from "Michal Trojnara <Michal.Trojnara@centertel.pl>"
   gpgv:                aka "Michal Trojnara <MichalT@centertel.pl>"
   gpgv:                aka "Michal.Trojnara <Michal.Trojnara@mirt.net>"
   gpgv:                aka "Michal.Trojnara <MichalT@PTK_PANSKA.PO_MAIN>"
   ```

4. **When you know you have the genuine article, compile and install stunnel:**

```
# cd /your-source-directory
# tar -xvzf stunnel-4.05.tar.gz.asc
# cd stunnel-version/
# ./configure
# make
# make install
```

Stunnel installs itself and its few components in the following paths by default:

```
stunnel - /usr/local/sbin/
stunnel.conf - /usr/local/etc/stunnel/
stunnel.pem - /usr/local/etc/stunnel/
man - /usr/local/man/man8/
```

If /usr/local/sbin isn't in your path, either modify your path or move stunnel to a directory that's in your path.

Configuring and running stunnel as a server

Once stunnel is installed, it's time to dig through a flat-text config file.

- ✔ **Good news:** You don't need a command-line startup with three lines of arcane switches to make stunnel work. Stunnel uses its configuration file instead of command-line options.

- ✔ **Bad news:** You must parse through a config file and configure a handful of arcane switches for stunnel to work.

Open stunnel.conf in your favorite text editor and look at the most important configuration options to run stunnel as a server, ready to decrypt incoming alerts from your Snort sensors and forward them to your database server.

Getting your hands dirty with stunnel.conf

As a server, stunnel cares about two things, and two things only:

- ✔ Its certification file
- ✔ The port it's supposed to monitor

Finding the pointer

To use the certification file pointer, follow these steps:

1. **Open** stunnel.conf **in your favorite text editor.**

2. **Find the following line in** stunnel.conf:

   ```
   cert = /usr/local/etc/stunnel/mail.pem
   ```

3. **Change the preceding line to use the actual name of the certification file,** `stunnel.pem`.

   If necessary, change this line to point to the location of the file. By default, the file is located in `/usr/local/etc/stunnel`. If yours is elsewhere, edit accordingly.

   When you're done, the cert line should look similar to this:

   ```
   cert = /usr/local/etc/stunnel/stunnel.pem
   ```

A `stunnel.conf` and `stunnel.conf-sample` file should be in the `/usr/local/etc/stunnel` directory. If either of these files aren't there, you can copy `/source-directory/stunnel-version/tools/stunnel.conf-sample` to your `/usr/local/etc/stunnel directory`. (`source-directory` and `stunnel-version` are the source directory and stunnel source directory where you expanded the stunnel distribution.) Make sure that you keep a backup of the `stunnel.conf` file in case it gets corrupted.

chroot

The `chroot` command changes the root directory of stunnel to the directory specified. The default directory `/usr/local/var/run/stunnel` doesn't normally exist. If you're on your system as root, set the `chroot` directory to `/var/run/stunnel`. (We create it and set up various file permissions next.)

As the comments in `stunnel.conf` say, set the PID of `stunnel` in your chroot jail by configuring the next three options. You don't want stunnel running as root, because that's a big fat security violation. You can leave the `pid` value to default, but set the `setuid` and `setgid` options both to stunnel. When you're done, this section of the conf file should look similar to this:

```
chroot = /var/run/stunnel/
# PID is created inside chroot jail
pid = /stunnel.pid
setuid = stunnel
setgid = stunnel
```

After you set up stunnel, you want to make sure that it's working, right? Well the stunnel developers gave you a perfect tool for that with a configuration switch within `stunnel.conf`. Add the line:

```
foreground = yes
```

This runs stunnel in the foreground, outputting messages to `stdout` (in this case) the terminal window. Any errors (or successes) display for you to see, curse, and go back and fix. Simply remove this line when everything seems to work, and stunnel runs as a daemon (in the background).

Hold the phone! I got no PEM!

Generating a certification file for stunnel is as easy as anything on Linux. We take that back; it's somewhat easier, especially because OpenSSL comes standard on most Linux distributions. To generate a certification file for stunnel with OpenSSL, type the following at the command line (either inside the stunnel directory or elsewhere):

```
openssl req -new -out
    stunnel.pem -keyout stun-
    nel.pem -nodes -x509 -days
    arg
```

The following table breaks down the command:

openssl	Launches the openssl process with the arguments described below.
req	Uses the X.509 signing request management. If you want egghead descriptions of encryption protocols, drink plenty of coffee and refer to: http://www.ietf.org/html.charters/pkix charter.html.
nodes	Creates the private key without encrypting it. Though it's rather dangerous, it's the only way stunnel can read the key.
out	Outputs the certificate to the filename specified (stunnel.pem in this case).
keyout	Outputs the private key to the filename specified (appends it to stunnel.pem, in this case).
x509	Uses X.509 to create the certificate.
days	Extends (or shrinks) the number of days that an OpenSSL certificate is valid. (The default number is 30 days.) Using a short number of days

increases privacy in case someone gets a hold of your certificate, while using a longer number of days means you won't need a new certificate as often. We set ours for 60 days, but you may be more or less paranoid.

Press enter and OpenSSL goes to work. You should see the message:

```
Using configuration from
            /etc/ssl/openssl.cnf
Generating a 1024 bit RSA private key
...................++++++
......................++++++
writing new private key to 'stunnel.pem'
```

Then, OpenSSL asks you a series of questions (such as country, state, and organization) to build your Distinguished Name (DN). Though it sounds lofty, the DN is the general information about you and your organization to use in your certificate request. Once OpenSSL finishes with the interrogation, the PEM file is created. Type **more stunnel.pem** to see the key and certificate, which looks something like the following gibberish:

```
-----BEGIN RSA PRIVATE KEY-----
MIICXAIBAAKBgQC/23Qz+1tRWuYhcNPlkart1xkFr
            d5YOQtEuuH4jVbFvaF7Kd2g
VYHOWwOaRKjKPzy2L8e6UaduvAQW5pH26J3iGr3dZ
            iVowdhzOx/KgTeC3iuTWF7Q
/eZ6gR86I7uOnrpA2FgYGeAIWSr7+yONrKsOXkBin
            HgKSNAk4BnRcLOwQwIDAQABto
-----END RSA PRIVATE KEY-----
-----BEGIN CERTIFICATE-----
MIIDWTCCAsKgAwIBAgIBADANBgkqhkiG9wOBAQQFA
            DCBgDELMAkGA1UEBhMCdHgx
DTALBgNVBAgTBGJsYWgxEzARBgNVBAcTCmJlYnVid
            WJ1YnUxETAPBgNVBAoTCGFo
aXAgcmkgMQ4wDAYDVQQLEwVmbmEgZjEPMAOGA1UEA
            xMGYWZ1bnMgMRkwFwYJKoZI
-----END CERTIFICATE-----
```

Skip down the file a ways, and you should see several uncommented services under Service-level configuration:

```
# Service-level configuration

[pop3s]
accept  = 995
connect = 110
```

Comment all these services out by inserting a # sign before each line with text on it. Thus, these lines should look like this:

```
# Service-level configuration

#[pop3s]
#accept  = 995
#connect = 110
```

Now, add the mysqls service:

```
[mysqls]
accept  = 3307
connect = 3306
```

This service-level configuration tells stunnel to listen on port 3307 and send decoded traffic to port 3306 (where mysql is listening).

Check everything:

- ✔ The `cert=` line is point to your `stunnel.pem` file.
- ✔ Are you running in the foreground? For testing purposes, you want to. Once everything is working, comment out or removed the `foreground =` configuration switch.
- ✔ The `chroot`, `pid`, `setuid`, and `setgid` lines are all pointing to valid directories and users.
- ✔ All service-level configurations are commented out except for mysqls.

If all those are true, save the file and exit.

Getting the server ready for the job

Before running stunnel, you must set up

- ✔ The stunnel user and group
- ✔ The root directory specified in `stunnel.conf`
- ✔ mysqls as a service

Follow these steps:

1. **Type the following at the command line:**

```
# groupadd stunnel
# adduser stunnel -g stunnel
# mkdir /var/run/stunnel
# chown -R stunnel /var/run/stunnel
# chgrp -R stunnel /var/run/stunnel
```

2. **Create the mysqls service:**

```
# echo "mysqls 3307/tcp" >> /etc/services
```

This command creates the mysqls service in the services file.

Stand back! I'm gonna fire up this thing!

You're ready for your first stunnel test.

At the command line, type the following:

```
# stunnel
```

The preceding command should produce something like this:

```
2004.02.22 05:09:41 LOG5[6376:16384]: stunnel 4.04 on i586-pc-linux-gnu
            PTHREAD+LIBWRAP with OpenSSL 0.9.6j 10 Apr 2003
2004.02.22 05:09:41 LOG5[6376:16384]: FD_SETSIZE=1024, file ulimit=1024 -> 500
            clients allowed
```

That means everything is working. If you receive error messages, go back and check your conf file. The error message should direct you to the problem.

Kill the stunnel server for now by pressing the Control and C keys at the same time. You return to the command line.

Running stunnel when it matters

Once you configure the Snort sensor client machines to send Snort's alert data to the mysqls service on the centralized database server, you can configure stunnel to run automatically at boot up as a daemon. To do so, complete the following steps:

1. **Open** `stunnel.conf` **and comment out** `foreground =` **by typing a #
   before the line.**

2. **Configure stunnel to run at boot up.**

   On most Linux systems, you just copy the *source-directory*/tools/
   `stunnel.init` into your /etc/init.d directory, where *source-directory*
   is the directory where you originally un-tarred stunnel for installation.

   When the server can accept connections on mysqls, start stunnel on the
   Snort sensors.

Configuring and running stunnel as a client

Configuring stunnel as a client is very much like configuring stunnel as a server. You download and install stunnel exactly the same, and the configuration is almost exactly the same as in the previous server section. The only differences are noted in the following sections.

Setting up the client in stunnel.conf

The configuration of `stunnel.conf` is exactly the same as the server, with the exceptions of the client switch and the mysqls service-level configuration.

To set stunnel up as a client, open the `stunnel.conf` file in your favorite text editor, configure the `cert`, `pid`, `setuid`, and `setgid` options for this installation of stunnel (see the previous section for details), and then find the following line:

```
#client = yes
```

Uncomment that line by removing the # sign from the beginning of the line.

The mysqls service-level configuration is slightly different. In this case, you send Snort alert data on port 3306 and then connect to 3307 on the remote database server. (This configuration has implications in the `snort.conf` file as well, and we cover that in detail following this section.) So, after you comment out all the other service-level configuration options, add the following line (where `server-ip-address` is the IP address of the database server running stunnel):

```
[mysqls]
accept = 3306
connect = server-ip-address:3307
```

The best way to test that stunnel is working correctly is to initially configure it to run in the foreground. To do so, add this line to the `stunnel.conf` file:

```
foreground = yes
```

When you're sure that stunnel is connecting, transmitting, and receiving properly, you can remove this line from the configuration file.

Save the `stunnel.conf` file and exit the text editor.

Getting the client system ready for the job

You must configure your system properly to make stunnel run correctly. Refer to the "Getting the server ready for the job" section for details. The client system configuration is exactly like the server configuration, with a few exceptions, which we detail below.

Once you complete all the file permissions, mysqls service, and other configuration tasks, you must configure Snort to communicate to the remote database using stunnel:

1. **Open the** `snort.conf` **file in your favorite text editor and find the following line:**

   ```
   # output database: alert, mysql, user=snort dbname=snort
   ```

2. **Change the** `output database:` **line for the configuration of your database (replacing the placeholders with your actual configuration information) and the new stunnel configuration:**

   ```
   output database: logging-method, mysql, user=snort-database-user
           password=snort-database-password dbname=snort-database,
           host=127.0.0.1, port=3306, sensor_name=your-sensor-name
   ```

   For example, our output database line looks like this:

   ```
   output database: alert, mysql, user=snorty password=shutup dbname=snortdb,
           host=127.0.0.1, port=3306, sensor_name=websensor1
   ```

3. **Save the configuration file and exit the text editor.**

Running Snort and stunnel

After you've checked the configuration on both the client and server system, tested that stunnel runs on both systems, and have the `foreground` switch on in `stunnel.conf` for both the client and server, you're ready:

1. **Start stunnel on the server and then on the client.**

2. **When everything looks happy, restart Snort on the client machine.**

3. **Launch stunnel on the server.**

4. **At the command line, type** stunnel **and press the Enter key.**

   You should get good information like this:

   ```
   2004.02.22 05:46:59 LOG5[6396:16384]: stunnel 4.04 on i586-pc-linux-gnu
           PTHREAD+LIBWRAP with OpenSSL 0.9.6j 10 Apr 2003
   2004.02.22 05:46:59 LOG5[6396:16384]: FD_SETSIZE=1024, file ulimit=1024 ->
           500 clients allowed
   ```

Launch stunnel on the client

1. **At the command line on the client, type** stunnel.

2. **Press the Enter key.**

   You should get good information like this:

   ```
   2004.02.21 04:38:25 LOG5[21948:1074092064]: stunnel 4.04 on i686-pc-linux-
           gnu PTHREAD+LIBWRAP with OpenSSL 0.9.7c 30 Sep 2003
   2004.02.21 04:38:25 LOG5[21948:1074092064]: FD_SETSIZE=1024, file
           ulimit=1024 -> 500 clients allowed
   ```

Launch Snort on the client

1. **Open another terminal to the client system.**

2. **Find Snort in the process list by entering the following command at the command line:**

   ```
   ps -ef |grep snort
   ```

   You should see something like this:

   ```
   snort  28088    1  0 Feb01 ?        00:54:17 [snort]
   ```

3. **Copy the process id (**28088 **in the preceding example) from the screen.**

4. **Use the process id in the following command to bounce (restart) the Snort process:**

   ```
   kill -1 process-id
   ```

   For example, the following command restarts our example:

   ```
   kill -1 28088
   ```

   Snort restarts and reads its newly configured snort.conf file.

   You should see results like these in the terminals running stunnel:

   - Where stunnel is running on the client:

     ```
     2004.02.21 04:43:16 LOG5[22499:1082531008]: mysqls connected from
             127.0.0.1:57889
     ```

   - Where you connected to the server:

     ```
     2004.02.22 04:43:16 LOG5[6398:16386]: mysqls connected from
             10.1.1.129:57890
     ```

It's working. You're done!

Getting it all running for real

On both the client and the server, press the Control and C keys to kill stunnel. Here's how to make stunnel run like a real Linux process:

1. **Open the** `stunnel.conf` **file on the server and comment out the** `foreground` **= line, like this:**

```
# foreground = yes
```

2. **Save and close the** `stunnel.conf` **file.**

3. **Open the** `stunnel.conf` **file for the client and comment out the** `foreground` **= line, like this:**

```
# foreground = yes
```

4. **Save and close the** `stunnel.conf` **file.**

5. **Check by running stunnel on both the server and the client (type stunnel at the command prompt and pressing the Enter key).**

   You should get no output from either.

6. **Bounce Snort on the client machine by typing the following command at the command line (replace** `pid-of-snort` **with the process id of the Snort daemon):**

```
kill -1 pid-of-snort
```

A few tests can confirm that everything is working as it should:

✔ Type **netstat** at the command line and press the Enter key.

  In addition to other network connections, you should see something like this:

```
tcp    0    0 10.1.1.1.pt:mysqls remote-192-16-22-1:58142 ESTABLISHED
```

  This shows that your client is connected to the server on the mysqls service.

Testing Snort

You need to test that Snort is actually working over the stunnel connection:

1. **Fire a Snort rule by running a program, such as Nmap (**`http://www.insecure.org/`**).**

2. **Confirm that the alert made it to its repository.**

   You can confirm by pointing your browser at the ACID console.

Chapter 14

Using the Barnyard Output Tool

*W*ant Snort to process more network data, faster? Barnyard lets Snort do what it does best: match network attack signatures to its rules. Barnyard takes over user-definable logging functions.

Barnyard for Fast Output

Like many open-source Unix-based applications, Snort allows many options. It's a piece of the security puzzle without any frills such as a GUI interface, but with hooks into other security tools and output options. Snort can format and push its alert logs to a database or a human-readable text file, but this process eats resources that Snort should be using to analyze network packets and match them to its security rules. When your network traffic is low, Snort does a fine job of analyzing packets formatting the output, and writing to a database. As network traffic increases, Snort must devote more time to formatting data than to analyzing packets. When this happens, Snort drops packets, meaning that Snort doesn't analyze every packet like it should. Barnyard eases these resource problems by

✔ Formatting Snort's unified output log data

✔ Writing logs to an output program, such as a database or syslog

What does Barnyard do?

Barnyard follows this sequence:

1. **Read Snort's unified output logging in binary format (ones and zeroes instead of text).**

2. **Parse the data into a human-readable format.**

   The pcap output plug-in writes to pcap format readable by network analysis tools.

3. **Write the data to your chosen output method.**

Seven Barnyard output plug-ins convert the unified log data into something else:

- ✔ **Alert_Fast:** Writes all Snort alerts to a single, flat text file that you specify.

- ✔ **Log_Dump:** Writes log output to flat text log files.

- ✔ **Alert_HTML:** Writes alert output to HTML Web pages.

- ✔ **Alert_CSV:** Writes alerts to a comma-separated values (CSV) flat text file.

   A CSV file can be read by many database and spreadsheet applications, including Access and Excel.

- ✔ **Alert_syslog:** Writes alerts to the flat text file syslog format in /var/log/ messages on a Unix-based OS.

   This format is the most portable between network and security management applications.

- ✔ **Output_pcap:** Writes alerts back to a binary pcap format.

   This format allows network analysis tools (such as Ethereal) to analyze the alert information and replay the network intrusion. This format isn't human-readable without another application.

- ✔ **ACID_DB:** Writes alerts to a database for use with the ACID console.

   This chapter covers configuring Barnyard for database output. Chapter 7 gives you all the information you need about ACID console.

In the section "Fitting Barnyard into your Snort environment" in this chapter, we present all the information you need on Barnyard's output plug-in options with some handy examples.

Unified logging with Snort

With ever-increasing network traffic and gigabit networks becoming more and more prevalent, the need for Snort to shed "unnecessary" processes became apparent. It is much faster for Snort to write its logs to a straight binary format, than for Snort to take the alert data it has already processed, parse that data to text, then format it to a human-readable output format (such as writing to a database or to a text log file). What unified logging buys you is a faster, more efficient Snort IDS system: Snort handles what it's supposed to, and Barnyard "prettifies" Snort's data.

Barnyard does what's known in the world of Snort as "post-processing."

Installing and Configuring Barnyard

The Barnyard source available on http://www.snort.org runs on Unix-operating system variants, such as Linux and BSD. Installing Barnyard on a Unix system is much like installing Snort itself. Unlike Snort, Barnyard Linux binaries aren't available on the http://www.snort.org Web site (though your particular Linux distribution may have created its own binary Barnyard package — you can check its Web site). We recommend you compile Barnyard from source.

The latest version of Barnyard is available from the Snort Web site:

```
http://www.snort.org/dl/barnyard/
```

Download the Barnyard archive to /usr/local/src, or another source directory of your choosing on the Unix system where Snort is running.

Prerequisites

✔ To run Barnyard "out of the box," Snort must be running and writing to a binary unified log. We present step-by-step instructions on installing Snort on your Linux system in Chapter 4.

In the section "Fitting Barnyard into Your Snort Environment" in this chapter, we present all you need to know to configure Snort to log to unified logging format.

✔ If you want Barnyard to write to a database, such as MySQL, you must have the database running with all the various tables formatted for Snort alerts.

Chapters 4 and 5 present all the information you need to run MySQL and configure it for Snort alerts on the Unix and Windows platforms.

✔ You need root-user access privileges on the Unix system where you'll install Barnyard. But you already knew that.

Barnyard is only distributed as un-compiled code, so you must compile and install it yourself. The basic process is

1. **Extract the archive.**

2. **Configure database options.**

3. **Compile and install Barnyard.**

The following sections cover each step of the installation process.

Extracting the archive

Extract the Barnyard archive by typing the following command at the command prompt:

```
tar -xvfz barnyard-version.tar.gz
```

The *version* variable is the actual version of Barnyard you downloaded. For example, when we extracted Barnyard, the command looked like this:

```
tar -zxvf Barnyard-0.1.0.tar.gz
```

The files in the archive extract to a directory called barnyard-*version*.

Configuring Barnyard

After extracting the Barnyard archive, you configure Barnyard.

To install Barnyard with database support, you must enable that support when you configure the code. Barnyard currently supports the MySQL and Postgres databases.

No database

To configure the Barnyard code without any database options, change to the barnyard-*version* directory and type the following command:

```
./configure
```

The default configure script, without option switches, simply configures the code for your system, placing the default install directories in the install script. For database support, consider the options in the following sections.

MySQL

The following commands configure the Barnyard installation with MySQL database support:

✔ To use all default MySQL directories, enter the following command:

```
--enable-mysql
```

This option provides support for MySQL by scanning your system and finding the default MySQL installation directory.

✔ If MySQL libraries or includes are installed in some directory other than the default, you must use one of the following options.

By setting both the includes and libraries configuration option, you automatically enable Barnyard's MySQL output module. This means you don't need to include the –enable-mysql setting.

✔ To use non-default directories for only MySQL includes code, insert the directory into the following command:

```
--with-mysql-includes=DIR:
```

For example, if your MySQL includes code is in the directory, enter the following command:

```
--with-mysql-includes=x
```

✔ To use non-default directories for only MySQL libraries, insert the directory into the following command:

```
--with-mysql-libraries=DIR
```

For example, if your MySQL libraries are in the directory, enter the following command:

```
--with-mysql-libraries=x
```

Configuring Barnyard with default MySQL support

To configure Barnyard with the default MySQL configuration support, type the following command at the command prompt:

```
./configure --enable-mysql
```

You must be in the barnyard-*version* directory to configure Barnyard before you compile.

Postgres

Barnyard has an output module for the Postgres database management system. The following commands configure Barnyard with Postgres database support:

✔ **–enable-postgres**

This option supports Postgres by scanning your system and finding the default Postgres installation directory.

To configure Barnyard to use Postgres, type the following if Postgres is installed in the default directory structure:

```
./configure --enable-postgres
```

✔ If Postgres libraries or includes are installed in a directory other than the default, you must use the `--enable-postgres` option plus at least one of the following configure options:

- **–with-postgres-includes=*DIR***

  This option sets the directory for Postgres includes code (replace the DIR variable with the actual directory path to your Postgres `include` directory).

  If you've installed Postgres in the default directory structure, you don't need this configure option.

- **–with-postgres-libraries=*DIR***

  This option sets the directory for the Postgres library files (replace the DIR variable with the actual directory path to your Postgres `lib` directory).

  If you've installed Postgres in the default directory structure, you don't need this configure option. By default, Postgres's lib directory is /usr/local/pgsql/lib.

  By setting both the includes and libraries configuration option, you automatically enable Barnyard's Postgres output module. This means you don't need to also use the –enable-postgres option.

Making and installing

To compile and install Barnyard, simply type the following command at the command prompt:

```
make && make install
```

The compiler reads the configuration script, and installs Barnyard components in the appropriate directories.

Where does it go?

The Barnyard executable and associated files install in the following directories by default:

```
barnyard - /usr/local/bin
```

```
barnyard.conf - /usr/local/etc/
```

```
gen-msg.map - /usr/local/etc
```

```
sid-msg.map - /usr/local/etc
```

The gen-msg.map and sid-msg.map files are included with Barnyard, but not necessarily intended to replace those already distributed by Snort. Both of these files are responsible for mapping Snort's rules to specific messages and signature IDs. If you've customized the gen-msg.map and sid-msg.map files that came with Snort, don't replace your files with the default versions distributed with Barnyard.

Fitting Barnyard into Your Snort Environment

Before you can get Barnyard running, you must configure Snort for unified logging and Barnyard to use Snort's binary log.

Setting up Snort for unified logging

Snort's unified logging feature allows Snort to write its alerts directly to a binary file, instead of converting that output to formatted text. The unified output plug-in is fast, efficient and easy to configure.

Configure the conf file

To configure Snort for unified logging, perform the following steps:

1. **Open snort.conf in your favorite plain-text editor, such as vi or pico.**

   Use `pico -w` to turn off word-wrap.

2. **Find the output section labeled:**

   ```
   # Step #3: Configure output plugins
   ```

3. **In the `# Step #3` output section, find the output plug-ins that you've enabled for Snort for plain-text or database alerting and logging.**

4. **Type a pound sign (#) in front of each output plug-in line you found.**

   Typing a # sign in front of the line makes it a *comment,* so the snort executable ignores the line.

   Examples of output lines that might need to be commented out include:

   ```
   output alert_fast: alert.ids
   output log_fast: log.ids
   output database: alert,mysql, user=snort dbname=snort
           host=127.0.0.1
   ```

5. **Remove the pound sign (#) from the following line in the output section:**

```
# output alert_unifed: filename snort.alert, limit 128
```

6. **Change the limit option number in the** output alert_unifed **line of the output section to the maximum size of the barnyard log file in megabytes.**

   The default is 128 megabytes ("128" in the output alert_unifed line), which should be fine unless you're short of disk space.

7. **Save the file and exit the text editor.**

Test Snort's output

To test whether Snort is writing to a binary file, follow these steps:

1. **Execute the following command at the command line:**

```
snort -dev -c path-to-snort-conf -l /var/log
```

2. **Change to the /var/log directory. You should see a file similar to the following:**

```
snort.alert.1074420820
```

The long number appended to the filename is a timestamp of when snort was started, so different log files with the same name don't get mixed up. The size of this file changes as Snort adds alerts.

Configuring Barnyard

To configure Barnyard to process Snort's unified alert logs, you must

✔ Make configuration settings changes to the System Configurations, Data Processor, and Output Plugins sections of the barnyard.conf file

✔ Start Barnyard with the proper command-line switches

Make a backup of the barnyard.conf file before you start modifying it. It's much easier than digging for the original in the install directory.

Configuration declarations

The first section to configure is labeled:

```
# Step 0: configuration declarations
```

1. **In the configuration declarations section, find these three lines:**

```
# set the hostname (currently only used for the acid db output plugin)
config hostname: hostname

# set the interface name (currently only used for the acid db output plugin)
config interface: fx1
```

The lines preceded by a pound sign (#) are comments and are not processed by the Barnyard executable. The three lines that start with "config" are the lines to change.

2. **On the** `config hostname` **line, replace the word "hostname" with the hostname of your computer.**

   If you don't know your computer's hostname, type the command `hostname` at the command prompt and press the Enter key.

3. **On the** `config interface` **line, replace "fx1" with the Ethernet network adapter on your computer.**

   On Linux systems, standard Ethernet cards are such x as eth0 and eth1.

As an example, our configuration declarations look like this:

```
# set the hostname (currently only used for the acid db output plugin)
config hostname: machine

# set the interface name (currently only used for the acid db output plugin)
config interface: eth0
```

Barnyard requires configuration settings for the type of data processor it is to use to process Snort's unified logs:

1. **Find the section in the barnyard.conf file labeled:**

   ```
   # Step 1: setup the data processors
   ```

2. **In this section, find the lines labeled:**

   ```
   # dp_alert
   # --------------------------
   # The dp_alert data processor is capable of reading the alert (event) 
           format
   # generated by Snort's spo_unified plug-in. It is used with output plug-ins
   # that support the "alert" input type. This plug-in takes no arguments.
   # processor dp_alert

   # dp_log
   # --------------------------
   # The dp_log data processor is capable of reading the log format generated
   # by Snort's spo_unified plug-in. It is used with output plug-ins
   # that support the "log" input type. This plug-in takes no arguments.
   #
   # processor dp_log
   ```

3. **Remove the pound sign (#) from in front of "processor dp_alert" and/ or "processor dp_log" depending on which method you use to write Snort's unified alerts or log files. Barnyard reads either Snort's unified logs or alerts, but not both at the same time.**

Output plug-ins

To configure Barnyard's output plug-ins, you must first decide how you want your output to appear. Do you want to view Snort alert logs in flat text format? How about HTML? Do you want the logs to go into a database? Or to comma-separated value text files? Barnyard can output Snort's logs to a variety of formats for a variety of applications.

Alert_Fast

To configure Barnyard to read Snort's unified alert file and output it to alert_fast format, follow these steps:

1. **Open barnyard.conf in your favorite text editor (such as vi or pico) and locate the following lines:**

```
# alert_fast
#----------------------------
# Converts data from the dp_alert plugin into an approximation of Snort's
# "fast alert" mode. Argument: <filename>

# output alert_fast:
```

2. **Remove the pound sign (#) from in front of the "output alert_fast:" line and type in a filename for Barnyard to output the alert log to. For example, the alert_fast section of our barnyard.conf file looks like this:**

```
output alert_fast: /var/log/snort/alert.ids
```

For the alert fast logging feature to function, the dp_alert data processor must be enabled earlier in the barnyard.conf file.

So, Barnyard takes Snort's incoming unified alert file, parses it into the alert_fast format and writes it to a file in /var/log/snort called alert.ids. If you change to that directory and issue the command "tail -f alert.ids", you see some juicy alerts:

```
-------------------------------------------------------------------
01/18/04-14:03:20.275942 {ICMP} 10.10.10.1 -> 10.10.10.2
[**] [1:483:2] ICMP PING CyberKit 2.2 Windows [**]
[Classification: Misc activity] [Priority: 3]
[Xref => http://www.whitehats.com/info/IDS154]
-------------------------------------------------------------------
01/18/04-14:03:20.455048 {ICMP} 10.10.10.1 -> 10.10.10.2
[**] [1:483:2] ICMP PING CyberKit 2.2 Windows [**]
[Classification: Misc activity] [Priority: 3]
[Xref => http://www.whitehats.com/info/IDS154]
-------------------------------------------------------------------
```

Log_Dump

To configure Barnyard to read Snort's unified log file and output it to log_dump format, follow these steps:

1. **Open barnyard.conf in your favorite text editor (such as vi or pico) and locate the following lines:**

```
# log_dump
#----------------------------
# Converts data from the dp_log plugin into an approximation of Snort's
# "ASCII packet dump" mode. Argument: <filename>

# output log_dump:
```

2. **Remove the pound sign (#) from in front of the "output log_dump:" line and type in a filename for Barnyard to output the log dump to. For example, the log_dump section of our barnyard.conf file looks like this:**

```
output log_dump: /var/log/logdump.ids
```

For the log_dump logging feature to function, the dp_log data processor must be enabled earlier in the barnyard.conf file.

So, Barnyard takes Snort's incoming unified log file, parses it into the log_dump format and writes it to a file in /var/log/snort called logdump.ids. Change to that directory and issue the command "tail -f logdump.ids" to see some juicy logs.

Alert_HTML

Sometime in the future, Barnyard will parse Snort's unified output log into an HTML file that you specify. In Barnyard version 0.1, the alert_html feature doesn't work.

If it ever works, you just find the alert_html section in your barnyard.conf file and uncomment one of the "output alert_html" configuration lines, then change the path and filename to where ever you want Barnyard to dump the HTML file.

Theoretically, the barnyard.conf file will look like this:

```
# alert_html (experimental)
#--------------------------
# Creates a series of html pages about recent alerts
# Arguments:
#   [webroot] - base directory for storing the html pages
#
# Example:
output alert_html:  /var/www/htdocs/op_alert_html
#   output alert_html:  /var/www/htdocs/op_alert_html
```

In the future, we'll all have jet-powered backpacks, and Barnyard will output to an HTML file that looks something like Figure 14-1.

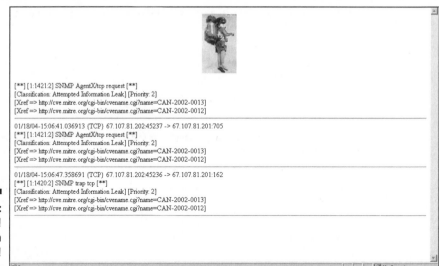

Figure 14-1:
Stand back!
I'm gonna
fire this up!

Alert_CSV

Unlike the alert_html, alert_csv actually works. Follow these steps to use it:

1. **Uncomment (remove the # sign from in front of) the alert_csv line in your barnyard.conf file.**

2. **Add a path and filename for Barnyard to dump the CSV formatted text file.**

Once it works, the configuration looks something like this:

```
# alert_csv (experimental)
#----------------------------
# Creates a CSV output file of alerts (optionally using a user specified format)
# Arguments:  filepath [format]
#
# Examples:
#   output alert_csv: /var/log/snort/csv.out
output alert_csv: /var/log/snort/csv.out
                  timestamp,msg,srcip,sport,dstip,dport,protoname,itype,icode
```

The additional switches (beginning with "timestamp," and ending with "icode") are formatting switches for the outputted data. Snort's alert information is generated in "buckets" like the timestamp of the alert, the source and destination IP addresses, and source and destination port numbers. The alert_csv output plug-in can configure how those "buckets" appear in the comma-separated value text file, so columns and rows line up correctly when the log file is imported into another format (such as Excel or a database). The following example shows a few of the more important buckets in the example that follows. The barnyard.conf file has a complete list of the buckets with descriptions.

The output from our example output_csv configuration looks like this:

```
"2004-01-18 22:27:54",SCAN SOCKS Proxy attempt, 10.1.1.1,59424,
           10.1.1.2,,"TCP",,
"2004-01-18 22:27:53",ICMP PING NMAP,10.1.1.1,, 10.1.1.2,,"ICMP",8,0
"2004-01-18 22:27:54",SNMP trap tcp, 10.1.1.1,59424,67.107.81.221,162,"TCP",,
"2004-01-18 22:27:54",SCAN Proxy \(8080\) attempt, 10.1.1.1,59424,
           10.1.1.2,8080,"TCP",,
```

Table 14-1 breaks down the first line of the preceding output, with a description of each bucket.

Table 14-1	Output Explained from the output_csv Plug-in	
Output	*Switch*	*Relevance*
"2004-01-18 22:27:54"	timestamp	Time of the Snort alert
SCAN SOCKS Proxy attempt	msg	Alert message text
10.1.1.1	srcip	Source IP of the alert
59424	sport	Source port of the alert
10.1.1.2	dstip	Destination IP of the traffic
"	dport	Destination port (there isn't one in this particular alert)
"TCP"	protoname	Network protocol of the suspect traffic
"	itype	ICMP type (none on this particular alert)

Alert_syslog

The alert_syslog feature outputs to the standard Unix syslog format. Typically this log is found in /var/log/messages. To configure Barnyard to process and parse Snort's unified log and write that to syslog, follow these steps:

1. **Find the following section of the barnyard.conf file:**

```
# alert_syslog
#----------------------------
# Converts data from the alert stream into an approximation of Snort's
# syslog alert output plugin. Same arguments as the output plugin in snort.
#
# Win32 can also optionally specify a particular hostname/port. Under
```

```
# Win32, the default hostname is '127.0.0.1', and the default port is 514.
#
# [Unix flavours should use these formats...]
# output alert_syslog
# output alert_syslog: LOG_AUTH LOG_ALERT
```

2. Remove the # sign from the line:

```
# output alert_syslog
```

3. Save the barnyard.conf file and restart Barnyard.

If you tail -f /var/log/messages, you see a pigpile of juicy alerts, interspersed with your normal system alerts:

```
Jan 18 08:27:47 elvis sshd[27332]: Did not receive identification string from
          10.1.1.1
Jan 18 08:30:00 elvis CRON[27334]: (root) CMD (test -x /usr/sbin/run-crons &&
          /usr/sbin/run-crons )
Jan 18 08:47:46 elvis sshd[27362]: Did not receive identification string from
          10.1.1.1
Jan 18 09:30:11 elvis barnyard: [1:1228:2] SCAN nmap XMAS [Classification:
          Attempted Information Leak] [Priority: 2] {TCP} 10.1.1.1:60196 ->
          10.1.1.2:1
Jan 18 09:31:00 elvis CRON[27349]: (root) CMD (test -x /usr/sbin/run-crons &&
          /usr/sbin/run-crons )
Jan 18 09:32:17 elvis barnyard: [1:469:1] ICMP PING NMAP [Classification:
          Attempted Information Leak] [Priority: 2] {ICMP} 10.1.1.2 ->
          10.1.1.1
```

This isn't the best or most intuitive way to read Snort alerts, but with network or security management packages, this information can be re-parsed and displayed as you want it. You can also use log-watching tools (such as Swatch) to notify you when an alert comes across the wire.

Output_pcap

The output_pcap configuration option allows Barnyard to read the Snort unified alert logs and output them to the binary pcap format. This format isn't human-readable in its raw form, but network analysis tools such as Ethereal can read it and display alert information in a graphical format.

To configure Barnyard to output to pcap format, follow these steps:

1. Find the section of the barnyard.conf file that looks like this:

```
# log_pcap
#----------------------------
# Converts data from the dp_log plugin into standard pcap format
# Argument: <filename>

#output log_pcap
```

2. **Remove the pound sign (#) from in front of the line "#output log_pcap."**

3. **After this line, add a colon (:) and a filename for Barnyard where you want to write the pcap log.**

   For instance, our log_pcap configuration line looks like this:

   ```
   output log_pcap: /var/log/snort/log.pcap
   ```

4. **Save the barnyard.conf file and exit the text editor, then restart Barnyard.**

To test Barnyard's pcap logging file, you can open the log.pcap file with tcp-dump with the "replay" switch from the command line like this:

```
tcpdump -r /var/log/snort/log.pcap
```

Database reporting

Barnyard can parse Snort's unified alerts and logs in to ACID database formats that you specify using the ACID_DB output option in the barnyard.conf file. Before you configure Barnyard to report to a database, you need to consider prerequisites, Snort's configuration, and Barnyard's configuration.

Prerequisites

Before you can run Barnyard to process Snort's unified alerts and output that to a database, you must have a database management system running with ACID tables created. We present all the information you need for database setup in Chapters 4 (for Linux) and Chapter 5 (for Windows).

You don't need ACID running for Barnyard to write to the database, but you need ACID or another database front end to see and manage the alerts in any meaningful way. Chapter 7 gives you all the information you need to set up ACID for your Snort IDS.

Configuring Snort for Barnyard database output

The only configuration change you need to make to Snort is to disable its database output option, if it is enabled. (If you've been following along in this chapter, we disabled it in the "Setting up Snort for unified logging" section.)

1. **Open snort.conf with your favorite text editor, such as vi or pico.**

2. **Find the following lines in the output section:**

   ```
   # database: log to a variety of databases
   # ----------------------------------------
   # See the README.database file for more information about configuring
   # and using this plugin.
   #
   # output database: log, mysql, user=snortman password=snortman dbname=snort
             host=127.0.0.1
   ```

```
# output database: alert, postgresql, user=snort dbname=snort
# output database: log, unixodbc, user=snort dbname=snort
# output database: log, mssql, dbname=snort user=snort password=test
```

3. **Ensure that each of the "output database:" lines have a pound sign (#) in front of them.**

   In the snort.conf file, find the lines that look similar to this:

```
output alert_unified: filename snort.alert, limit 128
# output log_unified: filename snort.log, limit 128
```

4. **Ensure that the # sign is removed from the "output alert_unified:" line and that there's a filename for Snort's unified alert log and a file size limit (maximum is 128MB).**

5. **Save the file and exit the text editor.**

Don't restart Snort yet, because we still need to make sure the database and Barnyard are properly set up.

Configuring Barnyard for database output

To configure Barnyard for database output, just enable the acid_db switch in the barnyard.conf file and ensure that it's properly configured:

1. **Open the barnyard.conf file in your favorite text editor, such as vi or pico.**

2. **Locate the acid_db section of the configuration file (it's located at the bottom):**

```
# acid_db
#-------------------------------
# Available as both a log and alert output plugin. Used to output data into
# the db schema used by ACID
# Arguments:
#       $db_flavor          - what flavor of database (ie, mysql)
#       sensor_id $sensor_id - integer sensor id to insert data as
#       database $database   - name of the database
#       server $server       - server the database is located on
#       user $user           - username to connect to the database as
#       password $password   - password for database authentication
# output alert_acid_db: mysql, sensor id 1, database snort, server,
#           localhost, database snort, user root
# output alert_acid_db: mssql, database snort, server localhost, user
#           snort, password test
```

3. **Enable the appropriate line (for either MySQL or MSSQL) by removing the # sign from in front of it, and configure the line with the proper information. This line should look very similar to the corresponding line in the snort.conf file that you just disabled.**

For example, our output alert_acid_db line looks like this:

```
output alert_acid_db: mysql, database snorty, server 127.0.0.1, user elvis,
                      password shutup, detail full
```

4. **Once it is configured, save the barnyard.conf file and exit the text editor.**

Starting Snort with the new configuration

To test our work, start Snort with its new snort.conf file.

1. **Type the following in the directory where the snort executable resides:**

```
snort -dev -c snort-conf -l /var/log/snort
```

The variable *snort-conf* is the path to the file snort.conf. For our configuration, this line looks like this:

```
snort -dev -c /usr/local/etc/snort.conf -l /var/log/snort
```

2. **Change to the /var/log directory, and you should see a file similar to the following:**

```
snort.alert.1074420820
```

The size of this file changes as Snort adds alerts. Until you run Barnyard, this is the only way to tell whether Snort's doing what it's supposed to.

The following section, "Starting Barnyard," starts Barnyard with the switches to read the Snort unified alert and parse that information to the database.

Starting Barnyard

We dedicate a section to starting Barnyard because it isn't as easy as it sounds. In typical Unix fashion, Barnyard has a multitude of switches that are somewhat less arcane than the Talmud. Once you understand what they do, it's easy to run Barnyard, process Snort's unified alerts and output them to the format that you want.

Barnyard command-line switches

Barnyard uses command-line switches to configure input, output and other administrative tasks. The following are valid Barnyard command-line switches, description and examples.

To view the command-line switches for Barnyard, type the following in the directory where the Barnyard executable resides:

```
barnyard -help
```

Input switches

Input switches tell Barnyard where to read Snort unified output logs.

- ✔ -d <directory>: This switch configures Barnyard to monitor a given directory where Snort spools its unified log. Without this switch, Barnyard fails to operate.

- ✔ -f <file>: This switch configures Barnyard to monitor a base spool filename. A spool filename is a fancy name for a file that's continually updated by a process or program. In this case, it's the Snort unified alert log file.

- ✔ -t <time>: This option sets the "starting unified filestamp" for Barnyard to look for when processing Snort unified logs. Snort unified logs output in this format: *filename.timestamp*. The *timestamp* is the <time> string you need for the -t switch.

The actual output filename is configured in Snort when you set the "output alert_unified" output option in the snort.conf file. See the section "Configuring Snort for Barnyard database output" earlier in this chapter for the specific configuration of this option.

The -d, -f and -t input switches operate in concert to direct Barnyard to the specific directory and Snort unified alert file. For example, to properly configure Barnyard to read the Snort unified filename snort.alert.1074463235 in the /var/log/snort directory, the command looks like this:

```
barnyard -d /var/log/snort -f /var/log/snort/snort.alert -t 1074463235
```

The preceding command requires some output options for Barnyard to write its parsed file.

Output switches

Barnyard's output switches direct Barnyard to a directory and file to output its processed Snort unified log file:

- ✔ -a <directory>: This switch archives the processed unified alert file to a specified directory.

  This switch isn't necessary if you've configured the barnyard.conf file with an output plug-in. It's useful for testing, or if you've written your own output plug-in and need the raw text file for further processing.

- ✔ -L <directory>: This switch configures Barnyard to output it's parsed unified alert log file to a specific directory. The actual filename for the parsed file is configured in the barnyard.conf file for the particular output plug-in you use.

✔ -w <file>: This switch configures Barnyard to output the text of the last alert Barnyard processed from Snort's unified alert log into a file.

In the world of Snort and Barnyard, this is called a "waldo" file. By checking the waldo file, Barnyard "remembers" where it was in the alert log processing so that if Barnyard is stopped and restarted, it doesn't need to re-process the entire Snort unified alert log. (A unified alert log can be as large as 128 megabytes of binary data. Barnyard requires a lot of resources to re-process the entire file if stopped and restarted.)

To configure Barnyard to process a Snort unified alert and output the data to a log file and output the last alert processed to a waldo file, the command at the command line for the example from the preceding section would look like this:

```
barnyard -w barn.waldo -d /var/log/snort -f /var/log/snort/snort.alert -t
        1074463235
```

This command still requires some configuration options must be set at the command line.

Configuration switches

Barnyard needs even more information for it to properly operate at the command line.

✔ - c <conffile>: The -c switch is used if either

- Your barnyard.conf file isn't in the default install directory (/usr/local/etc/snort/).

- You want to use a barnyard.conf file other than in the default location.

You must input the full path to the barnyard.conf file.

✔ -g <file>: The -g switch sets the location of the alert generator file that Snort uses to generate alerts (gen-msg.map).

You only must use this switch if the generator file isn't in the default location (/usr/local/etc/snort).

✔ -s <file>: The -s switch sets the location of the sid-msg.map file that Snort uses to map an attack's Signature ID to a description message. You only must use this switch if the sid-msg.map file isn't in the default location (/etc/snort).

We now have enough information to run Barnyard from the command line! We told you it was arcane. The following example scenario produces view Barnyard command-line execution success:

Snort unified alert file:

```
/var/log/snort/snort.alert.1074463235
```

Barnyard configuration file:

```
/usr/local/etc/barnyard.conf
```

Generator and SID files:

```
/usr/local/etc/gen-msg.map
/usr/local/etc/sid-msg.map
```

We want to output the processed Snort unified logs to the following directory:

```
/var/log/barnyard
```

And we want the waldo file to output to the directory where barnyard.conf resides with the following filename:

```
barn.waldo
```

With all that information, we construct the Barnyard command with switches at the command line, like so:

```
barnyard -w barn.waldo -c /usr/local/etc/barnyard.conf -d
         /var/log/snort/ -g /usr/local/etc/gen-msg.map -s
         /usr/local/etc/sid-msg.map -f
         /var/log/snort/snort.alert -t 1074463235
```

The output at the command line for our example command looks like this:

```
-*> Barnyard! <*-
Version 0.1.0 (Build 17)
By Andrew R. Baker (andrewb@snort.org)
and Martin Roesch (roesch@sourcefire.com, www.snort.org)

Loading Data Processors...
dp_alert loaded
dp_log loaded
dp_stream_stat loaded
Loading Built-in Output Plugins...
Fast Alert plugin initialized
AlertSyslog initialized
Log Dump plugin initialized
LogPcap initialized
AcidDb output plugin initialized
AlertCSV initialized
Parsing Config file: /usr/local/etc/barnyard.conf
Barnyard Version 0.1.0 (Build 17) started
```

If you missed a configuration option, fat-fingered a command-line switch, or otherwise made a mistake, Barnyard issues an error at or near the error point and exits the program.

To check your work, navigate to the directory where you output the parsed unified alerts and issue the "tail -f" command on the Barnyard alert file. You should see the alert file continually updating with Snort alerts.

Optional switches

Barnyard command-line switches can control these administrative tasks:

- ✔ -D: Use -D switch when you're ready for Barnyard to run in the background (after you've tested that your miles long Barnyard command actually will work). Simply add the -D switch to the Barnyard command, along with all the other switches.

  You can also configure Barnyard to start as a daemon in the barnyard.conf file.

- ✔ -o: The -o switch process a Snort unified log, outputs as directed by other output switches and then closes Barnyard. This command is useful when you want to test your configuration file, command-line switches and output file.

- ✔ -R: The -R switch directs Barnyard to run through its various configuration options and command-line switches, but then exit without processing a unified log or outputting to a log file. This switch tests your Barnyard configuration and command-line switches.

- ✔ -V: The -V switch simply outputs the Barnyard version information and exits. You don't need any other switches for this one to function.

- ✔ -X <file>: The -X switch specifies a process ID (pid) file when Barnyard runs in daemon mode.

- ✔ -h: The -h switch shows the help file with Barnyard usage information, switches and descriptions.

Finally, your barnyard.conf and snort.conf files are configured correctly, and Snort is writing its alerts to a unified alert log. Your database receives alerts, and you've constructed your Barnyard command with all the various switches. Congratulations! You now have Barnyard processing your alerts, letting Snort do what it does best: sniffing the network for attacks.

Part IV
The Part of Tens

The 5th Wave   By Rich Tennant

"The divorce was amicable. She got the Jetta, the sailboat and the recumbent bike. I got the servers and the domain name."

In this part . . .

This part points you to tools and resources to help you get the most out of your Snort IDS. It starts by showing you the top ten coolest tools for Snort, many of which help you visualize what Snort's telling you, or e-mail you convenient summaries of Snort's alert information. Finally, it tells you where you can go for extra Snort help and information.

Chapter 15

Ten Cool Tools for Snort

Developers are designing a ton of cool Snort tools. Some are actively supported, and some are left to the vultures. In this chapter, we present a quick rundown of a good mix of these up-and-coming tools.

Alert-Management Tools

The alert management tools in this section parse Snort log files and provide alert log viewing in a more convenient format. Most provide similar functionality to ACID (as discussed in Chapter 7) but either have less functionality or a slightly different approach.

SnortSnarf

SnortSnarf is a Perl script with more modules, installs in 5 minutes, and configures from the command line to do everything it needs. SnortSnarf parses Snort's alert or log data and outputs that data to handy HTML files.

What does it do?

SnortSnarf runs against Snort's alert and log files or, with a plug-in module, reads Snort data straight out of your MySQL database and outputs all that data to a stack of HTML files, similar to ACID console.

Where can I get it?

SnortSnarf is distributed from the Silicon Defenses Web site at http://www.silicondefense.com/software/snortsnarf/. All the information you need to run SnortSnarf is at the Silicon Defense site, in addition to some handy plug-ins for reading alerts out of a MySQL database.

What's cool about it?

SnortSnarf gives you a quick and easy way to transform those arcane Snort log files or database entries into easy-to-use, fully referenced Web pages. SnortSnarf can be run straight from the command line as either a one-off process or as a regularly scheduled process using the Linux `cron` utility.

SnortSnarf is a memory hog. Don't expect to run it directly on a high-traffic Snort sensor or a server with little memory to spare.

Figure 15-1 displays SnortSnarf's output.

Figure 15-1:
SnortSnarf's
handy Web-
page output.

Snort Alert Monitor

Snort Alert Monitor (SAM) is a Java-based console that gives you a quick look at the Snort alerts in your MySQL database.

Don't confuse this tool with SnortSam, the real-time attack blocker in Chapter 11.

What does it do?

SAM runs as a Java-console, so it's platform independent. SAM monitors your MySQL database and gives you a real-time view of incoming Snort alerts. SAM also gives you audible alerts (using a dictionary of sound files) for every alert you receive.

You can configure SAM to send you an e-mail when Snort alerts to an attempted exploit on your network. Although SAM hasn't been updated since 2002, it's still a pretty useful tool.

Where can I get it?

SAM is available from the SourceForge developer site at `http://sourceforge.net/projects/snortalertmon/`.

What's cool about it?

SAM takes all of 3 minutes to install and configure. You instantly have a window into your incoming Snort alerts. The audio alerts are taken from *2001: A Space Odyssey*, and who doesn't think HAL is cool?

SAM only outputs 60 minutes of Snort alerts to its console, and you don't get the drill-down detail and forensics options available for each alert (such as looking up an attacker's address via WHOIS) you get with ACID console or SnortSnarf.

Figure 15-2 is a screen shot of what SnortSnarf looks like.

Pig Sentry

Pig Sentry is a lightweight script that generates real-time alerts from a Snort alert log on a high-volume network.

What does it do?

Pig Sentry is a set of Perl scripts that monitors Snort's alert log and keeps a state table of recent alerts and then sends a notice for

- ✔ New alerts
- ✔ Increases in alert trending
- ✔ Patterns of existing alerts that indicate probable compromise

Pig Sentry's self-monitoring system keeps it "aware" of the state of your incoming alerts, even after it exits, making it easy to roll into a log rotation mechanism.

Where can I get it?

Pig Sentry is available at the Solv Web site at `http://web.solv.com/tools/pigsentry/`.

What's cool about it?

Instead of sitting in front of an ACID console waiting for an update, you can be out playing beach volleyball.

Pig Sentry was written to work with Snort 1.8.1 or earlier with full log output, so it may not be cool for you. But hey, beach volleyball is cool.

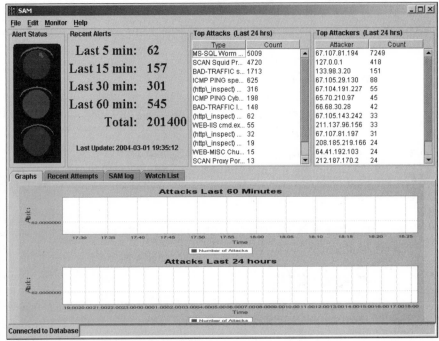

Figure 15-2:
"It's
puzzling.
I don't
think I've
ever seen
anything like
this before,"
says HAL.

Alert-Reporting Tools

For those who need those pretty graphics (especially those with managers who need the pretty graphics), these tools add some graphic capability to the Snort alert-logging functions.

RRD-Snort

RRD-Snort is a graphing utility that creates a graphic of alerts/events stored in a Snort database. RRD allows you to develop a graphic representation of the top attack methods detected by your Snort sensor.

What does it do?

RRD-Snort is a Perl script that reads stored alerts or events in the Snort database and converts that data to a distribution of top attack methods that the Snort sensor has detected. You choose the number of methods.

Where can I get it?

RRD-Snort is available at the Freshmeat Web site at `http://freshmeat.net/ projects/rrd-snort/`.

What's cool about it?

Who doesn't love cool 3-D graphics of flying X-Wings fighting the Emperor Zurg for control of the entire freakin' galaxy? Unfortunately, RRD-Snort outputs the most frequent attack methods detected by Snort in 2-D bar graphs. It's still pretty darn cool, though.

Snortalog

Snortalog is a Perl-based Snort log analyzer on steroids with output options to ASCII text, HTML, and graphs (formatted in JPEG, GIF, or PNG).

What does it do?

Snortalog is configured and managed from a GUI interface, and it runs on either Linux or Windows. It reads output from Snort in any format (no other tool that we've seen has this feature), including syslog, provides fast and full alerts, and then builds flat text or HTML summary reports. Snortalog's summary reports are similar to ACID's reports, but more compact. ACID is fully covered in Chapter 7.

In Linux, Snortalog outputs an impressive set of graphs based on the data it summarizes. The graphs are available in JPEG, GIF, and PNG formats.

Snortalog also reads log formats of Checkpoint FireWall-1 and Cisco PIX firewalls.

Where can I get it?

You can download the latest version of Snortalog from either

- ✔ The Snortalog author's homepage, which has all the information you need to run Snortalog: `http://jeremy.chartier.free.fr/snortalog/`
- ✔ The Snort Web site: `http://www.snort.org/dl/contrib/data_analysis/snortalog/`

What's cool about it?

Ever sit like a Pavlovian experiment waiting for little nuggets of data in your ACID console on a very busy network and database? Snortalog summarizes what you need to know about the state of your network security right now. It supports multiple sensors and produces pretty graphics for the management.

Alert-Response Tools

Everyone wants to press a button and launch a hundred Tomahawk missiles every time a real alert comes across the wire. Though these tools don't necessarily allow that functionality, they do allow you to update your firewall to block an incoming attack that Snort has alerted on.

SnortFW

Tired of hand-configuring `iptables` when an attacker fires a Snort alert? SnortFW does all that for you.

What does it do?

SnortFW analyzes incoming Snort alerts and (depending on the scan thresholds and danger level assignments) updates your `iptables` firewall to block the attacker. SnortFW also can e-mail alert information to any number of mailboxes for more intrusion response.

Where can I get it?

SnortFW is available at the Cipherdyne Web site at: `http://www.cipherdyne.org/fwsnort/download/fwsnort-0.6.1.tar.gz`

What's cool about it?

Though SnortFW code is still in the alpha development stage and has a few hitches, it's fast and effective at shutting down attacks as they happen.

Guardian

Guardian is an active response utility that updates firewall rules based on Snort alerts.

What does it do?

Guardian updates firewall rules on the fly off of Snort alerts, actively blocking all incoming data from an attacker's IP address. Other configuration options allow you to "whitelist" certain machines to prevent false positives from causing your firewall to go haywire. Guardian includes shell scripts for

- ✔ Commercial firewalls (Checkpoint Firewall-1 and Cisco PIX)
- ✔ Open source firewalls based on Unix, BSD, and Linux (`ipchains`, `iptables`, `ipfwadm` IPFW, and `ipfilter` firewalls and packet filters)

Where can I get it?

Guardian is available from the Chaotic Web site at `http://www.chaotic.org/guardian/`.

What's cool about it?

Guardian lets you strike back at your attackers by blocking their work before it can harm your systems. What could be cooler than that? Other than an automatic Tomahawk missile launch to the attacker's spider hole, we can't think of anything cooler.

Intrusion-Management Tools

Intrusion-management tools are considered the "whole package." The two tools covered here provide Snort configuration and management tools, reporting and some limited response capabilities. When you don't want to tickle 15 different configuration files, find some marginal Snort graphical utility, and tweak your firewall after every alert, these centralized management consoles are for you.

MIDAS

MIDAS is a centralized cross-platform network monitoring and network intrusion detection server that uses Snort as its base intrusion detection engine.

What does it do?

MIDAS stores the raw incoming Snort packet information locally and only sends specific packet information when an alert occurs. MIDAS features centralized configuration management, network monitoring, and built-in RRD graphics support.

Where can I get it?

MIDAS is available at the SourceForge Web site at `http://freshmeat.net/projects/midas-nms/`.

What's cool about it?

MIDAS is still in the alpha development stage, so it has some issues, but it's already shaping up as a solid, centralized intrusion detection server and manager, with nice support for distributed clients. Keep an eye on MIDAS. (We won't make a joke about gold, in case you were holding your breath.)

Demarc PureSecure

PureSecure is the total package when it comes to Snort tools. Integrating the Snort detection engine, PureSecure is a centralized intrusion detection and security suite. PureSecure is also a commercial product.

What does it do?

PureSecure combines major aspects of network security into a centralized management console. It uses the Snort IDS engine, a host-based System Integrity Verification system, and an Extensible Service Monitoring system to keep your network security under one all-seeing umbrella. And an all-seeing umbrella is as cool as fried taters.

Where can I get it?

Demarc PureSecure is available at the Freshmeat Web site at `http://freshmeat.net/projects/demarc/`.

What's cool about it?

Looking at one console for all your network security needs is cool unto itself. PureSecure also can generate reports, give you a host-based intrusion detection system, and use that work-pig Snort for the network IDS workload.

PureSecure is only free for non-commercial use.

IDScenter

IDScenter is a graphical front-end for managing Snort, alerts, and network security.

What does it do?

IDScenter touts the following features:

- ✔ Provides a centralized console for monitoring Snort alerts, managing rules and configuration files, and distributing updates
- ✔ Generates handy reports in HTML from your SQL database
- ✔ Includes an e-mail, audible alarm and visual alarm notification system
- ✔ Allows you to write your own plug-ins for your firewall

Where can I get it?

IDScenter is available on the Engage Security Web site at:
`http://www.engagesecurity.com/products/idscenter/`.

What's cool about it?

The coolest thing about IDScenter is that it's Windows-based! The fact that it's one of the few stable, extensible, and feature-rich centralized Snort consoles available for Windows propels it to "cool" status immediately.

Chapter 16

Ten Snort Information Resources

In This Chapter

▶ Tracking down information on Snort, intrusion detection, and incident response

▶ Knowing where to go when you need help with Snort

*T*his book gives you everything you need to know to run a fully functional Snort IDS on your network. If you want to go beyond this book, a number of resources are available to help you. Part of the beauty of Snort's open-source software model is its community support. If you run into a problem, someone else probably has found a solution.

The Snort.org Web Site

The Snort.org Web site at `http://www.snort.org/` is the first stop for all things Snort. This open-source, community-driven Web page is for the Snort IDS project and is also the home of Snort itself. At this site, you find

- ✔ The Snort source code, Linux pre-compiled binaries, and Windows pre-compiled binaries

- ✔ The latest and greatest Snort rules

- ✔ A Snort news Web log that gives you the latest news on Snort's development and identifies where Snort appears in the news on other sites

- ✔ Lots and lots of Snort documentation: official docs, FAQs, setup guides for specific platforms, and IDS deployment guides

If you don't know what you need, `snort.org` is a great place to start.

The Snort Mailing Lists

The Snort team maintains a number of Snort-related e-mail lists to which you can subscribe and post. Among the mailing lists are the following:

- **snort-announce** contains announcements of new releases and other official Snort news. This list has a pretty low amount of traffic — on average only a couple of posts per month. Because this list is moderated, your average Joe or Jane can't post directly to it without the message being approved.

- **snort-users** is a mailing list where you can post your Snort questions. An entire community of Snort users on this list can help you with your problem. This list is busy, sometimes exceeding 1,000 posts per month.

- **snort-sigs** is a discussion forum for the development of Snort rules. This list generally has a couple hundred posts per month.

If you're programming for Snort or running bleeding-edge Snort code (recommended for testing purposes only), you may want to check out a couple of other lists. You can subscribe by completing Web-based forms available at `http://www.snort.org/lists.html`. You can also find searchable archives at this site, which is a great start for help with Snort.

The SANS Institute

The security gurus at the SANS Institute have an excellent collection of white papers in their Web site's Reading Room, found at `http://www.sans.org/rr/`. Its Intrusion Detection section has a collection of papers on Snort and other IDS programs. An excellent section, "Incident Handling," of papers on responding to computer attacks and intrusions.

The Whitehats Security Forums

Whitehats is the home of the arachNIDS database of network attack signature information and a general security news site. Its URL is `http://www.whitehats.com/`. The Whitehats site contains a number of security forums, and no less than four forums devoted to intrusion detection, including one specifically for Snort.

The SecurityFocus IDS Mailing List

SecurityFocus is a respected computer security news site, as well as the home of a number of respected and popular computer security mailing lists. It has an IDS-specific section on its site at `http://www.securityfocus.com/ids/`. From there, you can subscribe to the Focus on IDS mailing list, which is a moderately busy list that mostly contains general IDS discussions, but also the occasional specific post about Snort.

The WINSNORT.com Web Site

WINSNORT.com is actually a company that creates its own Windows and Linux-based Snort sensor appliances that it offers for sale. This site also contains a lot of information on running Snort on Windows and Linux. Its URL is `http://www.winsnort.com/`.

The My-snort.org Web Site

My-snort.org is a Web log-style site that contains a lot of information on intrusion detection and Snort. Its URL is `http://www.my-snort.org/`.

The LinuxSecurity.com Web Site

While this site has "Linux" in its URL, it also contains a lot of great general information about security. It's constantly updated with the latest security news, with links to their sources, and has a number of original feature articles. Resources on IDS and Snort also are available at this site. Just point your browser to `http://www.linuxsecurity.com/`.

The Freshmeat.net Web Site

While not strictly a Snort or IDS-related site, Freshmeat.net is the best place to find out about open-source software releases and updates. The next time you say, "I wish Snort did *this*," or "I wish I had a tool to do *that* to my Snort logs, but I don't have the time or skills to program it," visit Freshmeat.net: Someone else probably has wished for the same things and programmed them for you. Simply go to `http://www.freshmeat.net/` and search on "snort". Almost every Snort-related open-source project shows up.

Our Web Site

Visit `http://www.vorpalmedia.com/` (run by the authors of this book). On it, you find informative updates on Snort and other topics we cover in *Snort For Dummies*. You can also use the mail form to ask us questions.

Appendix A

What's on the CD-ROM

*I*nstead of going to the Internet to install Snort, its components, and extra tools, feel free to use this CD-ROM. It may save you some time if you are setting up Snort to learn more about it. For putting Snort into production, however, we always recommend grabbing the latest and greatest stable versions of these programs off of the Web sites we point out in individual chapters. In addition to enhanced functionality, newer versions of these software packages may contain important security updates.

CD-ROM Contents

The CD-ROM includes the Snort IDS software, the ACID visualization console, the prerequisites to get them running, and other helpful tools.

JpGraph OO Graphic Library

The JpGraph OO Graphic Library is one of the many prerequisites for the ACID visualization console, covered in Chapter 7. This runs on both Linux and Windows.

SnortSam

SnortSam is a Linux-based real-time attack blocking utility covered in Chapter 11.

Snort

Snort is what this book's all about. We include versions for both Linux and Windows. We cover installing Snort for Linux in Chapter 4 and Snort for Windows in Chapter 5.

PHP

PHP is a scripting language parser that's required for the ACID console, covered in Chapter 7. We include versions for Linux and Windows.

MySQL

MySQL is a client/server database package that can accept Snort logs. We cover it in Chapters 4 (Linux), 5 (Windows), and 7 (using MySQL with ACID). We include versions for Linux and Windows.

WinPcap

WinPcap is a packet capture library and a prerequisite for Snort on Windows systems. We cover WinPcap in Chapter 5.

ACID

ACID is a Web-based visualization console for Snort alerts. ACID runs on Linux and Windows. We cover ACID in Chapter 7.

ADODB Database Library for PHP

ADODB Database Library for PHP lets PHP talk to databases such as MySQL. ADODB is a prerequisite for ACID, covered in Chapter 7.

Apache HTTPD Server

The Apache HTTPD Server is a popular Web server. We include the Linux version on the CD. Having a Web server is a prerequisite for ACID, which we cover in Chapter 7.

Barnyard

Barnyard is a helper application that takes the load off of Snort for log writing. We include the Linux version on the CD. Barnyard is covered in Chapter 14.

SnortSnarf

SnortSnarf is a Perl script that generates HTML pages from Snort logs. You must have Perl installed for SnortSnarf to run (see http://www.perl.com/ for information on obtaining Perl if you don't already have it). We cover SnortSnarf in Chapter 15.

PHPLOT

PHPLOT is a PHP add-on for generating graphs. PHPLOT is yet another prerequisite for ACID, which we cover in Chapter 7.

Swatch

Swatch is a system-log watcher that can be used to send you real-time Snort alerts. We include the Linux version of Swatch on the CD. We cover Swatch in Chapter 11.

Guardian

Guardian is an active response utility that updates firewall rules based on Snort alerts. We include the Linux version. We cover Guardian in Chapter 15.

PigSentry

PigSentry is a lightweight Perl script that generates real-time alerts from a Snort alert log on a high-volume network (see http://www.perl.com/ for information on obtaining Perl if you don't already have it). We include the Linux version on the CD-ROM. We cover PigSentry in Chapter 15.

Snortalog

Snortalog is a Perl-based Snort log analyzer on steroids with output options to text (ASCII) or HTML, as well as JPEG, GIF, and PNG formatted graphs. It should run on any system that has Perl (see http://www.perl.com/ for information on obtaining Perl if you don't already have it). We cover Snortalog in Chapter 15.

libpcap

libpcap is a packet capture library that is required for running Snort on your Linux system. We cover installing and using libpcap in Chapter 4.

OpenSSL

OpenSSL is an SSL library that is required for running OpenSSH and a number of other security tools. We include the Linux version on the CD-ROM. We cover installing OpenSSL in Chapter 4.

OpenSSH

OpenSSH is a secure remote-management utility. We include the Linux version on the CD-ROM. We cover installing OpenSSH in Chapter 4.

zlib

Zlib is a compression library, and is one of the many prerequisites for the ACID console. We cover installing zlib in Chapter 7.

libpng

Libpng is a graphics library for Linux and Windows, and is another prerequisite if you want ACID to graph your alert data. We cover installing it in Chapter 7.

Oinkmaster

Oinkmaster is a Perl script that can be used to update your Snort rules. It should run on any system that has Perl (see http://www.perl.com/ for information on obtaining Perl if you don't already have it). We cover Oinkmaster in Chapter 12.

CD-ROM Considerations

This CD-ROM was created in a format that should be readable by Microsoft Windows, Linux, and Macintosh OS X computers. Refer to your operating system's documentation for mounting and reading a CD-ROM, if necessary.

Some of the software on this CD-ROM requires un-archiving or un-compressing utilities to open them. Specifically, you might see software with the following filename extensions:

- **.tar**_These files are Unix TAR files.
- **.gz**_These files have been compressed using the GNU Zip algorithm.
- **.tar.gz** or **.tgz**_These formats are Unix TAR files that have also been compressed using the GNU Zip algorithm.
- **.zip**_These files have been compressed using the ZIP algorithm, supported by a number of utilities.

For Windows systems, the WinZIP utility (found at http://www.winzip.com) or WinRAR utility (found at http://www.rarlab.com/) can open all of these formats. Windows XP compressed file and folder feature will only handle files in the ZIP format, so you might need WinZIP or WinRAR, anyway.

For Linux systems, just make sure you have the *tar*, *gunzip*, and *unzip* utilities available on your system. The *whereis*, *locate*, and *find* utilities can help you locate them. Consult the documentation for your specific Linux distribution for more information on these utilities.

Index

• *O* •

• *P* •

• X •

• Z •

Notes

Wiley Publishing, Inc.
End-User License Agreement

GNU GENERAL PUBLIC LICENSE

TERMS AND CONDITIONS FOR COPYING, DISTRIBUTION AND MODIFICATION

0. This License applies to any program or other work which contains a notice placed by the copyright holder saying it may be distributed under the terms of this General Public License. The "Program", below, refers to any such program or work, and a "work based on the Program" means either the Program or any derivative work under copyright law: that is to say, a work containing the Program or a portion of it, either verbatim or with modifications and/or translated into another language. (Hereinafter, translation is included without limitation in the term "modification".) Each licensee is addressed as "you".

Activities other than copying, distribution and modification are not covered by this License; they are outside its scope. The act of running the Program is not restricted, and the output from the Program is covered only if its contents constitute a work based on the Program (independent of having been made by running the Program). Whether that is true depends on what the Program does.

1. You may copy and distribute verbatim copies of the Program's source code as you receive it, in any medium, provided that you conspicuously and appropriately publish on each copy an appropriate copyright notice and disclaimer of warranty; keep intact all the notices that refer to this License and to the absence of any warranty; and give any other recipients of the Program a copy of this License along with the Program.

You may charge a fee for the physical act of transferring a copy, and you may at your option offer warranty protection in exchange for a fee.

2. You may modify your copy or copies of the Program or any portion of it, thus forming a work based on the Program, and copy and distribute such modifications or work under the terms of Section 1 above, provided that you also meet all of these conditions:

a) You must cause the modified files to carry prominent notices stating that you changed the files and the date of any change.

b) You must cause any work that you distribute or publish, that in whole or in part contains or is derived from the Program or any part thereof, to be licensed as a whole at no charge to all third parties under the terms of this License.

c) If the modified program normally reads commands interactively when run, you must cause it, when started running for such interactive use in the most ordinary way, to print or display an announcement including an appropriate copyright notice and a notice that there is no warranty (or else, saying that you provide a warranty) and that users may redistribute the program under these conditions, and telling the user how to view a copy of this License. (Exception: if the Program itself is interactive but does not normally print such an announcement, your work based on the Program is not required to print an announcement.)

These requirements apply to the modified work as a whole. If identifiable sections of that work are not derived from the Program, and can be reasonably considered independent and separate works in themselves, then this License, and its terms, do not apply to those sections when you distribute them as separate works. But when you distribute the same sections as part of a whole which is a work based on the Program, the distribution of the whole must be on the terms of this License, whose permissions for other licensees extend to the entire whole, and thus to each and every part regardless of who wrote it.

Thus, it is not the intent of this section to claim rights or contest your rights to work written entirely by you; rather, the intent is to exercise the right to control the distribution of derivative or collective works based on the Program.

In addition, mere aggregation of another work not based on the Program with the Program (or with a work based on the Program) on a volume of a storage or distribution medium does not bring the other work under the scope of this License.

3. You may copy and distribute the Program (or a work based on it, under Section 2) in object code or executable form under the terms of Sections 1 and 2 above provided that you also do one of the following:

a) Accompany it with the complete corresponding machine-readable source code, which must be distributed under the terms of Sections 1 and 2 above on a medium customarily used for software interchange; or,

b) Accompany it with a written offer, valid for at least three years, to give any third party, for a charge no more than your cost of physically performing source distribution, a complete machine-readable copy of the corresponding source code, to be distributed under the terms of Sections 1 and 2 above on a medium customarily used for software interchange; or,

c) Accompany it with the information you received as to the offer to distribute corresponding source code. (This alternative is allowed only for noncommercial distribution and only if you received the program in object code or executable form with such an offer, in accord with Subsection b above.)

The source code for a work means the preferred form of the work for making modifications to it. For an executable work, complete source code means all the source code for all modules it contains, plus any associated interface definition files, plus the scripts used to control compilation and installation of the executable. However, as a special exception, the source code distributed need not include anything that is normally distributed (in either source or binary form) with the major components (compiler, kernel, and so on) of the operating system on which the executable runs, unless that component itself accompanies the executable.

If distribution of executable or object code is made by offering access to copy from a designated place, then offering equivalent access to copy the source code from the same place counts as distribution of the source code, even though third parties are not compelled to copy the source along with the object code.

4. You may not copy, modify, sublicense, or distribute the Program except as expressly provided under this License. Any attempt otherwise to copy, modify, sublicense or distribute the Program is void, and will automatically terminate your rights under this License. However, parties who have received copies, or rights, from you under this License will not have their licenses terminated so long as such parties remain in full compliance.

5. You are not required to accept this License, since you have not signed it. However, nothing else grants you permission to modify or distribute the Program or its derivative works. These actions are prohibited by law if you do not accept this License. Therefore, by modifying or distributing the Program (or any work based on the Program), you indicate your acceptance of this License to do so, and all its terms and conditions for copying, distributing or modifying the Program or works based on it.

6. Each time you redistribute the Program (or any work based on the Program), the recipient automatically receives a license from the original licensor to copy, distribute or modify the Program subject to these terms and conditions. You may not impose any further restrictions on the recipients' exercise of the rights granted herein. You are not responsible for enforcing compliance by third parties to this License.

7. If, as a consequence of a court judgment or allegation of patent infringement or for any other reason (not limited to patent issues), conditions are imposed on you (whether by court order, agreement or otherwise) that contradict the conditions of this License, they do not excuse you from the conditions of this License. If you cannot distribute so as to satisfy simultaneously your obligations under this License and any other pertinent obligations, then as a consequence you may not distribute the Program at all. For example, if a patent license would not permit royalty-free redistribution of the Program by all those who receive copies directly or indirectly through you, then the only way you could satisfy both it and this License would be to refrain entirely from distribution of the Program.

If any portion of this section is held invalid or unenforceable under any particular circumstance, the balance of the section is intended to apply and the section as a whole is intended to apply in other circumstances.

It is not the purpose of this section to induce you to infringe any patents or other property right claims or to contest validity of any such claims; this section has the sole purpose of protecting the integrity of the free software distribution system, which is implemented by public license practices. Many people have made generous contributions to the wide range of software distributed through that system in reliance on consistent application of that system; it is up to the author/donor to decide if he or she is willing to distribute software through any other system and a licensee cannot impose that choice.

This section is intended to make thoroughly clear what is believed to be a consequence of the rest of this License.

8. If the distribution and/or use of the Program is restricted in certain countries either by patents or by copyrighted interfaces, the original copyright holder who places the Program under this License may add an explicit geographical distribution limitation excluding those countries, so that distribution is permitted only in or among countries not thus excluded. In such case, this License incorporates the limitation as if written in the body of this License.

9. The Free Software Foundation may publish revised and/or new versions of the General Public License from time to time. Such new versions will be similar in spirit to the present version, but may differ in detail to address new problems or concerns.

Each version is given a distinguishing version number. If the Program specifies a version number of this License which applies to it and "any later version", you have the option of following the terms and conditions either of that version or of any later version published by the Free Software Foundation. If the Program does not specify a version number of this License, you may choose any version ever published by the Free Software Foundation.

10. If you wish to incorporate parts of the Program into other free programs whose distribution conditions are different, write to the author to ask for permission. For software which is copyrighted by the Free Software Foundation, write to the Free Software Foundation; we sometimes make exceptions for this. Our decision will be guided by the two goals of preserving the free status of all derivatives of our free software and of promoting the sharing and reuse of software generally.

NO WARRANTY

11. BECAUSE THE PROGRAM IS LICENSED FREE OF CHARGE, THERE IS NO WARRANTY FOR THE PROGRAM, TO THE EXTENT PERMITTED BY APPLICABLE LAW. EXCEPT WHEN OTHERWISE STATED IN WRITING THE COPYRIGHT HOLDERS AND/OR OTHER PARTIES PROVIDE THE PROGRAM "AS IS" WITHOUT WARRANTY OF ANY KIND, EITHER EXPRESSED OR IMPLIED, INCLUDING, BUT NOT LIMITED TO, THE IMPLIED WARRANTIES OF MERCHANTABILITY AND FITNESS FOR A PARTICULAR PURPOSE. THE ENTIRE RISK AS TO THE QUALITY AND PERFORMANCE OF THE PROGRAM IS WITH YOU. SHOULD THE PROGRAM PROVE DEFECTIVE, YOU ASSUME THE COST OF ALL NECESSARY SERVICING, REPAIR OR CORRECTION.

12. IN NO EVENT UNLESS REQUIRED BY APPLICABLE LAW OR AGREED TO IN WRITING WILL ANY COPYRIGHT HOLDER, OR ANY OTHER PARTY WHO MAY MODIFY AND/OR REDISTRIBUTE THE PROGRAM AS PERMITTED ABOVE, BE LIABLE TO YOU FOR DAMAGES, INCLUDING ANY GENERAL, SPECIAL, INCIDENTAL OR CONSEQUENTIAL DAMAGES ARISING OUT OF THE USE OR INABILITY TO USE THE PROGRAM (INCLUDING BUT NOT LIMITED TO LOSS OF DATA OR DATA BEING RENDERED INACCURATE OR LOSSES SUSTAINED BY YOU OR THIRD PARTIES OR A FAILURE OF THE PROGRAM TO OPERATE WITH ANY OTHER PROGRAMS), EVEN IF SUCH HOLDER OR OTHER PARTY HAS BEEN ADVISED OF THE POSSIBILITY OF SUCH DAMAGES.

FOR DUMMIES®

The easy way to get more done and have more fun

PERSONAL FINANCE

0-7645-5231-7

0-7645-2431-3

0-7645-5331-3

Also available:

Estate Planning For Dummies
(0-7645-5501-4)

401(k)s For Dummies
(0-7645-5468-9)

Frugal Living For Dummies
(0-7645-5403-4)

Microsoft Money "X" For Dummies
(0-7645-1689-2)

Mutual Funds For Dummies
(0-7645-5329-1)

Personal Bankruptcy For Dummies
(0-7645-5498-0)

Quicken "X" For Dummies
(0-7645-1666-3)

Stock Investing For Dummies
(0-7645-5411-5)

Taxes For Dummies 2003
(0-7645-5475-1)

BUSINESS & CAREERS

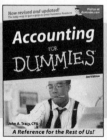

0-7645-5314-3

0-7645-5307-0

0-7645-5471-9

Also available:

Business Plans Kit For Dummies
(0-7645-5365-8)

Consulting For Dummies
(0-7645-5034-9)

Cool Careers For Dummies
(0-7645-5345-3)

Human Resources Kit For Dummies
(0-7645-5131-0)

Managing For Dummies
(1-5688-4858-7)

QuickBooks All-in-One Desk Reference For Dummies
(0-7645-1963-8)

Selling For Dummies
(0-7645-5363-1)

Small Business Kit For Dummies
(0-7645-5093-4)

Starting an eBay Business For Dummies
(0-7645-1547-0)

HEALTH, SPORTS & FITNESS

0-7645-5167-1

0-7645-5146-9

0-7645-5154-X

Also available:

Controlling Cholesterol For Dummies
(0-7645-5440-9)

Dieting For Dummies
(0-7645-5126-4)

High Blood Pressure For Dummies
(0-7645-5424-7)

Martial Arts For Dummies
(0-7645-5358-5)

Menopause For Dummies
(0-7645-5458-1)

Nutrition For Dummies
(0-7645-5180-9)

Power Yoga For Dummies
(0-7645-5342-9)

Thyroid For Dummies
(0-7645-5385-2)

Weight Training For Dummies
(0-7645-5168-X)

Yoga For Dummies
(0-7645-5117-5)

FOR DUMMIES®

A world of resources to help you grow

HOME, GARDEN & HOBBIES

0-7645-5295-3

0-7645-5130-2

0-7645-5106-X

FOOD & WINE

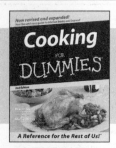

0-7645-5250-3

0-7645-5390-9

0-7645-5114-0

TRAVEL

0-7645-5453-0

0-7645-5438-7

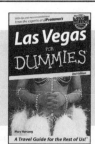

0-7645-5448-4

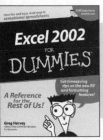

FOR DUMMIES®

Helping you expand your horizons and realize your potential

INTERNET

0-7645-0894-6

0-7645-1659-0

0-7645-1642-6

Also available:

America Online 7.0 For Dummies
(0-7645-1624-8)

Genealogy Online For Dummies
(0-7645-0807-5)

The Internet All-in-One Desk Reference For Dummies
(0-7645-1659-0)

Internet Explorer 6 For Dummies
(0-7645-1344-3)

The Internet For Dummies Quick Reference
(0-7645-1645-0)

Internet Privacy For Dummies
(0-7645-0846-6)

Researching Online For Dummies
(0-7645-0546-7)

Starting an Online Business For Dummies
(0-7645-1655-8)

DIGITAL MEDIA

0-7645-1664-7

0-7645-1675-2

0-7645-0806-7

Also available:

CD and DVD Recording For Dummies
(0-7645-1627-2)

Digital Photography All-in-One Desk Reference For Dummies
(0-7645-1800-3)

Digital Photography For Dummies Quick Reference
(0-7645-0750-8)

Home Recording for Musicians For Dummies
(0-7645-1634-5)

MP3 For Dummies
(0-7645-0858-X)

Paint Shop Pro "X" For Dummies
(0-7645-2440-2)

Photo Retouching & Restoration For Dummies
(0-7645-1662-0)

Scanners For Dummies
(0-7645-0783-4)

GRAPHICS

0-7645-0817-2

0-7645-1651-5

0-7645-0895-4

Also available:

Adobe Acrobat 5 PDF For Dummies
(0-7645-1652-3)

Fireworks 4 For Dummies
(0-7645-0804-0)

Illustrator 10 For Dummies
(0-7645-3636-2)

QuarkXPress 5 For Dummies
(0-7645-0643-9)

Visio 2000 For Dummies
(0-7645-0635-8)

Available wherever books are sold. Go to www.dummies.com or call 1-877-762-2974 to order direct.

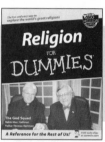

FOR DUMMIES®

We take the mystery out of complicated subjects

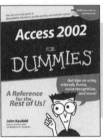